ECONOMIC ISSUES TODAY

Alternative Approaches

ECONOMIC ISSUES TODAY

Alternative Approaches
Second Edition

Robert B. Carson
State University College, Oneonta, New York

St. Martin's Press
New York

This book is dedicated to my mother,
Catherine Postlewaite Carson

Library of Congress Catalog Card Number: 80–51674
Copyright © 1980 by St. Martin's Press, Inc.
All Rights Reserved.
Manufactured in the United States of America.
4321
fedcb
For information, write: St. Martin's Press, Inc.,
175 Fifth Avenue, New York, N.Y. 10010

cover design by Joseph Notovitz

cloth ISBN: 0–312–23424–4
paper ISBN: 0–312–23425–2

ACKNOWLEDGMENTS

Tables 8.1 and 8.2 from Roger A. Herriot and Herman P. Miller, "The Taxes
We Pay," *Conference Board Record* (May 1971), p. 40, used by permission of
THE CONFERENCE BOARD.

P. 212: E. Y. Harburg and Jay Gorney, "Brother, Can You Spare a Dime?"
Lyrics by E. Y. Harburg. Music by Jay Gorney. © 1932 by Warner Bros., Inc.
Copyright renewed. All rights reserved. Used by permission.

Preface

The adoption of *Economic Issues Today* in hundreds of principles of economics and economic issues courses has occasioned the publication of a second edition. Needless to say, I am immensely gratified by such a response. Preparing a second edition is any author's rare privilege.

Without altering the basic format of the original edition, I have made a number of changes for the second edition that will be evident to earlier readers. It is somewhat more extensive; sixteen issues are examined compared to thirteen in the first edition. Moreover, a number of the original issues have been extensively rewritten, and all have been updated to consider events and policy shifts that have occurred during the past three years. New issues—depression, structural unemployment, and international trade and finance—have been added to broaden and deepen the macroeconomic coverage. *Economic Issues Today* is also available in two volumes: *Microeconomic Issues Today* and *Macroeconomic Issues Today*.

Let me explain why I undertook this project in the first place. All too frequently, students begin their study of economics with the impression that economists as a group are bland, dull, and monolithic in the discussion of important issues confronting the general society. We may as well admit that the profession sometimes exhibits a tendency to be rather bland in its public utterances, but surely any supposed unanimity toward social policy questions has vanished. With the rise of a large radical caucus within the discipline, beginning in the late 1960s, and the recent resurgence of variations of laissez-faire ideology, the facade of consensus has clearly been broken down. The application of economic theory to issues of public policy more and more reflects a range of choice from Conservative, to Liberal, to Radical on the political spectrum.

For the student struggling with basic theory and analytic tools, as well as for the ordinary citizen overwhelmed by economic data in the newspapers and on the TV evening news, it is hard to avoid confusion about what economists really think about the problems facing the nation. This book begins with the assumption that the answers economists give to policy questions can usefully be compared and analyzed according to the particular biases of their arguments and the probable outcomes of their proposals. In other words, differences in economic logic and interpretation of evidence are not so much a function of skill mastery as they are the expression of strongly held social and political opinions. The book also assumes that economics as a body of knowledge takes on greater meaning and is more readily comprehended when it is viewed in this way.

Readers should understand that this is a very "arbitrary" kind of book. Its arbitrariness, however, is not one-sided. On each issue, Conservative, Liberal, and Radical analyses and proposals are presented independently and in a first-person advocacy manner. On one page, there may be a vigorous and unyielding defense of laissez faire and the market economy; on another, a program for the elimination or modification of the free market. This is not the way economic analysis and theory is usually taught, but it is what the practice of economics is about. In the real world, the citizen and the economist make public policy choices that protect, attack, or modify the market mechanism. We may defend our positions in terms of economic logic, but behind our proofs lies our political and ideological view of the world. This book attempts to examine the relationship between ideological values and the economic theories and policies that are their outcome.

Since the book presents a wide range of views on a number of currently sensitive issues, it should provoke disagreement, controversy, and discussion. In itself, the book does not urge a particular ideological position or a particular variety of economic analysis. The decision to select or reject this or that point of view is left, as it should be, to the reader.

While I was writing, a curious colleague asked me to explain what exactly I was trying to do. I obliged him as best I could, and he observed, "If you're really successful, you'll have written a book that will be at least two-thirds objectionable to every reader." Although I hadn't thought of it that way before, I suppose that is precisely the goal—to constructively anger a reader two-thirds of the time.

The arguments are presented in plain language, with as little use of economic jargon as possible. The chapters are self-contained and may be assigned in any order the instructor chooses. (The Instructor's Manual provides a grid correlating the chapters here with the chapters in the leading principles textbooks.) There are relatively few footnotes or direct references to particular economists, although the ideas of many contemporary economists and schools of economic thought will be apparent. The bibliography at the end is offered for anyone wishing to dig a little deeper into an issue or a particular economic perspective or approach.

The decision to minimize the explicit discussion of technical terms and specific economic concepts in the discussion of contemporary policy issues does not mean the author rejects the importance of formal economic analysis. For instructors using *Economic Issues Today* along with a conventional principles of economics textbook, the formal analysis will be supplied by the principles text and classroom instruction. For instructors using the book without a conventional text, the Instructor's Manual supplies an outline of the pertinent economic concepts and provides graphical analyses. Even instructors using this book as a collateral reading may find the manual quite useful.

The basic outline of this book grew out of discussions with Irving Rockwood and my own earlier experience with two collections of readings in economics. As the work developed, I received further encouragement in very early stages from Tony Dick and Murray Curtin, and at a later, and most critical juncture, from Bertrand Lummus of St. Martin's Press. Indeed, Bert Lummus' steady encouragement in the writing and final preparation of the manuscript was crucial. No author could wish for a more stimulating and congenially demanding editor. The editorial and production work of the St. Martin's staff, especially the help given by Emily Berleth, deserves special recognition.

A fair number of colleagues have made important contributions. Some offered explicit suggestions for changes in style and content. Others' contributions were less direct and perhaps not even known at the time. Their help came from their critical skills and their ordinary activities as teachers, scholars, and friends. Without differentiating the particular contributions, I would like especially to thank George Webster and David Ring of Hartwick College, Natalie Marshall of Vassar College, and Alfred Lubell, Daniel Fine, Guy C.Z. Mhone, and Robert Moynihan of State University College at Oneonta, New York. Kevin O'Donnell and Harold Dodt served courageously and well as research assistants.

For typing, research, important "go-for" work, and other support in preparing the manuscript, I am indebted to Ruth Wheeler, Barbara Lifgren, Sheila Reynolds, Sue Lapine, Michael McKeon, Diane Collin, Riva Daniels, Joann Gorko, Peter Granger, Brian Schmid, and, of course, my wife, Marjorie Gale Carson. A special debt is owed Charlize Fazio for typing from my impossible scrawl and meeting equally impossible deadlines. My son, James, and my daughter, Sarah, were also helpful as they cheerfully adapted to their father's preoccupation with writing.

Finally, but most importantly, a book of this kind comes out of classroom experiences and learning from the students themselves. Students are always the instructor's and author's best teachers and critics. During a decade and a half of teaching, I have incurred too many debts of this kind to begin to list names. However, without the thoughtful and demanding ideas and skepticism of hundreds "on the other side of the desk," I would not have been prepared to undertake this effort.

Of course, the aid given by all those named above by no means shifts responsibility or implies their agreement with all or any of the finished manuscript.

Robert B. Carson

Contents

PART 1

INTRODUCTION

Alternative Economic Philosophies

A Survey of Conservative, Liberal, and Radical Critiques

> The ideas of economists, both when they are right and when they are wrong, are more powerful than is commonly understood. Indeed, the world is ruled by little else. Practical men, who believe themselves to be quite exempt from any intellectual influences, are usually the slaves of some defunct economist. Madmen in authority, who hear voices in the air, are distilling their frenzy from some academic scribbler of a few years back.
>
> *John Maynard Keynes, 1936*

The Ideological Basis of Economics

"More government spending for jobs!" "Less spending to halt inflation!" "More overseas business expansion to help profits!" "Stop American imperialism!" "End government meddling with business!" "Make the corporations pay for their damage to the environment!" All around us we hear the steady clatter of noisy political recipes offering solutions to the economic problems haunting the United States. The competing arguments and policy proposals coming from political parties, public figures, and the news media seem endless. Ordinary citizens are quite understandably confused as to what course of public policy to support.

No wonder that practically every economist has been asked by at least one earnest relative, friend, student, businessperson, or labor leader "what *the economists* think and recommend" on a particular issue. Such a question usually reflects a certain naiveté on the questioner's part about what economists as a group really think and do. Most people—including beginning economics students—have a tendency to assume that economists somehow agree. After all, it would seem logical that a man or woman whose professional interest is, say, studying the problem of unemployment should be able to tell exactly how the unemployment problem can be solved. Once upon a time, economists would shrink from such a question by pointing out that they only studied unemployment; solving it was a political problem. Over the past several decades, though, economics and economists have moved far beyond classroom teaching and debate. No longer do they occasionally consult with presidents, business executives, and labor leaders; now they advise them. However, the advice given on any particular problem varies among economists. This is often quite a surprise to the citizen questioner who, although paying due professional respect to the economists, still sees him or her as a kind of mechanic. When one's car does not start, the car owner expects (at least hopes) that the diagnosis of mechanical trouble given at one garage is exactly the same as what he will hear at any other. If there is one mechanical problem, there should be one mechanical solution. The moral of this comparison is that economics is more than studying a repair manual and economists are not mechanics.

Once, an exasperated President Kennedy, trying hard to find a politically acceptable route out of a national recession, exclaimed, "If you laid all economists head to feet, all you would reach is confusion." The president missed the point. Really what you would reach wouldn't be confusion but different points of view. While practitioners of conventional economics rarely like to admit their differences, the facts of disagreement override professional courtesy. The economist who urges tight money to stop inflation as a requirement for dealing with unemployment is miles apart from a colleague who advocates a massive public works program to reduce unemployment.

How is such disagreement possible? Isn't economics a science? Economists' answers to that question vary. A common and reasonable enough response is simply that scientists disagree, too. While there is much truth to such an answer, it really begs the question. Plainly, the "dismal science" of economics is not a science like physics. While economists may sometimes talk about the laws of supply and demand as if they were eternal verities like the law of gravity, there is abundant anthropological and historical evidence that many societies have behaved quite contrary to the laws of supply and demand. Outside of science fiction, however, there is no denying the law of gravity.

To be sure, economists employ (or at least they should) the rigor of scientific method and quantitative techniques in collecting data, testing hypotheses, and offering reasonable conclusions and predictions. However, economists deal with different "stuff" from that of their colleagues in the exact sciences. Their data involve human beings and their laboratory is a world of behavior and perception that varies with time and place. On top of this, economists, like all social scientists, are called upon to answer a question not asked of those in the "pure" sciences: "What *ought* to be?" Astronomers, for instance, are not asked what *ought* to be the gravitational relationships of our universe. That would be a nonsense question. Economists, however, cannot evade making some determinations about optimal prices, optimal income distribution, and so forth. Their decisions, while perhaps based upon a genuine effort at neutrality, detachment, and honest evaluation of the available evidence, must finally be a matter of interpretation, a value judgment based upon their own particular world views. To put the point directly: Economics, as a study of human behavior, cannot avoid value judgments. Struggle as it may, economics as a discipline is never free from ideology.

Until recent years, most economists haven't talked much about ideology, or their individual political views of the world. "Ideology" has been somehow a dirty word, or unprofessional, or it has been too troublesome to deal with. But, as the pressure of crises within the economy and society heightened in the 1960s and 1970s, the economics profession more and more found itself shifting from debate over merely "theoretical" questions to those centering on concrete political issues. The *Newsweek* editorials of the Conservative Milton Friedman and the Liberal Paul Samuelson show that leaders of the profession now fearlessly parade their politics as they offer their particular analyses of economic problems. Meanwhile, the shrill debate between conventional economists and those of a more radical persuasion has forced increased attention to political economic alternatives.

The significance of these trends should not be lost on the beginning student of economics. The above arguments hold that the content and application of economic reasoning are finally determined by the force of what people believe, not by an independent and neutral logic. But to say that economics is a matter of opinion is not to say that it is just a study of relatively different ideas: Here's this view and here's that one and each is of equal value. In fact, opinions are not of equal value. There are good opinions and there are bad ones. Economic ideas have different consequences when adopted as policy. They have different effects, now and in the future. As we confront the various policy solutions proposed to deal with the many crises now gnawing deep into our economy and society, we must make choices. This one seems likely to produce desired outcomes. That one does not. No other situation is consistent with a free and reasoned society. Granted it is a painful situation, since choice always raises doubts and uncertainty and runs the risk of wrong judgment, but it cannot be evaded.

This short book is intended to focus on a limited number of the hard choices that we must make. Its basic premise is that economic judgment is basically a matter of learning to choose the best policy solution among all possible solutions. This book further assumes that failure to make this choice is to underestimate the richness and importance of the economic ideas we learn and to be blind to the fact that ideas and analysis do indeed apply to the real world of our own lives.

On Sorting Out Ideologies

Assuming we have been at least partially convincing in our argument that economic analysis is permeated by ideological judgment, we now turn to examine the varieties of ideology common to American economic thought.

In general, we may characterize the ideological position of contemporary economics and economists as Conservative, Liberal, or Radical. These, the same handy categories that evening newscasters use to describe political positions, presumably have some meaning to people. The trouble with labels, though, is that they can mean a great deal and, at the same time, nothing at all. At a distance the various political colors of Conservative, Liberal, and Radical banners are vividly different. Close up, though, the distinctiveness blurs, and what seemed obvious differences are not so clear. For instance, there is probably *not* a strictly Liberal position on every economic issue, nor are all the economists who might be generally termed "Liberal" in consistent agreement. The same is true in the case of many Radical or Conservative positions as well. Unless we maintain a certain open-endedness in our categorizing of positions, the discussion of ideological differences will be overly simple and much too rigid. Therefore, the following generalizations and applications of ideological typologies will attempt to isolate and identify only "representative" positions. By doing this we can at least focus on the differences at the center rather than on the fuzziness at the fringes of schools of thought.

We are still left with a problem. How do you specify an ideological position? Can you define a Radical or a Liberal or a Conservative position? The answer here is simple enough. As the British economist Joan Robinson once observed, an ideology is like an elephant—you can't define an elephant but you should know one when you see it. Moreover, you should know the difference between an elephant and a horse or a cow without having to resort to definitions.

There is a general framework of thought within each of the three ideological schools by which we can recognize them. Thus we will not "define" the schools but merely describe the salient characteristics of each. In all the following, the reader is urged to remember that there are many varieties of elephants. Our specification of a particular ideological view on any issue is a representative model—a kind of average-looking elephant (or horse or cow). Thus, the Conservative view offered on the problem of inflation, for instance, should not be thought of as the only possible expression of Conservative thought on this question. However, it should be sufficiently representative so that the basic Conservative paradigm, or world view, can be distinguished from the Radical or Liberal argument.

THE CONSERVATIVE PARADIGM

What is usually labeled the Conservative position in economic thought and policy making was not always "Conservative." Conservative ideas may be traced to quite radical origins. The forebears of modern Conservative thought—among them England's Adam Smith (1723–1790)—were not interested in "conserving" the economic order they knew but in destroying it. In 1776, when Smith wrote his classic *Wealth of Nations*, England was organized under a more or less closed economic system of monopoly rights, trade restriction, and constant government interference with the marketplace and with an individual's business and private affairs. This system, known as mercantilism, had been dominant in England, and, with slight variations, elsewhere on the Continent, for over 250 years.

Smith's remedy was simple enough: Remove all restrictions on commercial and industrial activity and allow the market to work freely. The philosophical basis of Smith's argument rested on his beliefs that (1) all men had the natural right to obtain and protect their property; (2) all men were by nature materialistic; and (3) all men were rational and would, by their own reason, seek to maximize their material well-being. These individualistic tendencies in men would be tempered by competition in the marketplace. There men would have to compromise with one another to gain any individual satisfaction whatsoever. The overall effect of these compromises would ultimately lead to national as well as individual satisfaction. Competition and self-interest would keep prices down and production high and rising. They would also stimulate product improvement, invention, and steady economic progress. For this to happen, of course, there would have to be a minimum of interference with the free market—no big government, no powerful unions, and no conspiring in trade. Smith's position and that of his contemporaries and followers was known as "Classical Liberalism." The Conservative label now applied to these views seems to have been affixed much later, when Smith's heirs found themselves acting in the defense of a status quo rather than opposing an older order.

Thus, modern capitalist economic thought must trace its origins to Adam Smith. While this body of thought has been built upon and modified over the past 200 years, the hand of Adam Smith is evident in every conventional economics textbook. Common sense tells us, however, that a lot has changed since Smith. Today business is big. There are labor unions and big government to interfere with his balanced free market of equals. His optimistic view of a naturally growing and expanding system is now replaced by growth problems and by a steady dose of pessimism in most glances toward the future. Nevertheless, modern Conservatives, among contemporary defenders of capitalism, still stand close to the ideals of Adam Smith.

Modern Conservative thought is anchored to two basic philosophic ideas that distinguish it from Liberal and Radical positions. First, the market system and the spirit of competition are central to proper social organization. Second, individual rights and freedoms must be unlimited and uninfringed.

Conservatives oppose any "unnatural" interference in the marketplace. In particular, the Conservative views the growth of big government in capitalist society as the greatest threat to economic progress. Milton Friedman, Nobel Laureate and preeminent figure in the Conservative Chicago school, has argued that government has moved from being merely an instrumentality necessary to sustain the economic and social order and become an instrument of oppression. Friedman's prescription for what "ought to be" on the matter of government is clear:

> A government which maintained law and order, defined property rights, served as a means whereby we could modify property rights and other rules of the economic game, adjudicated disputes about the interpretation of the rules, enforced contracts, promoted competition, provided a monetary framework, engaged in activities to counter technical monopolies and to overcome neighborhood effects widely regarded as sufficiently important to justify government intervention, and which supplemented private charity and the private family in protecting the irresponsible, whether madman or child—such a government would clearly have important functions to perform. The consistent liberal is not an anarchist.*

The antigovernment position of Conservatives in fact goes further than merely pointing out the dangers to individual freedom. To Conservatives, the growth of big government itself causes or worsens economic problems. For instance, the growth of elaborate government

*Milton Friedman, *Capitalism and Freedom* (Chicago: University of Chicago Press, 1962), p. 34.

policies to improve the conditions of labor, such as minimum-wage laws, social security protection, and the like, are seen as actually harming labor in general. A wage higher than that determined by the market will provide greater income for some workers, but, the Conservative argument runs, it will reduce the total demand for labor and thus dump many workers into unemployment. As this example indicates, the Conservative assault on big government is seen not simply as a moral or ethical question but also in terms of alleged economic effects.

Another unifying feature of the representative Conservative argument is its emphasis on individualism and individual freedom. To be sure, there are those in the Conservative tradition who pay only lip service to this view, but for true Conservatives it is the centerpiece of their logic. As Friedman has expressed it:

> We take freedom of the individual . . . as the ultimate goal in judging social arguments. . . . In a society freedom has nothing to say about what an individual does with his freedom; it is not an all-embracing ethic. Indeed, the major aim of the liberal [here meaning Conservative as we use the term] is to leave the ethical problem for the individual to wrestle with.*

Modern Conservatives as a group exhibit a wide variety of special biases. Not all are as articulate or logically consistent as Friedman's Chicago school. Many are identified more readily by what they oppose than what they seem to be for. While big government, in both its microeconomic interferences and its macroeconomic policy making, is the most obvious common enemy, virtually any institutionalized interference with individual choice is at least ceremonially opposed.

Some critics of the Conservative position are quick to point out that most modern-day Conservatives are not quite consistent on the question of individual freedom when they focus on big business. In fact, until comparatively recently, Conservatives usually did demand the end of business monopoly. Like all concentrations of power, it was viewed as an infringement upon individual rights. The Austrian economist Joseph Schumpeter argued that "Big Business is a half-way house on the road to Socialism." The American Conservative Henry C. Simons observed in the depressed 1930s that "the great enemy to

*Ibid., p. 12.

democracy is monopoly." Accounting for the change to a more accommodating position on big business is not easy. Conservatives seem to offer two basic reasons. First, big business and the so-called monopoly problem have been watched for a long period of time, and the threat of their power subverting freedom is seen as vastly overstated. Second, by far the larger problem is the rise of big government, which is cited as the greatest cause of business inefficiency and monopoly misuse. Another factor that seems implied in Conservative writing is the fear of communism and socialism, both internal and external. To direct an assault on the American business system, even if existing business concentration were a slight impediment to freedom, would lay that system open to direct Radical attack. How serious this supposed contradiction in Conservative logic really is remains a matter of debate among its critics.

Lest some readers rashly dismiss the Conservative position as mere "crackpot economics" having nothing to do with the real world of concentrated economic power, it should be pointed out that Conservatives have recently spoken in a very loud voice. Friedman, for instance, acted as an economic adviser to presidential candidate Barry Goldwater in 1964 and to President Richard Nixon, and he contributes a widely read editorial column in *Newsweek* magazine. Meanwhile, business enterprise, reacting to public (particularly youthful) distrust of the business system, embarked on a "reeducation" campaign in the mid-1970s. While not all of the efforts of such agencies as the Institute for Small Business or the National Association of Manufacturers can, strictly speaking, be called "Conservative," the overall stress on individualism and private enterprise has supported the Conservative argument. Although the Conservative position was badly eroded in the several decades after the 1929 crash and later by the virtually total victory of Keynesian ideas, Conservatism now claims a growing constituency among businesspeople, ordinary citizens, and economics students. Without much doubt, Conservatives have benefited from the antigovernment attitude that has grown up following Vietnam, Watergate, and chronic stagflation.

THE LIBERAL PARADIGM

According to a national opinion poll, Americans tend to associate the word "Liberal" with big government, Franklin Roosevelt, labor unions, and welfare. Time was, not too long ago, when "Liberal" stood not just as a proud appellation but seemed fairly to characterize the natural drift of the whole country. At the height of his popularity and before the Vietnam war toppled his administration, Lyndon Johnson, speaking of the new "Liberal" consensus, observed:

> After years of ideological controversy, we have grown used to the new relationship between government, households, businesses, labor and agriculture. The tired slogans that made constructive discourse difficult have lost their meaning for most Americans. It has become abundantly clear that our society wants neither to turn backward the clock of history nor to discuss our present problems in a doctrinaire or partisan spirit.

Liberals speak less certainly now. Some might argue that they are a lot less visible in the American economics profession, or at least that they are a lot less vocal in identifying theirs as a "Liberal" position. Although what we will specify as the Liberal position in American economic thought still dominates the teaching and practice of economic reasoning, Vietnam, the recessions of 1970 and 1974–1975, and persistent inflation have dented the seemingly invincible Liberal armor of a decade ago.

While Conservatives and Radicals are comparatively easily identified by a representative position, Liberals are more difficult. In terms of public policy positions, the Liberal spectrum ranges all the way from those favoring a very moderate level of government intervention to those advocating broad government planning of the economy.

Despite the great distance between the defining poles of Liberal thought, several basic points can be stated as unique to the Liberal paradigm. First, like their Conservative counterparts, Liberals are defenders of the principle of private property and the business system. These, however, are not categorical rights as we observed in the Conservative case. Individual claims to property or the ability to act freely in the marketplace are subject to the second Liberal principle—that social welfare and the maintenance of the entire economy supersede individual interest. In a vicious condemnation of what we would presently call the Conservative position, John Maynard Keynes directly assaulted the philosophical grounds which set the individual over society. Keynes argued:

> It is not true that individuals possess a prescriptive "natural liberty" in their economic activities. There is no "compact" conferring perpetual

rights on those who Have or on those who Acquire. The world is not so governed from above that private and social interest always coincide. It is not a correct deduction from the Principles of Economics that enlightened self-interest always operates in the public interest. Nor is it true that self-interest generally is enlightened; more often individuals acting separately to promote their own ends are too ignorant or too weak to attain even these. Experience does not show that individuals, when they make up a social unit, are always less clear-sighted than when they act separately.*

To the Liberal, then, government intervention in, and occasional direct regulation of, aspects of the national economy is neither a violation of principle nor an abridgement of "natural economic law." The benefits to the whole society from intervention simply outweigh any natural right claims. The forms of intervention may vary but their pragmatic purpose is obvious—to tinker and manipulate in order to produce greater social benefits.

Government intervention and regulation go back several decades in American history. The Progressives of the early twentieth century were the first to support direct government regulation of the economy. Faced with the individual and collective excesses of the giant enterprises of the era of the Robber Barons, the Progressives followed a number of reformist paths in the period from 1900 to 1920. One was the regulation of monopolistic enterprise, to be accomplished either through direct antitrust regulation or by stimulating competition. Pursuit of these policies was entrusted to a new government regulatory agency, the Federal Trade Commission (created in 1914), an expanded Justice Department and court system, and greater state regulatory powers. Second, indirect business regulation was effected by such Progressive developments as legalization of unions, the passage of social legislation at both the federal and state levels, tax reforms, and controls over production (for example, laws against food adulteration)—all of which tended to circumvent the power of business and subject it to the public interest.

Although the legislation and leadership of the administrations of Theodore Roosevelt, William Howard Taft, and Woodrow Wilson went a long way in moderating the old laissez-faire ideology of the previous era, actual interference in business affairs remained slight un-

*John M. Keynes, "The End of Laissez Faire," in *Essays in Persuasion* (New York: Norton, 1963), p. 68.

til the Great Depression. By 1933 perhaps as many as one out of every three Americans was out of work (the official figures said 25 percent), business failures were common, and the specter of total financial and production collapse hung heavy over the whole country. In the bread lines and shantytowns known as "Hoovervilles" as well as on Main Street, there were serious mutterings that the American business system had failed. Business leaders, who had always enjoyed a hero status in the history books and even among ordinary citizens, had become pariahs. Enter at this point Franklin Roosevelt, the New Deal, and the modern formulation of "Liberal" government-business policies. Despite violent attacks upon him from the Conservative media, FDR pragmatically abandoned his own conservative roots and, in a bewildering series of legislative enactments and presidential decrees, laid the foundation of "public interest" criteria for government regulation of the marketplace. *Whatever might work was tried.* The National Recovery Administration (NRA) encouraged industry cartels and price setting. The Tennessee Valley Authority (TVA) was an attempt at publicly owned enterprise. At the Justice Department, Attorney General Thurman Arnold initiated more antitrust actions than all of his predecessors. And a mass of "alphabet agencies" was created to deal with this or that aspect of the Depression.

Intervention to protect labor and extensions of social welfare provisions were not enough to end the Depression. It was the massive spending for World War II that finally restored prosperity. With this prosperity came the steady influence of Keynes, who had argued in the 1930s that only through government fiscal and monetary efforts to keep up the demand for goods and services could prosperity be reached and maintained. Keynes's arguments for government policies to maintain high levels of investment and hence employment and consumer demand became Liberal dogma. To be a Liberal was to be a Keynesian and vice versa.

Alvin Hansen, Keynes's first and one of his foremost proponents in the United States, could scarcely hide his glee in 1957 as he described the Liberal wedding of Keynesian policies with the older government interventionist position this way:

> Within the last few decades the role of the economist has profoundly changed. And why? The reason is that economics has become operational. It has become operational because we have at long last developed a mixed public-private economy. This society is committed to the

welfare state and full employment. The government is firmly in the driver's seat. In such a world, practical policy problems became grist for the mill of economic analysis. Keynes, more than any other economist of our time, has helped to rescue economics from the negative position to which it had fallen to become once again a science of the Wealth of Nations and the art of Political Economy.*

Despite the Liberal propensity for tinkering—either through selected market intervention or through macro policy action—most Liberals, like Conservatives, still rely upon supply and demand analysis to explain prices and market performance. Their differences with Conservatives on the functioning of markets, determination of output, pricing, and so forth lie not so much in describing what is happening as in evaluating how to respond to what is happening. For instance, there is little theoretical difference between Conservatives and Liberals on how prices are determined under monopolistic conditions. However, to the Conservative, the market itself is the best regulator and preventive of monopoly abuse. To the Liberal, monopoly demands government intervention.

As was noted before, the Liberal dogma covers a wide spectrum of opinion. For most Liberals, Hansen's description of the mixed economy is accurate enough. However, among "left-wing" Liberals, such as Robert Heilbroner or John Kenneth Galbraith, there is considerable support for the position that capitalism as described in conventional theory either must be ended or has in fact ceased to exist.

Robert Heilbroner points to the crisis within capitalism as basic to capitalism itself. He argues: "The persistent breakdowns of the capitalist economy, whatever their immediate precipitating factors, can all be traced to a single underlying cause. This is the anarchic or planless character of capitalist production."** This planlessness, according to Heilbroner, sets the stage for government to act as a necessary regulator.

To the left-leaning and always iconoclastic John Kenneth Galbraith, who sees problems of technology rather than profit dominating the giant corporation, a more rational atmosphere for decision making must be created. In brief, the modern firm demands a high

*Alvin H. Hansen, *The American Economy* (New York: McGraw-Hill, 1957), p. 175.

**Robert Heilbroner, *The Limits of American Capitalism* (New York: Harper & Row, 1966), p. 88.

order of internal and external planning of output, prices, and capital. The interests of the firm and state become fused in this planning process, and the expanded role of Liberal government in the whole economy and society becomes obvious. While Galbraith currently maintains that he is a socialist, the Liberal outcome of his program is obvious in that (1) he never explicitly takes up the expropriation of private property, and (2) he still accepts a precarious social balance between public and private interest.

While Galbraith's Liberalism leads to the planned economy, most Liberals stop well before this point. Having rejected the logic of self-regulating markets and accepted the realities of giant business enterprise, Liberals unashamedly admit to being pragmatic tinkerers—ever adjusting and interfering with business decision making in an effort to assert the changing "public interest." Yet all this must be done while still respecting basic property rights and due process. Under these arrangements business regulation amounts to a protection of business itself as well as the equal protection of other interest groups in pluralist American society.

The effect of this position has not been lost on business. Most large businesses have accommodated to and, to a large extent, are dependent upon governmental intervention in the economy. The Conservative depiction of most Liberals as being antibusiness does not withstand the empirical test. For instance, in 1964 Henry Ford organized a highly successful businessmen's committee for the Liberal Johnson while Conservative Goldwater, with Friedman as his adviser, gained little or no big business support.

THE RADICAL PARADIGM

Specifying a Radical position would have been no problem a decade or two ago. Outside of a handful of Marxist scholars, some socialists left over from the 1920s and 1930s, and a few unconventional muckrakers, there was no functioning Radical tradition in American economic thought. However, the two-sided struggles of the 1960s over racism and poverty at home and the war in Vietnam produced a resurgence of Radical critiques. By the mid-1970s, the Radical caucus within the American Economic Association had forced on that body topics for discussion at annual meetings that directly challenged conventional economic thought. The Union of Radical Political Economy

(URPE) could boast over 2,000 members and its own journal. Meanwhile, basic textbooks in economics began to add chapters on "Radical Economics."

Radical economics had arrived—but what, precisely, was it? To many non-Radicals it was simply Marxist economics warmed over, but this explanation, though basically true, is too simple. To be sure, the influence of Marx, the leading critic of capitalism, is pervasive in most Radical critiques. But Radical economics is more than Marx. His analysis of capitalism is over a hundred years old and deals with a very different set of capitalist problems. With this qualification in mind, we will argue, however, that no study of current Radical thought is possible unless one starts with, or at least touches upon, the ideas of Karl Marx. Although a few iconoclastic Radicals will reject a close association with Marxism, the evidence is overwhelming that Marxist analysis is central to understanding the representative Radical position in America today.

Since the Marxist critique is likely to be less familiar to many readers than the basic arguments of Conservatives or Liberals, it is necessary to be somewhat more detailed in specifying the Radical position. As will be quickly apparent, the Radical world view rests on greatly different assumptions about the economic order than those of the Conservatives and the Liberals.

In brief, Marx's scenario for capitalist progress was the following: Depending as they do on the steady accumulation of profit to expand capital and output, capitalists will appropriate surplus labor value from the worker. To capitalists this is a normal and necessary course. If workers were paid, or in any way received, the full value of their labor, capital accumulation, and thus economic growth, would be impossible. However, as this accumulation proceeds, with the steady transference of living labor into capital (what Marx called "dead labor"), capitalists face a crisis. With more and more of their costs reflecting dependence upon capital and with surplus labor value their only source of profits, capitalists are confronted with the reality of not being able to expand surplus. Unless they can exploit labor further by intensifying work, lowering real wages, lengthening the working day, or making similar changes, they face a falling rate of profit on their capital investment. Moreover, with markets limited and workers' ability to consume being constantly reduced, there is a tendency among capitalists to overproduce.

These trends set certain systemic tendencies in motion. Out of the chaos of capitalist competitive struggles for profits in a limited market, there develops a drive toward "concentration and centralization." In other words, the size of businesses grows and the number of enterprises shrinks. However, the problems of the falling rate of profit and chronic overproduction create violent fluctuations in the business cycle. Each depression points ever more clearly toward capitalist economic collapse. Meanwhile, among the increasingly impoverished workers, there is a steady growth of a "reserve army of unemployed"—workers who are now unemployable as production decreases. Simultaneously, increasing misery generates class consciousness and revolutionary activity among the working class. As the economic disintegration of capitalist institutions worsens, the subjective consciousness of workers grows to the point where they successfully overthrow the capitalist system. In the new society the workers themselves take control of the production process, and accumulation for the interest of a narrow capitalist class ceases.

Marx, of course, recognized that these developments would not be perfectly lineal. Capitalists could and would undertake counteracting policies. Greater exploitation, profitable foreign trade, and technological advances could temporarily head off the tendency for profits to fall. Lenin was to add later that imperialism, which amounted to exporting the surplus production problem to underdeveloped nations, could also buy time.

More recently, Paul Baran and Paul Sweezy have argued that the development of monopoly capitalism (along with the imperialist thrust) has allowed the system a respite from the accumulation and profit crisis. According to this neo-Marxist interpretation, modern capitalism is monopoly capitalism.* The key institution in the accumulation process remains the business firm, but unlike its predecessors, the modern giant enterprise is an effective "price maker," able to set prices through collective actions so as to maximize total income. However, ending capitalism's tendency toward falling prices is only half the problem. Enough goods must still be sold for a firm to realize income beyond its production costs. In other words, the surplus must rise *and* it must be absorbed. In Keynesian terms, it would be said that

---

*See Paul Baran and Paul Sweezy, *Monopoly Capital* (New York: Monthly Review Press, 1966). This "revising" of orthodox Marxist theory of capitalist development is, in one form or another, accepted by most modern Radicals.

effective demand must remain high. According to Baran and Sweezy, monopoly capital has been able to accomplish this in the following ways: (1) by highly effective manipulation of consumer tastes for functionally useless and irrational goods ("the sales effort"), (2) by encouraging a high and increasing government expenditure in both the civilian and military sectors, and (3) by the imperialist domination of overseas markets and sources of raw materials. In all this activity, government is seen as an agent for monopoly capital, shaping its social, fiscal, and foreign policies in order to legitimize the monopoly order and enhance monopoly profits.

While the old capitalist crisis of falling surplus value has been replaced by a tendency for the surplus to rise, most Radicals see this as a temporary development. The old contradictions between capital and labor remain, state actions to maintain demand and to uphold order are not without limits, and the internal crisis of the capitalist economy has exploded into a world struggle among nations. Despite its recent history of success, monopoly capitalism, say the Radicals, will not halt the overall suicidal trajectory of capitalist development. Only the forms and the timing of crisis have changed.

To followers of the Baran and Sweezy critique, probably the most significant of these changes is the alteration of Marx's predictions of proletarian revolution. Revolutionary pressures, rather than rising first from the traditional class of industrial workers, are now greater at the periphery of capitalism—among the exploited populations of Third World nations and the growing subproletariat at home. Monopoly capital may have slowed the growth of exploitation for some workers, but it has greatly increased it for others. Class struggle still looms as the eventual vehicle for capitalism's destruction—but not precisely as Marx had argued.

Marxist analysis is, of course, more penetrating than this short resume can indicate. One further point that should be examined briefly is Marx's view of the relationship between a society's organization for production and its social relations. To Marx, capitalism was more than economics. Private values, religion, the family, the educational system, and political structures were all shaped by capitalist class domination and by the goal of production for private profit. It is important to recognize this tenet in any discussion of how Marxists—or Radicals with a Marxist orientation—approach contemporary social and economic problems. Marxists do not separate economics from politics or private belief. For instance, racism cannot be abstracted to the level of an ethical question. Its roots are seen in the capitalist production process. Nor is the state ever viewed as a neutrality able to act without class bias. Bourgeois democracy as we know it is seen simply as a mask for class domination. The state is quite simply the tool of dominant interests. To the Marxist, the problem with the system is the system; no resolution of capitalist crises is really possible short of changing the system itself.

Marx, in his early writings before his great work, *Capital*, had emphasized the "qualitative" exploitation of capitalism. Modern Radicals have revitalized this early Marx in their "quality of life" assaults on the present order. In these they emphasize the problems of worker alienation, commodity fetishism, and the wasteful and useless production of modern capitalism. The human or social problems of modern life are seen as rooted in the way the whole society is geared to produce more and more.

In addition to their Marxist heritage, modern Radicals derive much of their impulse from what they see as the apparent failure of Liberalism. Liberal promises to pursue policies of general social improvement are perceived as actions to protect only *some* interest groups. In general, those benefiting under Liberal arrangements are seen as those who have always gained. The corporation is not controlled. It is more powerful than ever. Rule by elites has not ended nor have the elites changed. Moreover, the national goals of the Liberal ethic—to improve our overall national well-being—have stimulated the exploitation of poor nations, continued the cold war, and increased the militarization of the economy.

Quite obviously the Marxist prediction of capitalism's final collapse has not yet come to pass. For critics of the Radical position, this fact, along with certain internal analytic problems, is quite sufficient to consign their critique to the garbage heap. Such a view is somewhat unenlightened. First of all, Marx's ideas in one form or another are more prominent in the world today than the other two ideologies discussed here. Second, Marxism—at least as American Radical scholars have developed and used it—is more a way of looking at the world than a prophecy of things to come. It is the technique of analysis rather than the century-old "truth" of Marx's specific analysis that counts.

As noted before, not all Radicals subscribe to all Marxist doctrine, but Marx in one form or another remains the central element of the Radical challenge. His fundamental contention that the system of private production must be changed remains the badge of membership in the Radical ranks. This sets them apart from mainstream Conservative and Liberal economists.

Critics of Radicalism usually point out that Radical analyses are hopelessly negativistic. Radicals, they say, describe the problems of capitalism without offering a solution other than the end of the whole system. While there is some truth to this charge, we shall see in the following sections that some solutions are indeed offered. But even if their program were vague, Radicals would argue that their greatest contribution is in revealing the truth of the capitalist system.

Applying the Analysis to the Issues

We have identified the representative paradigms; now we will put them to use. The following selected issues by no means exhaust the economic and political crises troubling the nation. Nevertheless this book should still provide a good-sized sampling of the social agenda confronting us. The issues presented here were selected because of their immediacy and representativeness in illustrating the diverse ideological approaches of Conservative, Liberal, and Radical economic analyses.

In each of the following issues, the representative paradigms are presented in a first-person advocacy approach. The reader might do well to regard the arguments like those in a debate. As in a debate, one should be careful to distinguish between substantive differences and mere logical or debating strategies. Thus, some points may be quite convincing while others seem shallow. However, the reader should remember that, shallow or profound, these are representative political-economic arguments advanced by various economic schools.

The sequence in presenting the paradigms is consistent throughout the text: first Conservative, then Liberal, and finally Radical. In terms of the logical and historical development of contemporary economic ideologies, this sequence is most sensible. However, it is certainly not necessary to read the arguments in this order. Each one stands by itself. Nor is an ideological position intentionally set out as a straw man in any debate.

Readers should look at each position critically. They should test their own familiarity with economic concepts and their common sense against what they read in any representative case. Finally, of course, as students of economics and as citizens, they must make their own decisions. They determine who, if anyone, is the winner of the debate.

Because of space limitations, the representative arguments are brief, and some important ideas have been boiled down to a very few sentences. Also, within each of the three major positions there is a wide variety of arguments, which may sometimes be at variance with one another. Conservatives, Liberals, and Radicals disagree among themselves on specific analyses and programs. For the sake of simplicity, we have chosen not to emphasize these differences but arbitrarily (although after much thought) have tried to select the most representative arguments. Each paradigm's discussion of an issue presents a critique of present public policy and, usually, a specific program proposal.

In all of the arguments, the factual and empirical evidence offered has been checked for accuracy. It is instructive in itself that, given the nature of economic "facts," they can be marshaled to "prove" a great variety of different ideological positions. Different or even similar evidence supports different truths, depending on the truth we wish to prove.

PART 2

PROBLEMS
IN THE
MARKETPLACE

Part 2 focuses upon issues generally accepted by economists as *microeconomic* in their analysis. Microeconomics examines specific economic units—households, firms, industries, labor groups—and how these individual units behave.

The focal point of formal microeconomic analysis since its nineteenth-century origins has been the market. Accordingly, the organization of Part 2 is to look at selected problems in the marketplace. The topics include problems of agricultural supply and demand, consumer market behavior, energy-environment tradeoffs, firm size, government regulation, international business development, labor unions, and income distribution. Each topic presents some important dimension of market performance; each has been selected for its representative qualities in developing a broadened understanding of microeconomic problems within the contemporary American economy.

ISSUE 1

Agriculture After the Russian Grain Deals

A New Era or the Same Old Mess?

Farmers should raise less corn and more Hell.
Mary E. Lease, Kansas, 1890s

There's nothing evil about exporting food.
Earl Butz, Secretary of Agriculture, 1975

It's the criticism of these sales to the Russians that'll bring on higher food prices, not the sales. All those complaints amount to an open invitation to jack up prices.
Don Woodward,
National Association of Wheat Growers, 1975

As a farmboy, I can remember my dear old Hoosier grandmother telling me to watch out for some American businessmen; they will trade with the Devil if they can make a profit.
Congressman John Rarick, 1972

Farmers are motivated by just old-fashioned greed.
Robert Bergland, Secretary of Agriculture, 1979

THE PROBLEM

In 1972 the United States and the Soviet Union secretly negotiated the sale of 19 million metric tons of American grain. Ironically, this sale was completed precisely as the United States was mining Haiphong Harbor in North Vietnam and bombing rail lines north of Hanoi in an effort to stop the flow of Russian goods into the war zone. Although critics were to attack the sale as the "Great Grain Robbery," Secretary of Agriculture Earl Butz defended it as a boon to the American farmer. When accused of being willing to trade with the devil if it meant a profit, the feisty Butz replied, "If he has dollars."

Contrary to general opinion, the Russians' decision to purchase almost a quarter of the 1972 American wheat crop, as well as a large amount of corn and soybeans, resulted only partially from the failure of their grain harvest. For a number of years Soviet leadership had been yielding to consumer pressure to produce more meat protein. Of necessity, this meant providing greater amounts of grain for beef in feeding lots. When the 1971 and 1972 crops failed to reach expectations, the Soviet leaders decided not to slaughter their beef herds or tell their people to eat potatoes and beets. They chose instead to buy United States grain and to allow their "protein program" to continue.

The Russian purchase in 1972–1973 was not a one-shot affair. Some 8 million metric tons of grain were sold to the Soviet Union in 1974 and about 3 million tons the next year. The Russians experienced crop failures again in 1975 and negotiated another sale—this one for 13 million tons—for 1976. Although this sale was temporarily suspended when world-wide prospects of underproduction caused world and domestic grain prices to skyrocket, it was reinstituted when the bumper 1975 harvest came in. Meanwhile, the Soviet Union and the United States concluded a five-year agreement for Russian purchase of 6 to 8 million tons of corn and wheat each year, with the American government reserving the right to curtail sales if reserves or domestic output fell too sharply.

To growers and sellers, the "discovery" of the Russian market was a critical new direction for American agriculture, an end to the long era of chronic excess production, depressed prices, and dependence upon varieties of government subsidy programs. By selling the equivalent of one quarter of the 1972 crop, the Russian grain deal literally emptied American storage bins and grain elevators. This additional demand drove the prices of wheat from $1.70 per bushel in mid-1972 to $5.00 in 1973. Farmers were ecstatic, and there was talk that the old problem of overproduction had finally been eliminated.

The boom, however, was not permanent. Sales to the Russians and other importers did hold up prices through 1976; but with the bumper crop of 1977, wheat prices tumbled all the way down to $2.50 per bushel. Farmers again agitated for enlarged government aid, and many believed that "the new era of farm prosperity" supposedly heralded by the Soviet grain sales had permanently evaporated. Consumers, meanwhile, tended to view the agricultural events of the 1970s somewhat differently than the farmers. Whether the grain sales were the cause or not, they marked the end of comparatively low food prices in the United States. Although inflation gripped the economy after 1972, food prices led general price increases, accelerating at about twice the overall consumer price advance. They went up more than 14 percent per year in 1973, 1974, and 1975. To many, farmer prosperity came to be understood as consumer misery. However, as the immediate agricultural boom ebbed in 1977 and 1978, consumers noticed no change in food price tendencies. Ironically, as grain bins again overflowed, prices of food advanced at annual rates in excess of 10 percent for 1978 and 1979.

Looking back at the developments in agriculture as the 1970s drew to a close, there was wide disagreement among economists about how to interpret the Russian grain deals and subsequent events affecting farm output and prices. The issue became increasingly blurred in 1980, when the United States responded to the Russian invasion of Afghanistan by embargoing agricultural sales to the Soviets. With that market closed, the surplus problem seemed certain to worsen. Political pressure for direct governmental action has increased accordingly, but economists are not of one mind about returning to the policies of the past.

On the matter of food prices, however, there is more general agreement on trends if not on causes. The era of low food prices in the United States is over. Quite simply, you can't take eating for granted any more.

SYNOPSIS The Conservative argument holds that the free operation of supply and demand is the correct and most efficient determinant of agricultural prices. The Liberal argument anticipates a general upward movement of food prices due to increased world demand but still argues for some governmental regulation to protect consumers and farmers from wild market fluctuations. Radical arguments hold that the rising food prices are mostly "contrived," held up by agribusiness and middleman profits.

The Conservative Argument

Americans generally recognize that there is a "farm problem," but its nature and causes are incorrectly understood. Consumers are aware of rising prices, and many see this price trend as directly traceable to the massive sales of grain abroad in the early and mid-1970s, thus simplifying the issue into a false cause-and-effect relationship. They have forgotten the disastrous price policies of the past which are the basis for current problems. As a result they also overlook the real advances in agricultural policy evidenced in the Russian grain sale.

POLICY FAILURE IN TIMES OF SURPLUS

Although many politicians and some economists may believe and act to the contrary, supply and demand remain the determinants of prices and resource allocation. Of course, it is possible to contrive "desired" prices and output through a manipulated agricultural policy, but, regardless of short-run successes, such policies must produce serious misallocations and costs in the long run.

For a considerable period of time, at least since World War I, most economists understood the American farm problem as a matter of rising productivity with comparatively stable or modestly increasing demand. The result in the marketplace has been a downward pressure on farm prices and the production of agricultural surpluses. The economic options under such conditions were either to let prices fall to whatever level they might reach or to maintain prices artificially. Due largely to political pressure from the farm lobby in the depressed 1930s the goverment devised a variety—really a potpourri—of farm programs to keep prices up and supposedly guarantee a living income to the American farmer. Tariffs were slapped on foreign farm products. Certain "basic" farm products were guaranteed a government-paid "parity" price well above the going market price. Bureaucrats worked out production controls and acreage allotments, with the curious economic aim of paying producers not to produce. Except for the interlude of World War II, when vast overseas demand for United States agricultural products briefly restored farm prosperity, farm prices have been held up only by government price manipulation.

As a result, Americans have paid much more for their food than was necessary, and they have paid more than they realized. Most

Americans probably did not notice the higher prices. Due to the phenomenal productivity of American agriculture and the steadily rising standard of living in the United States, these artificially higher prices seemed quite tolerable. Food expenditures, as a share of total consumer purchases, actually declined in the postwar years.

However, few consumers realized that they were paying an additional price. Consumers are also taxpayers, and as such they had to bear the cost of expensive government subsidies paid to farmers and of maintaining the bureaucracy set up to administer various farm programs. By 1970 these expenses were directly costing $6.3 billion per year. Since the early 1930s they have cost a minimum of $100 billion. If the taxpayer cost of food is added to the consumer cost of food, we then get a clearer picture of our food bill. And, it is not as inexpensive as we might have imagined.

These artificial prices, moreover, interfered with the flow of human resources out of agriculture that otherwise might have been expected. The "gentle" Liberals were supposedly interested in cushioning the declining income of millions of American farmers. In fact, many of these farmers were functionally redundant. Many who might have moved off their relatively unproductive family farms were enticed to stay by the promise (but not reality) of higher farm incomes. These farmers, though unable to take advantage of increasingly expensive farm technology, stayed on their farms when, for their own benefit, they should have moved to other jobs.

Meanwhile, higher American farm prices closed off American food products from world markets. Due to climate, soil, technology, and agricultural science, American agriculture had an enormous advantage over the rest of the world in food production. This advantage and the export income it would have created was frittered away by programs aimed at keeping domestic prices relatively high. Precisely at a time when the United States faced a worsening balance of international payments (after World War II), the government pursued an agricultural program that denied the nation earnings it could have been making by exporting food.

THE NEW OUTLOOK

The vast increase in world population, the growing scarcity of food, and the rising cost of food production as a result of energy costs had pushed world prices upward even before the Russians opted for more steak and less borscht. The Russian grain purchases, because of their timing and size, have been overdramatized as the cause of buyer misery at the checkout counter. The worldwide increase in food prices had simply caught up with American agricultural prices. Thus the laws of supply and demand and not an enlightened Congress eliminated the costly farm subsidy program of the American government.

With world prices higher and world markets opening up to American agriculture, Des Moines consumers may find themselves competing with those in Minsk for a loaf of bread or a steak. Lest this observation cause panic, it should be recalled that food purchases still amount to only 17 percent of American disposable income. That leaves a great deal more discretionary income in Des Moines than it does in Minsk.

For the future, though, Americans should expect a long-run gentle rise in food prices (although there may be extreme short-range ups and downs). This does not mean imminent starvation in the United States. First of all, much of our present food costs are the result of buying convenience items (TV dinners, for instance) or purely luxury food goods (exotic gourmet specialties). Rising prices will require some households to reduce this type of consumption, to reshuffle their specific food demands, and to forgo some nonfood purchases, but this will hardly lower the quality of food consumed or have much effect on our standard of living. The recent trend toward home baking, cooking, and canning is a consumer reaction to the market, not a sign of national economic decay.

Second, many consumer complaints about rising food prices do not comprehend the structure of food costs. The farm prices themselves account for only 40 percent of the grocery store price of processed food. The bulk of food costs come from middlemen charges. Fuel and labor charges are the principal elements in the rising expenses of moving food from field to tabletop. With this evidence before us, it is clear that the Russian grain deals' impact on prices, even with their effects of vastly and quickly increasing demand, has not been the most significant factor in the rising cost of food. In other words, foreign trade should not be singled out as the basic cause of higher food prices.

At any rate, food prices must reflect actual production and distribution costs. The political need for tax subsidies will then disappear and tax bills should be lowered. Capital and human resource allocation in agriculture will respond to actual and not manipulated market conditions of demand and supply. If the Russian grain deal stands for anything, it stands for the end of ill-advised and inefficient paternalism and protection for American agriculture. It also marks the economic revitalization of that industry and the beginning of full exploitation of our comparative advantage in this area.

The significance of overseas sales of American farm products should not be minimized. As the following chart shows, the foreign food market grew from about $2 billion in 1972 to over $12 billion by 1976. Without these gains, our trade balance for total exports ("all products") would be disastrous. Whether Americans realize it or not, our revitalized agricultural sector is our best, perhaps our only, hedge against Arab oil "stickups" and the dwindling efficiency of our nonagricultural production. Looked at this way, recent cost increases to consumers have been a small price to pay.

FIGURE 1.1   U.S. BALANCE OF TRADE, 1954–1975

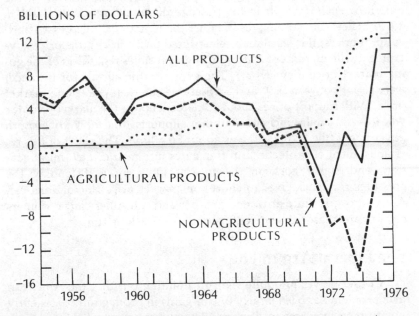

Source: Foreign Agricultural Trade of the United States, U.S. Department of Agriculture, as cited in Monthly Review of the Federal Reserve Bank of Kansas City, April, 1976.

There are those, of course, who will still point to the Russian grain deals as special taxes that were levied on the consumer because the price of food did rise abruptly between 1972 and 1975. Most of this increase, however, resulted from the inelastic nature of agricultural supply in the short run. That is, there could not be an immediate production reaction to the Russian wheat deal or other foreign sales. Wheat, soybeans, and corn cannot be produced as quickly as automobiles. By 1976 agricultural producers had greatly increased their supply and, as the law of supply and demand would have it, food prices began to level off and even come down a bit. While small variations in price will be common as supply and demand falter and rise from time to time, the variations will be a small price to pay for restoring market-directed order to agriculture. Food prices overall will likely rise as the demands of a hungry world grow. That, however, will not be the fault of the Russians, then-Secretary Butz, or American farmers.

The political effort to withstand farm interest-group pressures when periodic excess production or slack demand forces prices down demands great courage. Regrettably, the Carter administration did not show such strength in the passage of a new agricultural act in 1977. Instead of standing fast against the temporarily depressed agricultural prices, this legislation reinstituted target prices (the price government will guarantee farmers through subsidies regardless of the going market price they sell at). The supports for wheat, for instance, were set at between $.50 and $.75 above the then prevailing market price. With support prices about 25 percent above the market price for wheat—and similar increases in other supports—the 1977 price tag to government (the taxpayers) was about $6 billion. The result of this re-establishment of protectionism translates into inefficiency, misallocation, and higher costs in the future. Only by withstanding the pressures for quick fixes to short-run market price fluctuations can American agriculture grow and prosper and can American consumers pay fair and reasonable prices for food over the long run.

The Liberal Argument

Conservatives are quite right in pointing out that the American farm problem has been largely one of gains in production consistently outstripping increases in demand. Throughout most of this century, food demand was essentially a function of domestic population increase. Until recently the United States has exported large quantities of food abroad only in time of war. Meanwhile, steady advances in agricultural technology and science have produced greater output, reducing human employment. Table 1.1 puts these gains in perspective.

RISING PRODUCTION AND GROWING CRISIS

Each unit of land has been producing greater yields as a result of new fertilizers and hybrid strains. At the same time, the application of greater capital has substantially reduced the number of manhours needed in production. By the 1930s American farmers were the most productive in the world—and also going broke the fastest. It is easy enough for the Conservative devotee of the laws of supply and de-

Table 1.1   U.S. Agricultural Productivity: 1800–1950

Crop	1800	1880	1920	1950
Wheat				
yield/acre (bu)	15	13	14	17
manhours/ 100 bu	373	152	87	28
Corn				
yield/acre (bu)	25	26	28	39
manhours/ 100 bu	344	180	113	39
Cotton				
yield/acre (bu)	147	179	160	283
manhours/bale	601	318	269	126

Source: U.S. Bureau of the Census, *Historical Statistics of the United States,* Series K 83–97, Washington, D.C., 1960.

mand to say: "Leave things alone and let the devil take the hindmost." The fact is, excess agricultural production and falling prices affected people—a great number of people.

In 1930 about 44 percent of the American population was still classified as rural. About 57 million people still lived on farms or in small towns dependent on agriculture. At least 31 million were full-time farmers. To have adopted the Conservative proposal of letting these human resources "drop out" of farming if it didn't pay and find alternative employment would have been inhumane and stupid. In the Great Depression decade, there was no alternative employment. The exodus from farming (which did reduce the farm population to less than 10 million by 1972) would have been faster and would have created even greater employment problems for the general economy.

With this in mind, the New Deal policies of reducing farm migration through price supports, direct payments, and other subsidies (easy credit, electrification, and so on) were created. To be sure, these programs *did* artificially hold up farm prices and, in terms of subsidy costs, *did* pass the cost of the farm program on to taxpayers at large. But they also brought a degree of order to the agricultural sector and improved the income distribution inequities between farmers and nonfarmers. For example, in 1934 farm income was only about a third that of nonfarm income ($163 per year per person compared to $469 per year per person). By 1964, after nearly thirty years of New Deal-type "tinkering," annual farm income per person stood at $1,405 and nonfarm income at $2,318. Moreover, the supposed costs of federal farm subsidy programs are vastly overstated. The $6.3 billion paid in 1970 was less than a tenth of all federally paid subsidies to the private sector; of this total about $4 billion was paid out for just three agricultural products—feed grains, wheat, and cotton.

Before concluding this topic, it must be conceded that past American agricultural policy has had its failures. For instance, the improved income situation of the farm sector, a noteworthy achievement, masks some other problems. The farm programs of the 1930s, 1940s, and 1950s could not halt the eventual decline of the family farm or the regional small farm in the Northeast. With greater application of technology and changes in farm production, farm employment (mostly family workers) fell from 7 million in 1960 to 4.5 million in 1977. Although average farm income did improve relative to nonfarm income during the 1960s and 1970s, maldistribution of earnings within the farm sector increased.

As Figure 1.2 shows, the large farms ($100,000 or more per year of gross income) grew from a 17.3 percent share of farm earnings in 1960 to a 46.8 percent share in 1976. These figures are even more impressive when we look at the number of farms in each income category. As the data shows, these large enterprises amount to only 3.9 percent of all farms. Over 80 percent of American farms are comparatively small (gross earnings of less than $40,000).

We can easily conclude then that the few big farms have been getting bigger but that most remaining farmers still earn very modest incomes. In such a situation, it is quite likely that past farm subsidy

FIGURE 1.2   THE RISE OF LARGE FARMS, 1960–1976

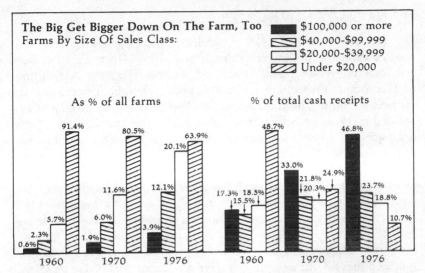

Source: Reprinted by permission from Sales & Marketing Management magazine. Copyright 1977.

programs and payments for nonproduction have provided the greatest gains for the large farm producer. However, even with such shortcomings, the earlier farm policies are defensible. They did raise and maintain average farm earnings above what a purely laissez-faire solution would have produced, thus strengthening agriculture in general. They mitigated the impact of the Depression on many farmers, and when farm out-migration did occur after World War II, it was more easily absorbed into a growing economy. The Conservatives' laissez-faire policy would have emptied rural America sooner, encouraged the growth of only the largest farms, and led to unacceptable human costs.

While past Liberal farm policies are historically defensible, it is apparent that America has moved into a new agricultural era demanding policy changes. The capital-intensive nature of agriculture is everywhere apparent and the day of the small family farm has passed. At the same time, the long-run future growth in world food demand is undeniable. These trends, however, are misunderstood by the free market advocates.

DEVELOPING A NEW FARM PROGRAM

Between 1972 and 1975, agricultural prices generally rose. As long as that was the case, price supports and any effort to restrict output were unnecessary and ill-advised. However, as the Agriculture and Consumer Protection Act of 1973 anticipated, high prices paid to farmers would not hold permanently. The 1973 act, renewed and expanded in 1977, introduced the concept of target pricing. Under this arrangement, government announces a target price on a specified list of commodities. If the market price is below the target price, the government pays the farmer the difference between what they would receive for selling their goods in the market and the targeted figure. According to such a plan, consumers would still enjoy the benefits of the lower market price, but farms would be guaranteed a reasonable return on their crops. To prevent the very large producers from tapping the public treasury for outrageous subsidy payments, the 1973 law specified that no farmer should receive more than $20,000 in payment for any crop.

The Liberals' expectation that pure supply and demand solutions to the agricultural problem would fail were proven by 1977, as farm prices fell precipitously. The agricultural act of that year updated the target prices to adjust for inflation and again provided a floor to farm income. Many farmers argued that the floor was too low. Farmers demonstrated in Washington, and held mildly effective strikes; but the farm sector was protected from the far greater agonies that a Conservative free market program would have created. This, however, is not the last word on the farm problem. In addition to these recent policy changes, others might be considered. For instance, a crop reserve should be established. This would provide a market for certain storable crops in good years as a hedge against drastic price increases in bad times. Finally, farmers might need some help as prices for machinery, fertilizer, and the like continue to rise. This could mean direct government action against monopolistically maintained supplier prices or provision for low-cost loans to help farmers pay for these items.

These efforts should bring stabilization to agriculture for the next decade and beyond. While food prices may go up and down over time, it must be expected that, in general, they will remain higher than

Americans were accustomed to a decade ago. This upward tendency is very likely as production costs rise and American food products become more directly affected by growing world demand. In all this, government must be prepared to intervene to aid the consumer as well as the farmer. The laws of supply and demand can, in fact, be regulated to improve market outcomes.

The Radical Argument

The American farm problem has changed over the past decade from that of surplus production to one of occasional shortages and constantly rising retail prices. The situation for most farmers and all consumers has not changed at all. Under federal agricultural policy, the little guy remains the loser.

THE OLD POLICY: HELP THE BIG GUYS

While most farm programs between 1920 and 1973 were supposedly aimed at protecting the family farm and supporting the agricultural sector in general, they utterly failed to halt the concentration of agriculture into fewer and fewer hands. Programs of price supports and payments for nonproduction stimulated this concentration since small farmers could not possibly reap many gains from them. Between 1930 and 1970, land under cultivation actually increased, but the number of farms declined from 6.5 to 2.9 million. While Liberals reluctantly note this tendency, they do not understand that it has meant higher prices to consumers with few, if any, benefits to most individually owned farms.

The market power of farmers, never very strong anyway, was further eroded during the 1950s and 1960s as marketing procedures were increasingly affected by the entrance of large business corporations into agriculture—*agribusiness*. Food chains bought orchards and feed lots and integrated their operations all the way from planting and slaughtering to store counter. Cereal producers, dairy product firms, baking companies, and other farm purchasers became more concentrated. At the same time suppliers of farm machinery became increasingly integrated. As a result, farmers paid high, monopoly-established prices for equipment and had to sell their produce to a comparatively few buyers. These buyers rarely had to pay more than the support price or "take-it-or-leave-it" prices for nonsupported commodities. Contract production with big companies replaced the old market relationships. For instance, half of all fresh vegetables are grown under contract.

By the early 1970s, agriculture had been "discovered" by the large industrial conglomerates. Agribusiness grew and matured as ITT absorbed Wonder Bread and Smithfield Hams, Ling-Temco-Vought took control of Wilson Meats, Greyhound joined with Armour Packing, and similar mergers took place. Basically, this phenomenon extended and accentuated the "price taker" situation of American farmers, even large farmers. Whether selling to the government, A&P, or General Foods, farmers had long been accustomed to dealing with buyers that set their own prices. The real power of this new and rejuvenated agribusiness would, however, be felt by the consumer as well. The new conglomerate middlemen in food production and distribution had the potential capacity to extract enormous profits. By 1972 the structure for increasing food prices and middlemen profits had been laid down. The only restraint was that posed by general overproduction in American agriculture. The Russian grain deal soon changed this situation. By eliminating both the fact and the psychology of overproduction and comparatively low prices in agricultural goods, the deal paved the way for agribusiness to assert its power over table food prices.

THE NEW POLICY: KEEP PRICES UP

The Russian grain deals reflect a highly calculated effort at creating super-profits out of the anguish of farmers and the general public. Since the government itself lacks the legal authority to export goods, the grain sales have been consummated by some half-dozen leading American grain-trading firms. The steps in the selling process are something like this: First, the harvest comes in and cannot be altered by farmer action. Second, the Department of Agriculture's Commodity Credit Corporation (CCC) grants the Russians exceptionally low credit arrangements. Third, the companies purchase the wheat owned and stored by the government in CCC bins and sell it to the Russians at a price significantly below the prevailing domestic price. Fourth, the companies, over and above their sales fees, receive millions in subsidies from the government (the difference between the domestic price and the sale price).

The effects of the sales were injurious to practically all Americans except the grain companies and a few insiders who were able to make extraordinary profits by speculating on grain futures. Farmers were unable to take advantage of the resulting rise in wheat prices, since most had sold their grain to the government or at the going market price. The American grain reserve was eliminated. Wheat prices and prices of substitute products went up, and so did the prices of beef and bread, both dependent upon grain prices. Restive consumers were told it was just the law of supply and demand.

The Conservative prediction that growing world agricultural sales would eventually bring prosperity back to farming, although creating some hope in 1973–1974, had turned to ashes by 1978. Four years after Secretary Butz promised a new era for farming by opening American agriculture to the world, farmers had become dependent on world demand to get rid of two-thirds of their wheat, a quarter of their corn, and half their soybeans. While American overseas grain sales remained fairly high, world grain prices (indeed, most world agricultural prices) tumbled.

Did lower farm prices translate into significantly lower food prices? Hardly. With large food corporations and agribusiness controlling the final goods prices for most United States food consumption, lowered per-unit farm prices meant higher profits, not lower prices at the grocery store. Grocery chain profits soared as farmers groaned and consumers cursed. Consumers blamed farmers. Farmers blamed unions for rising equipment costs, and Arabs for higher energy and fertilizer bills. Almost no one has placed the responsibility where it really belongs—with the grain trading companies and their agents at the Department of Agriculture and with agribusiness monopolies, which are well represented in Washington.

Those who argue that world population pressures and scarcity are the cause of higher food prices are simply not telling the truth. During the past decade the United States has reduced the amount of food it makes available annually for the Food for Peace program (directed at the starving nations). It sells less to the poor nations, precisely as it sells more to fatten Russian beef. High food prices do not reflect absolute or relative scarcity of food, but super-profits by agribusiness. Any program attempting to unravel the food price problem must begin by directing its attention at the real culprits—American business, or at least the part of it that dominates food production and pricing.

To be sure, Americans will be forced to live with higher food prices—but *not* because of shortages.

FOOD EXPORTS AND BALANCING THE INTERNATIONAL BUDGET

Another aspect of the decision to trade with the Russians was its favorable effect on the American balance of payments. Quite apart from the domestic profits for agribusiness, increased overseas sales of American grain offset to some degree the American trade deficit. The rising trade imbalances of the 1960s and early 1970s, stimulated by Vietnam War costs, had to be halted to protect the American dollar in world markets. Nixon's strategy of devaluation in 1971 was intended to enhance the appeal of American goods and thus stimulate American trade. It made American farm products particularly attractive in world markets. The result was to increase demand for our farm output and force higher domestic prices. What this actually meant was that, by relatively lowering farm prices in world markets through the devaluation strategy and improving farm sales overseas, Americans had to pay more for their own food. Ironically, the Russian grain deals were a means to offset the impact of the Vietnam War on our international payments balance; essentially it amounted to a further (albeit quite disguised) war tax on the American consumer.

ARE BOYCOTTS A USEFUL STRATEGY?

From a Radical perspective, short-run strategy to deal with price gouging by monopolies or by those who reap extraordinary profits from favorable supply-and-demand situations is limited mainly to the boycott. Short of the expropriation of private enterprise, which is of course the only long-run solution, organized consumer actions against the high price of food must be in the form of not buying. It should be understood, however, that these actions are rarely successful in terms of their immediate objective. First, they demand exceptional organization by consumers. Second, they face formidable opponents who are willing to "tough it out" so that the principle of the boycott does not catch on. Third, in the case of specific food boycotts, consumers usually face a situation where there are few, if any, substitutes. The decision not to eat beef, for instance, has a serious effect on our normal diets. Even in the case of coffee, which has little food value, the 1977 boycotters found that the boycott caused them great discomfort.

Thus, choosing not to eat in order to bring food prices down is not likely to be an effective strategy. Even if boycotts do not win, however, they do have some beneficial side effects. They serve an educational purpose for consumers, demonstrating the potential power of mass political organization, a lesson that can be applied later in more effective ways. A threat of greater mass social organization that will take direct action on prices, jobs, inflation, or any other problem is, of course, a direct challenge to the existing economic order.

ISSUE 2

Consumer Protection
The Matter of Automobile Safety

Consumption is the sole end and the purpose of all production; and the interest of the producer ought to be attended to, only in so far as it may be necessary for promoting that of the consumer.

Adam Smith, 1776

The upshot of consumer protection, when it succeeds, is simply to hold industry to higher standards of excellence, and I can't see why they should object to that kind of incentive.

Ralph Nader, 1967

Let me emphasize: competition does not protect the consumer because businessmen are more softhearted than bureaucrats or because they are more altruistic or because they are more generous, but only because it is in the self-interest of the entrepreneur to protect the consumer.

Milton Friedman, 1978

Originally, the idea of consuming more and better things was meant to give man a happier, more satisfied life. Consumption was a means to an end, that of happiness. It now has become an aim in itself.

Erich Fromm, 1955

THE PROBLEM

According to the time-honored doctrine of consumer sovereignty, the final authority in determining production and prices is the consumer. In this view, consumers vote with their dollars in the marketplace. Their decisions, presumably intelligently formed, are expressed by their final selection and willingness to pay for goods. Since the mid-1960s, however, the theory of consumer sovereignty has been challenged by *consumerism*—the consumer protection movement.

To consumer protectionists, consumer sovereignty is really *caveat emptor*, let the buyer beware. Their argument, in simple terms, holds that consumers cannot possibly know the quality or possible detrimental effects of the goods they purchase. Consumer demand is manipulated by television, advertising, and an uncritical desire to "keep up with the Joneses" by copying other people's consumption habits. Accordingly, consumers have become increasingly exploited by sellers of shoddy and dangerous commodities.

The consumerist movement was launched in 1965 with the publication of Ralph Nader's *Unsafe at any Speed*, an effective muckraking attack on a popular General Motors car, the Corvair. Nader argued persuasively that the sporty rear-engined auto had a number of defects, among them a dangerous habit of flipping over when cornering, even at low speeds. He also claimed that General Motors engineers and managers knew about the car's engineering deficiencies but had kept quiet about them. Corvair sales dropped after Nader's attack, although General Motors disputed his influence. The company made its last Corvair in 1969.

Spurred by Nader and his activists and by the sobering fact that auto fatalities had grown by about 1 percent a year since 1960, Congress enacted the National Traffic and Auto Safety Act in 1966. This legislation required that the auto industry begin to install certain specific safety features in all new cars. The first requirements (which went into effect in 1968) specified seat belts for all occupants, energy-absorbing steering columns, increased windshield resistance, dual braking systems, and padded instrument panels. Over the years, additional safety requirements have been mandated by the National Highway Safety and Traffic Safety Administration (also established in 1966) and, like it or not, American consumers began to adjust to the concept of legislated auto safety standards.

Meanwhile, Nader's consumer advocate activities soon spread to other areas, and his popularity and political effectiveness grew. Within a few years, state and federal laws were introduced to give consumers greatly expanded power in product liability and class action suits. By 1975 over a million such suits were being initiated each year. More important, perhaps, has been the creation of governmental protection agencies. The Federal Trade Commission now includes a Bureau of Consumer Protection and a Bureau of Deceptive Practices. The executive branch boasts a special assistant for Consumer Affairs and a Consumer Advisory Council. By 1976 over 400 separate units in forty different government agencies were operating to advance consumer interests or protect consumer rights. While the effective power of many of these offices might be questioned, the numbers at least reflect the rise in interest in consumer problems.

Probably the best known of the activities of consumer groups and governmental agencies remains those initiated in the "birthplace" of the consumer movement, automobile safety. Whatever their actual success in producing safer automobiles, consumer activities have certainly had economic effects in the automobile industry. Precisely what these economic effects have been is a matter of considerable disagreement among economists.

SYNOPSIS The Conservative argument takes the position that consumers are best able to determine for themselves what they should buy, and that any effort to improve upon consumer rationality diminishes consumer satisfaction, raises prices, and interferes with economic efficiency. The Liberal argument contends that consumers do not have sufficient protection against the manipulative power of giant enterprises. The Radical argument wonders whether consumerism raises the right questions, pointing out that consumption is accepted uncritically as an end in itself.

The Conservative Argument

How safe should an automobile be? How safe can it be? Should all cars be built like M-16 tanks? Should speed limits be reduced to a much safer twenty miles per hour? Indeed, wouldn't the safest car be no car at all? We have started from a fairly intelligent question and proceeded to absurdity. And that is precisely the direction of the present consumerist thrust into auto safety.

The past decade's agitation by a few consumer groups and rulings by growing layers of federal and state bureaucracies have forced auto makers to undertake serious engineering changes in car production. From seat belts to bumpers to impact resistant frames, auto manufacturers have had to meet a series of deadlines in installing safety devices. If we were in a joking mood, we might wonder how a satirist like Bob Newhart would have handled a crowd of consumer safety advocates a hundred years ago if they had turned their attention to the horse. The trouble is that the auto safety freaks—and practically all consumer advocates—are not funny. In point of fact, they are an economic and social expense. They interfere with the free functioning of supply and demand and infringe on social and individual freedoms.

THE ECONOMIC EFFECT

The required installation of auto safety equipment adds to the cost of cars, in terms of both actual equipment and research and engineering. These costs obviously must be paid for in higher automobile prices. Since most studies have shown that automobile demand is moderately elastic, the rising price of autos must reduce total sales. Many consumers will hold on to their present cars longer, own fewer family cars, or shift to alternative means of transportation. Additional costs may cause consumers to rearrange their preferences so that, to get a needed auto, they will forgo some other commodity. Higher priced cars may actually be traded off against clothes or even food. In any case, aggregate consumer benefits are diminished by the price increase.

Meanwhile, the incomes and profits for automobile makers are also adversely affected. For many small foreign car makers, the bumper requirements alone were more than they could adapt to, and production of certain makes had to be halted altogether. Although it may be argued that American manufacturers were able (quite happily) to take up the slack created by this decrease in foreign cars, it is obvious that continuing increases in safety costs will sooner or later have serious effects on profits. The burden will be particularly great on AMC, Chrysler, and many foreign makers. Being comparatively small, they are less able to adjust their productive efficiency and profits to dwindling demand than are the giants, General Motors and Ford. Thus auto safety not only raises prices, lowers demand, and reduces overall corporate profitability, but may also have the wholly undesired effect of increasing industrial concentration in the auto business. As we shall argue later, such undesired monopoly effects are almost always the result of interference with the market mechanism rather than of a latent tendency within business.

In addition to adding direct costs to consumers and producers, consumer protection increases taxes. Federal and state protection agencies spend $500 to $750 million annually. There appears to be no end to the proliferation of public consumer protection agencies and programs; as consumerism grows, the cost will be passed on to the ordinary citizen.

THE SOCIAL EFFECT

The decision to enforce most auto safety standards denies consumers the right to own unsafe autos if they want to. Safety standards to protect second parties—pedestrians and other drivers—are probably justifiable on the grounds of community protection. But the thrust of practically all safety efforts has been aimed at car owners and occupants (who are there, after all, as a matter of choice) . The owner who wants safety should be able to buy it—collapsible steering wheels, padded dashboards, air bags, and the whole works. However, the consumer who values personal safety less than some other purchase should be free to make the choice. How far is enforced self-protection to go? Will each home have a food inspector peering into the kitchen pots and checking for cholesterol and fat intake? Beyond the obvious economic effect of making consumers pay more and thus compelling them to rearrange their budget choices, rigid auto safety standards subtract from personal freedom.

The dismal record of consumers' voluntary interest in auto safety is fairly well documented. When the Ford Motor Company voluntarily added certain safety options to its cars in the 1950s, it met with public apathy. There was no rush to buy autos with seat belts and padded dashes. Ford quickly abandoned its experiment. Meanwhile, National Safety Council surveys of auto seat belt usage indicate that less than half of all drivers and occupants use them regularly. Although speed limits have been lowered and are observed by many drivers (because of fuel costs, not safety), speeding remains such a serious problem that New York State recently organized a $6-million state police task force to enforce speed laws. Quite simply, broad social concern for auto safety is nonexistent.

A DIGRESSION ON COST-BENEFIT

A frequently cited proof of the efficacy of auto safety rules is that the fatality and injury rates have fallen since the passage of the Vehicle Safety Act of 1966. While Conservatives will accept the fact of lowered fatalities, they believe that it deserves careful study before concluding a causal connection with enforced safety standards. Indeed, factors other than safety devices may explain this trend.

For instance, the age profile of the population might be considered. The birth rate peaked around 1950, and this led to a slower growth of under twenty-five-year-old drivers, the most accident prone age group. Also, we might look at income and cost trends. Since the late 1960s, real income growth has slowed and the cost of repairs and medical bills has risen greatly. Would not these tendencies act as a deterrent to risk taking while driving? We might also ask: Have driving patterns changed so as to reduce travel and risk, especially with the rising price of gasoline? A whole range of additional factors similar to these might be considered. What have been the effects of smaller cars, radial tires, new highways, driver education, and so on?

The point of this digression should be obvious. The well-known Liberal argument that social benefits of reduced injury and death outweigh the dollar cost of safety equipment can simply not be proved so long as there is no way to be certain that the safety equipment has had any significant effect on the reduction of injuries and death. The true value of safety equipment cannot be ascertained.

Ironically, from a social point of view, the auto safety movement may produce the opposite of its desired results: auto safety may in fact decline. Indeed, it could be argued (but not proved) that safety equipment could actually increase accidents since drivers with supposedly safer autos would be willing to take increased chances while driving.

Meanwhile, as the price of automobiles increases and consumers (at least the majority, with an elastic demand for autos) determine to forgo new car purchases, older and less safe machines will make up a larger share of the nation's private vehicles. The repair expense to keep an old car on the road is now less than the expense of buying a new car. Regardless of federal indifference to supply and demand in its auto safety programs, federal authority cannot repeal all the laws of market behavior. To be sure, the government could enact more stringent inspection requirements for old vehicles, but human ingenuity and a few dollars to friendly gas station inspectors would likely blunt tighter inspection efforts. Meanwhile, whether successful or not, the inspection effort would represent one more layer of bureaucratic control.

We can see, therefore, that consumerist programs do not improve on the market's own defense of "consumer sovereignty." The Conservative position is to halt government interference. No consumer program is the best program.

The Liberal Argument

The classical economic assumption that buyers and sellers bargain equally in the marketplace and that buyers, acting with restraint and wisdom, are sovereign falls into the same intellectual category as belief that the world is flat. As in the case of the "flat worlders," a great many compelling reasons can be mustered to "prove" the argument, but they fly in the face of virtually all available evidence.

From the Liberal point of view, interference in the private production of goods is justifiable and necessary for several reasons. First of all, average consumers have had great difficulty in obtaining accurate information about the goods they buy. Almost daily, the Food and Drug Administration and other research-oriented government and private agencies reveal a new atrocity: Thalidomide, Red Dye No. 2, Tris, and so on. These goods have been sold or used without the consumer's knowledge of their effects.

Second is the matter of external costs—costs paid by the society that are not accounted for in the selling price of a good. Conservatives may argue that people have the right to drive an unsafe car if they choose. Auto accidents, however, affect more people than those who are injured. They lead to higher insurance rates, greater court costs and heavier expenditures on roads, accident prevention, and enforcement. Nor are injuries or deaths simply "personal" matters. These human losses mean the dollar loss of present wage earnings and the loss of productive workers (now and in the future), and thus a greatly expanded social cost to the whole society.

SPEED VERSUS SAFETY

The extraordinary growth of giant enterprises over the past century, along with the development of huge advertising budgets and sophisticated selling techniques, has created immense power on the sellers' side of the market. Economic concentration has given producers great freedom in establishing and maintaining their own price and quality standards. Massive advertising, meanwhile, has moved well beyond an informational function to one of actually creating and manipulating consumer wants. In such a situtation, it is essential that government intervene on behalf of consumers to protect them from false advertising and poorly made or dangerous merchandise.

The past decade's efforts in the areas of automobile safety are an example of how governmentally supported consumer protection actions can improve the quality of an important consumer good. Outside of a house, an auto is usually the largest single outlay made by a consumer. Americans own about 120 million cars. Once considered a rich man's luxury (and, after the Model T, the poor man's luxury), the auto has today become everyone's necessity. The vast majority of citizens are dependent on the auto to get to work, school, stores, and many recreational activities.

However, just as consumers began to buy more and more autos after World War II, the auto makers began to shift consumer attention from a car's serviceability and economy to its size, horsepower, and styling. (This trend had actually begun with General Motors in the early 1930s, but depression, war, and generally poor highways did not allow it to blossom until the late 1940s and 1950s.) The "ideal" car became one with speed, internal comfort, and annual style changes that could quickly distinguish it from last year's model or from other manufacturers' offerings. While social critics sneered at Americans' fancies and fantasies in automobiles, very few paid much attention to safety hazards. Autos had probably never been very safe, but by 1965, 55,000 Americans were dying each year on the roads. New highways, along with greater horsepower and more weight, had made automobiles lethal weapons. The auto industry, which had shrunk from ten producers to just four, paid no attention to safety standards. Their advertising and their research emphasized speed and comfort, and the buying public had accepted these values. Until Ralph Nader and a few others focused attention on safety inadequacies, rarely did car dealers have to respond to queries about how safe their products were.

In the past decade, all this has changed. Government, working through Congress and administrative rulings by new protection agencies (such as the National Highway Safety Administration), created minimum safety requirements for all cars: safety belts, bumper improvements, window defrosters, stronger glass, and the like. Careful monitoring of autos has led to massive recalls to remedy specific safety deficiencies. Speed, the great killer in most cases, has been de-emphasized in product advertising. The latter development has of course been aided by the rising cost of gasoline, which has induced consumers to value performance over horsepower.

THE SAVINGS FROM SAFETY

Government safety requirements have no doubt added to the price of automobiles, although much less than the industry has argued. Safety belts, for instance, which (when used) have radically reduced serious injuries in collisions, added less than 1 percent to the price of a $5,000 automobile. The problem, of course, is to measure the increases in costs to consumers against the savings to society from reduced auto hazards. It would be inaccurate to stress only increased auto prices in a survey of auto safety costs and benefits.

Using the crudest kind of calculations, the dollar cost per year of auto safety could be estimated as high as $3.1 billion. This assumes an extraordinary 10 percent safety add-on to the average manufacturer's cost of $3,500 per car and further assumes annual auto sales to be 9 million cars. The benefits are more difficult to calculate. We do know, though, that each life unnecessarily lost is also a loss to society in earned wages for the period of the victim's work life. We also know that auto related deaths have declined by about 10,000 per year since the first significant safety features were added to the 1969 model cars. Using a recent U.S. Department of Transportation "interrupted earning stream" estimate of $400,000 value per victim's life and calculating that at least three-quarters of the 10,000 reductions in fatalities is the direct or indirect result of improved safety standards, we can demonstrate at least $3 billion in social savings from reduced fatalities alone. Additional savings from reduced or less serious injuries and the psychic gratification of feeling safer in one's auto would more than cover the liberally estimated dollar cost of the safety equipment. In a more complicated and extensive benefits model, the U.S. Department of Transportation estimated in 1977 that presently mandated auto requirements would reduce fatalities by 24,000 by 1990, producing social savings of $9.5 billion. Doubtless, other models could be constructed but even the most conservative should easily prove that auto safety pays for itself.

Meanwhile, manufacturers complain that enforced recalls of autos to remedy defects constitutes an assault on their profits, and there is probably some truth to this. The answer to the problem, however, is better workmanship and engineering on the industry's part, not relaxed consumer protection. The costs for shoddy construction must be borne by industry, not by society at large.

If there is any serious defect in the government's efforts to protect auto buyers, it is that not enough has been done. The Highway Safety Bureau, for instance, operates on a yearly budget of about $100 million and employs a staff of about a thousand. That is a very small bureaucracy indeed to watch over safety standards in the nation's largest consumer-oriented industry.

Greater efforts in auto safety as well as protection in other areas of consumer interest are essential. Consumer protection will not be attained until *caveat emptor* is replaced by *caveat venditor* (let the seller beware) as the dominant motto of the marketplace.

The Radical Argument

The relevant issues in the controversy over improved auto safety are rarely raised. Conservatives approach the question as a matter of maintaining free markets and free choice, and Liberals argue for the improvement of market conditions and the protection of buyers, but these are really evasions of what the auto safety question highlights. Why, in an advanced and supposedly civilized society such as ours, is automobile safety a problem at all? Is it that we lack the resources and the technology to build safe vehicles? On the contrary, we all know that technology has nothing to do with the problem. Unsafe autos, like unsafe food and dangerous drugs, are just "there." They are part of our economic and social system—to be tolerated or, when things get bad enough, to be reformed. Auto hazards and the like are the necessary but unwanted effects of an irrational social order.

WHY "CONSUMER SOVEREIGNTY" DOESN'T EXIST

Capitalist economic systems are organized to make profits, not to make people happy or life safer. For a capitalist enterprise to make large profits, it has to sell in quantity, and it must obtain as great a surplus over costs as possible. Obviously that simple calculation nowhere contains any estimate of social costs and benefits. Insofar as the production-for-profit system is concerned, satisfaction is maximized simply if we have *more*. Irrespective of the time-honored tradition of consumer sovereignty, it is not really the consumers' power to choose among goods that is important. What is important is that they consume, period. Citizens in a capitalist society are taught from birth to accept uncritically that the object of life is to obtain goods; the more goods, the better their lives.

Looked at this way, it is easy to see why modern capitalism periodically becomes absorbed in such developments as the auto safety issue. The social costs of the mass consumption of dangerous automobiles and even private concerns about the problem have finally developed to such a point where reformist action must be taken. The auto safety movement is merely another step in the long progression of product reform movements. It differs very little from the public outcry against adulterated food which created the Food and Drug Administration in 1906. The FDA has certainly improved food cleanliness, and probably the current consumer movement will make cars safer to drive (or at least we will believe so). However, the "success" of such reforms deflects us from questioning the reasonableness of an economic system that sells poisoned food or hazardous vehicles in the first place.

Conservatives and Liberals may bicker over whether "consumer sovereignty" is best expressed in free or regulated markets, but both are committed to encouraging high levels of essentially irrational consumption. No traditional economist has ever proposed that consumer sovereignty be defined as the rational and coordinated control of production by the users of goods. That of course would lead to the abolition of the capitalist system. However strongly Conservatives and Liberals seem to disagree on the extent of government interference with production, both hold firmly to the principles of maintaining high levels of output as well as the primary goal of production for profits.

THE PERVERSION OF THE SAFETY IDEA

When it comes to consumer protection, it is difficult, perhaps politically impossible, for Radicals to oppose such a reform effort as automobile safety, even if it does blunt concern for the underlying crisis. Radicals, after all, are interested in the genuine well-being of American citizens even if their choices and values are distorted by an irrational market structure. The fact is that Americans do drive automobiles, and no useful political or social objective would be attained by having them drive unsafe ones. Nevertheless, it is instructive to see that even a socially desirable good like auto safety can be used to exploit consumers.

Although the American auto industry has complained vigorously about the intrusion of the safety experts, they would be hard pressed to show real economic loss as a result of the safety efforts. Higher prices for cars have probably had some effect on reducing demand, mostly by putting autos out of reach of the lower income groups. The corporate profits of auto makers, however, have remained high. In fact, if the recent recessionary conditions could be discounted, profits would have been much higher since the passage of the safety standards than before.

In 1977 General Motors reported a record-breaking net income of about $4 billion on sales of $55 billion. GM ranked thirty-seventh among all American corporations in net income as a percentage of stockholders equity. More important, paid earnings per share were two-thirds higher than stockholder earnings a decade earlier, in preconsumerist 1966. Ford and Chrysler also ranked in the top 200 firms in earnings ratio, and their earnings-per-share record was also better than it had been a decade earlier (Ford's had increased almost 100 percent). Not only have manufacturers passed on to consumers all safety costs through monopolistic price setting, but their own profits have continued to rise. They have used higher safety costs as a pretext to obtain price increases which represent more than the safety features actually cost. Consumers, warned by the media that auto safety costs money, have accepted higher auto prices almost unquestioningly. In fact, no data on actual safety costs is available except what the manufacturers choose to release. The evidence, however, clearly indicates that whatever the costs, they have not eaten into manufacturers' profits.

Despite their public opposition most American automobile corporations have collaborated with the safety people because one of the corporate benefits of the safety program has been to limit foreign competition. The "safe bumper" codes, for instance, promptly eliminated many small foreign makes from American markets or else imposed serious engineering costs that raised their prices. By taking some of the price advantages away from the "foreigners," the safety regulations enabled the highly concentrated American automobile industry to increase its monopolistic control over prices, output, and quality.

Ironically, the promise of better and safer cars is thus twisted to produce better profits. And where is the "government of the people" during all this? The answer is simple. While millions have been spent to promote automobile safety, the Justice Department has spent scarcely a penny to investigate price collusion among the car makers. Consumer protection is not to be extended to the pocketbook.

It is hard to oppose automobile safety, but, under a monopolistic production-for-profit system, it is hard to take it very seriously either. At any rate, a Radical program must go deeper than the auto safety question. When looking at consumption and consumer behavior, the Radical sees the underlying exploitative nature of the capitalist system. Consumer safety will never be possible as long as production for profit remains the objective.

ISSUE 3

The Energy Crisis and the Environment

Can We Eat Our Cake and Have It, Too?

The fuel industry has been warning . . . for the past decade that if government regulations continued to keep oil and natural gas prices too low to generate capital needed to find oil and gas, our nation would eventually run short.

Gulf Oil Corporation Advertisement, 1973

It's sort of like sex. Everybody's going to get all the gasoline they need but they're damn sure not going to get all they want.

R. W. Baldwin, President,
Gulf Refining and Marketing, 1979

If we have to have people literally freezing to death because segments of the business community don't think they're enjoying a sufficient rate of profit—a highly questionable premise in the oil and gas industry, to say the least—then what is the Federal Power Commission for?

Congressman John Conyers, 1977

We cannot for the life of us understand why so many liberals in this country are hostile to business. . . .

Mobil Oil Company, 1977

Out of Work? Hungry? Eat an Environmentalist!

Bumper Sticker, 1975

THE PROBLEM

In the late 1960s Americans were made increasingly aware of the dangers of pollution by a small but growing band of environmentalists and ecologists. Schoolchildren planted trees, "Earth Days" were proclaimed, and, more important, citizens' lobbies pressed successfully for environmental protection acts. The high-water mark of environmentalist activity probably came on December 2, 1970, when the Environmental Protection Agency was established as an independent regulatory agency of the federal government. The EPA was charged with coordinating government action "to assure protection of the environment by abating and controlling pollution."

Meanwhile, in a related but contradictory set of circumstances, Americans were vastly increasing their energy consumption. While trees were being planted and schoolchildren being warned of a future world without green grass and blue water, Americans bought more and more television sets and air conditioners, and Detroit built bigger gas-guzzling automobiles. Precisely as the nation learned to believe that the environment was in danger, it was increasing its energy consumption. In fact, energy use was going up at about 3 percent per year, or a little faster than the growth of real GNP. Overall, Americans, totaling only about 5 percent of the world's population, were consuming 35 percent of the world's energy production.

The paradox of growing energy usage in a time of environmentalism is obvious now, but it went largely unnoticed until crises occurred. The first crisis came in the winter of 1973–1974, when the gasoline pumps went dry and automobiles sat lonely in garages in numbers unmatched since the World War II shortages. Because of what has come to be known as the Arab oil embargo, Americans suddenly learned that there was an energy shortage. The second crisis appeared in the frigid winter of 1977, when the nation quite literally ran out of available natural gas supplies. Schools closed, industries and commercial enterprises shut their doors for lack of fuel, and home consumers warily watched their thermostats and listened for their furnaces.

A third crisis began to take shape in early 1979 when the heretofore "stable" government of oil rich Iran collapsed into civil war. The resulting economic and political instability created grave doubts that Iran could or would continue to contribute its 10 percent share to world oil production. Even with the passage of a national comprehensive energy program a few months earlier, the collapse of Iran and a general growth of political tension in the Middle East created expectations of future oil shortfalls. While federal plans for gasoline rationing were being weighed, the pump price of gasoline pushed upward.

Conceivably, a growing energy shortage at a time of exceptional environmental concern could be thought of as complementary tendencies, both leading to the lowering of fuel emissions into the atmosphere. In fact, the result was quite the opposite. The apparent shortage of oil and gas spurred concern and action that was often in opposition to environmental objectives. Indeed, the ecologists, along with the Arabs and other oil producing nations, were seen by many as the enemies of continued American economic growth and the standard of living to which the nation had become accustomed. Although environmentalists' concerns were both broader and deeper than the question of energy fuels, their well-known efforts to protect the Alaskan tundra and marine life from oil drillers and their opposition to nuclear power and the burning of high-sulfur coal made them the bad guys to many proponents of economic growth. For numerous Americans, the environment, and not energy, was the luxury item.

The great debate had begun with the early rounds going to the energy advocates. Just four years after the EPA was established, the Energy Research and Development Administration was created. In 1977, with the winter's crisis clear in everyone's mind, the energy administrator was elevated to cabinet rank. Meanwhile, the Alaskan pipeline was completed, offshore drilling reinstated, and plans laid for more nuclear power—all to the horror of environmentalists. In late 1978, Congress approved President Carter's energy program after a year of intense debate. While this legislation did emphasize conservation of energy, the supply aspects of the bill were not victories for environmentalists. Great stress was laid on exploiting America's plentiful but environmentally dirty coal stocks, and only a token effort was undertaken to developing "clean" solar energy.

All in all, the energy crisis seemed to be overwhelming public concern for matters of ecology. However, beneath the rancorous moral and ethical arguments over priorities, in what has come to be called the energy-environment tradeoff, there remain serious economic issues and choices that affect public policy making.

SYNOPSIS The Conservative argument presents the energy and environmental crises as basically the result of not following a "full-cost" pricing policy. The Liberal argument maintains that government regulation is essential to develop a rational energy program and make sure that polluters pay their clean-up costs. The Radical argument sees the "energy crisis" as a planned effort to raise energy company profits and halt environmental concern.

The Conservative Argument

Contrary to some rumors and allegations, Conservatives are not in favor of exorbitant oil product prices or excessive oil company profits. Neither are they indifferent to blue sky and clean water. To put Conservative opinion on the side of the energy users (understood in Liberal and Radical logic as big business) and against the environment and people in general is plainly false.

The market system did not invent pollution and interference with the ecological balance. That was done by the first *homo sapiens* who found he (or she) could cut down a tree or burn off a jungle to trap and kill animals. Neither are market economies the worst violators of the environment today. A visitor to many Russian industrial centers will probably note that the air quality of Donora, Pennsylvania, is better.

Of course, given the contrived choices between energy and economic growth versus environmentalist demands, Conservatives would support the former. However, such a choice of tradeoffs would not be necessary if the market were permitted to work freely.

ENERGY COSTS MUST RISE

The rising dollar price of energy and the environmental cost of high energy usage are facts that Americans should have anticipated. They are part of the costs that should be balanced against the benefits of a mass production–mass consumption industrial economy. Energy fuels are not a renewable or free resource, and the earth has no interplanetary garbage collection. Thus rising demand and dwindling supplies of energy must raise energy prices. Meanwhile, the by-products of high energy use must produce some social or environmental costs. Heretofore Americans have not been forced to face these costs and calculate them in pricing goods. The days of 19-cents-a-gallon gas (plus a free set of dishes for a full tank) are, like the passenger pigeon, gone forever.

The proper energy-pricing policy must be composed of two parts. The first should, for the sake of continued economic growth, encourage the development of new energy sources. The second part must include in final prices the burden of associated environment costs in energy usage. Up to this point, there would probably be little disagreement from Liberals and even Radicals. However, both groups will reject the Conservative solution—reliance on the market mechanism.

Until recently, energy has been underpriced in terms of a simple supply-and-demand analysis. Publicly financed electrical power, tax-subsidized domestic oil, virtually free overseas oil, price-fixed natural gas, and publicly subsidized nuclear power have all tended to increase demand through artificially low prices. While it is hard to calculate the elasticity of demand for energy fuel, it seems a reasonable assumption that, if prices had tended to rise as scarcity actually developed or if these prices had included all production costs, the use of energy would have declined. The market would have provided an accurate rationing system. Moreover, competitive price advantages would have stimulated private research in energy-saving machines and in lower-cost fuel substitutes (for example, coal for oil in thermal electric power production, or hydroelectric or nuclear power instead of oil). The two-ton gas-devouring "torpedo 8" would never have become the standard measure of American private opulence if the market had set the real price of automobiles. (Note: in the case of a car's real costs, we would also have to include hitherto uncharged highway construction costs.)

The pricing policies of government have produced a real problem. Since the late 1960s, energy use in the United States has grown at a phenomenal rate. As Table 3.1 indicates, the development of American energy sources has lagged dangerously during this same period, creating a growing gap between what we produce and what we use.

The natural gas crisis in the winter of 1977 painfully demonstrated the ultimate effect of government interference in the marketing of energy resources. Court and Federal Power Commission decisions since the 1950s held down the price of natural gas. At the same time, gas grew from a virtually untapped energy source before World War II to a source of about 30 percent of American energy by 1976. Artificially low prices made gas more attractive than other fuels. Meanwhile producers, faced with low, fixed rates for gas, reduced their efforts to find new fields. Natural gas reserves finally fell to the point where gas was unavailable at any price. The entire economy paid dearly as industrial layoffs ran into the millions and home users shivered in cold houses.

Table 3.1 U.S. Energy Consumption Produced Domestically, 1965–1985

Year	% energy produced in U.S.
1965	90
1967	88
1969	84
1971	82
1973	81
1975	83
1977	77
1978	75
1985 (est.)	74

Source: U.S. Department of Energy.

The natural gas shortage did have an educational effect, albeit a moderate one. In President Carter's omnibus Energy Bill of 1978, the laws of supply and demand were at least partially recognized by the legal specification that natural gas price control should be phased out by 1985.

A few months after the passage of his energy legislation, a new round of OPEC price increases induced the President to announce that price controls over "old" domestic crude (oil discovered before 1973) would similarly be phased out by 1981.* These actions amounted to a grudging admission that government maintenance of low energy prices was a major cause of any energy shortage. However, this was only a beginning at best. Much more needs to be done to restore market pricing.

A POLICY FOR THE FUTURE

Since Americans do not want nor should they have economic stagnation or negative growth, we should allow the market to set the price of fuel at such a level as to induce the development of alternative energy sources. In general, this will mean higher production costs in all industries. It will also have income redistribution effects, but these

*New oil discovered since 1973 was not controlled.

will not be so great as is popularly imagined. In the world at large, this policy will probably cause some damage to European economies that lack virtually any fuel reserves, and it will probably create windfall profits in oil-producing nations (until their resources are gone). However, the technological superiority of the former and the absence of either sizable populations or technical skills in the latter will maintain the existing economic balance in the long run. The Arabs, after all, cannot eat their oil nor can they turn it into machines of their choosing. Meanwhile, America's plentiful supply of coal, its offshore oil reserves, and nuclear and solar power will provide a strong energy base if our energy gluttony is reduced somewhat by higher fuel prices. The effects on our standard of living would be negligible.

The development of alternative energy sources and the further utilization of our own gas and oil resources is also desirable from the viewpoint of world politics. As long as the United States remains dependent on foreign supplies for as much as 60 percent of its oil, and as long as oil remains our crucial energy source, we are always vulnerable to international blackmail. Our national security is threatened. However, the strength of the OPEC cartel would soon end if energy alternatives to Arab oil were to be encouraged by market forces. The possibility (and reality) of shifting our demands to these substitutes would check outrageous oil price increases.

With regard to developing alternative energy sources, the oil companies have already moved toward becoming energy companies. Exxon and others have begun extensive research into oil shale, coal, nuclear, and solar solutions. This is the proper market response to the oil price increase, and it should not be interfered with.

The other side of the energy-environment question, pollution costs, can also be solved in the marketplace. Here we must remember the old saw that there is no such thing as a free lunch. If we want cleaner fuels, cleaner industry, or cleaner air, we must pay for them. The only way to attain these goals is in full-cost pricing of goods. That is, the price of all goods must reflect both internal costs and externalities resulting from the production process. We must begin to calculate these external costs. While this process probably entails the setting of scientifically determined minimums for clean air and water standards, it is justifiable as a community response and does not impair the working of the market. Industries could opt to pay the cost of meeting minimum requirements on emissions, and add such expenses to their normal production costs, or they could pay a tax or fee for someone else to do the cleaning up for them. This too would be an added production cost.

Compared to what Americans have been used to, the Conservative solution *does* cost more, although probably not so much as is generally believed. The relative price of energy-consuming and pollution-creating goods must rise. This will necessitate consumer reshuffling of choices and changed consumption patterns. However, since nothing is free, it is the only possible solution this side of the Kingdom of Oz. Liberals and Radicals may dress up their panaceas by creating impressive regulatory agencies or by calling for national resource and economic planning, but they cannot avoid the reality of higher priced goods. This can be the only logical outcome to the present pulling and hauling over the energy-environment crisis. And the Conservative solution still relies on the market and advocates individual freedom.

Regrettably, the general public, through their elected representatives, still supports the myth that only government can bring energy and environmental costs below what a market solution would dictate. Although the above arguments have sought to prove that this is analytically and practically impossible, perhaps a final piece of evidence is worth offering. In 1978 the Carter administration succeeded in obtaining congressional approval for the Department of Energy to police energy affairs and to create a "rational" costing of energy fuels. This was a critical point of Carter's energy plan. The initial budget for this 20,000 person agency was $12 billion, or more than the annual profits of all American oil companies. Taxpayers cannot long afford these so-called savings resulting from government efforts to protect us from the cost of a market economy.

The Liberal Argument

Given the hard (and actually unreasonable) choice between sustained national economic growth and meeting all ecological priorities, the former would have to be selected as the more vital immediate national goal. In an economy already hard hit by unemployment and inflation, further economic sacrifices resulting from a failure to obtain enough inexpensive energy would simply be too great for the nation to bear. This does not mean abandonment of the national environmental commitment begun in the 1960s, but it does mean relaxation of that commitment for the time being.

Apart from the economics of the energy problem, there is also the political question: Can we afford to continue our dependency on foreign sources of oil? The possibilities of "oil blackmail" or dangerous political instability in oil-producing nations such as Iran only add to our need to develop a comprehensive energy program that guarantees adequate energy and eventual self-sufficiency.

THE NEED FOR CONTROLS

While Conservatives argue that national energy and national environmental policies can be determined by simple reliance on a pure market mechanism, there is quite enough evidence to dispute this point. First of all, there is no known case of individual corporations undertaking expensive but unremunerative social betterment programs. We cannot expect any corporation to undertake programs to save energy or the environment for their own sake. The nature of the market is to maximize profits in the comparatively short run, not to balance long-run social costs and benefits. Thus any program aimed at resolving the energy-environment crisis must emanate from the federal government, where the power of law and the inducements of taxes and subsidies can direct the private sector toward desired objectives.

Proof that corporate decision making is aimed at maximizing profits rather than social benefit is abundant as more information is obtained on the oil embargo and crisis of 1973. While Americans waited in line for a few gallons of high-priced gasoline, corporate balance sheets showed no signs of distress. Precisely as the OPEC nations were supposedly putting the squeeze on the oil companies in 1972 and 1973, after-tax profits for the nine largest oil producers averaged a whopping 45-percent increase. For Exxon and Gulf the profit increase was 60 percent. Moreover, additional evidence from several government reports now shows that the real scarcity of oil and gasoline was not nearly so great as the corporations maintained. Although there was a scarcity of certain fuel types in certain regions, this was largely the result of bad business decision making. Moreover, many companies had actually been cutting back overseas production before 1973 in an attempt to raise prices by reducing supplies. Even during the height of the shortage hysteria, as fuel prices edged upward daily, some oil importers reported shortfalls when they actually had sufficient supplies on hand. The effect, of course, was to kick prices and profits up even more. With such a record, it would be unsound to rely on corporate wisdom to solve the energy problem or deal with environmental problems in a socially desirable way.

TOWARD AN ENERGY AND ENVIRONMENT POLICY

As Americans staggered through the winter of 1977, the weather finally caught up with the nation's long unwillingness to face its energy problem. The technique of voluntary energy conservation advocated by the Ford administration and supported by the energy companies, along with certain limited federal efforts to spur production, proved inadequate. The failure of voluntarism is evident in Table 3.2. After the crisis of 1974, consumption went down but it soon rose again.

Table 3.2   U.S. Energy Consumption by Source, 1973–1976 (in millions of barrels of oil per day, equivalent)

	1973	1974	1975	1976
Oil	17.3	16.6	16.3	17.2
Natural Gas	10.8	10.5	9.6	9.4
Coal	6.7	6.0	6.1	6.5
Nuclear Power	0.4	0.6	0.8	1.1
Hydroelectric Power	1.4	1.5	1.5	1.5
	36.1	35.2	34.3	35.7

Source: Chase Manhattan Bank, Business in Brief, No. 127, April, 1976.

Even more striking is the evidence offered in Table 3.3. Per capita consumption of energy units, after a brief decline in the mid-1970s, again began to increase. In fact, the Department of Energy estimated that per capita consumption would grow at nearly 2 percent a year through 1985.

The evidence was clear: The United States needed a firm and effective federally administered energy policy. Reliance upon purely pri-

Table 3.3   Per Capita Energy Consumption in the U.S.
(in million British Thermal Units)

Year	BTU
1970	328
1971	328
1972	338
1973	361
1974	342
1975	332
1976	351
1977	354
1978	364
1980 (est.)	375
1985 (est.)	406

Source: U.S. Department of Energy.

vate solutions could not assure that the whole nation would receive the energy that was essential in amounts and rates that did not create regional economic dislocations. Moreover, a federal policy, besides maintaining equity, would be the only way to deal with problems posed by OPEC's price rulings and with the "profits first" bias of American energy companies. Experience showed us that the days of depending upon the market laws of supply and demand were over. Supply and demand controls were too important to be left to the market to resolve.

An overall energy policy must be aimed at the following objectives: (1) end American dependence on foreign energy sources, (2) encourage the development of alternative energy fuels, (3) develop programs and policies to lower energy demand, (4) retain price-control power over fuels, and (5) rely on tax-subsidy mixes to direct or encourage business actions in meeting the above objectives (for example, subsidies for firms carrying out alternative energy research).

THE CARTER ENERGY PROGRAM

Given these policy requirements, what is the Liberal evaluation of the energy bill that passed Congress with great fanfare in late October 1978?

At best, the energy package received mixed reviews. First of all, it was much too late in coming, almost a year and a half after President

Carter had sounded a national alarm about the energy crisis. By October 1978, American payments for oil imports had reached $42 billion per year (they were a mere $7.6 billion in 1973) and were the largest single contributor to imbalance in the nation's balance of payments and the resulting deterioration of the dollar. Second, the bill as it passed in its final form was a patchwork of compromises, in some cases producing victories for the enemies of a national energy policy.

On the positive side, the bill did seek to lower energy demand and to shift emphasis away from oil and gas. Tax credits were offered to owners who insulate their homes and/or who install solar heat equipment. So-called gas guzzling automobiles, those getting 14 m.p.g. and less, would be hit by a special tax beginning in 1980 (the tax threshold would rise to 22.5 m.p.g. by 1986 and could cost as much as $3,850 per year per car). Except where environmental conditions demanded, public utilities were directed to plan to burn coal by 1980, and industries were to be awarded a 10 percent tax credit if they installed coal-burning facilities in place of oil and natural gas. Among other efforts to reduce demand was the ending of discounts for large users of natural gas and the implementation of incremental pricing (so that big users pay proportionately more).

On the negative side, the energy producers obtained significant gains at the expense of the public. Natural gas controls were to be phased out by 1985, allowing 10 percent increases per year until that time. Under a complicated arrangement, newly discovered gas would rise from $1.50 to $2.00 per thousand cubic feet, effectively creating an immediate 33 percent price increase for many consumers. Permanent tax reductions were also to be offered to energy producers for risking the expense of new oil and gas drilling and the development of oil shale production.

From many Liberals' point of view such legislation will enhance the power of the energy giants, Exxon and other huge oil companies. These firms have become involved in all stages and fields of energy production and distribution, and they have the market power to exploit any of the above concessions to producers in the energy bill, as well as to pervert some of the better intended parts of the legislation. For instance, the act's effort to develop alternative fuel sources may be offset by their actions. The reason is obvious. An oil company's innovative plans in, say, the field of solar development, while serious if they see profit possibilities, will still be limited by the desire to protect their existing oil markets and their capital investment. As a rule of thumb, the energy crisis should not be used as a pretext for greater monopolistic integration in the energy business.

It might be added, parenthetically, that some Liberal economists (particularly in the AFL-CIO) would end all subsidy benefits to the oil giants and move to break up their virtual control of markets from wellhead to gas pump. This reaction grew out of the pricing behavior of some of the companies during the crises of the 1970s.

Perhaps the biggest disappointment of the Carter program was its failure to plan for the development of mass transportation systems.* Since private autos account for about half of our oil requirements and 18 to 20 percent of our total energy use, one obvious way to lower gasoline demand is to substitute mass transit for autos. One bus can eliminate fifty cars and a suburban train can substitute for a thousand. The redevelopment of mass transportation offers perhaps the greatest opportunity to lower our energy demand without painfully changing our life styles. It should also be noted that investment in building a new mass transportation system would provide a great stimulus to jobs and to the economy.

Liberals' doubts about the fairness and effectiveness of the Carter approach to the energy problem were heightened in mid-1979 when the President announced his decision to permit price decontrol of "old" domestic crude oil over the next two years. According to Carter, this would increase U.S. output and reduce the effectiveness of the OPEC cartel. Few Liberals were convinced. What it would do, most believed, would be to provide enormous profits for the oil companies as they raised prices of domestic crude from six or eight dollars per barrel to the going OPEC price ($20 or more per barrel). The President's proposal for a moderate "windfall" profits tax on these earnings did not make his action more palatable. Any windfall to the oil companies could only swell their bloated profits, thus diminishing their interest in developing cheaper oil substitutes.

As the second "Great Gasoline Shortage" developed in the summer of 1979, the President made yet another energy address, this time stressing synthetic fuel production, reaffirming his commitment to nuclear and solar development, and requesting gasoline rationing authority. To those standing in gasoline lines, the shortage was real

---

*Although at this writing specific legislation to aid mass transportation has not been enacted, the President's July 1979 "Energy and the Nation" speech did grudgingly admit the need to upgrade mass transit facilities.

enough, but many cynics, including many Liberals, still believed that fuel would be readily available when prices got high enough. Environmentalists, meanwhile, were horrified by the emphasis on synfuel and nuclear power.

ENERGY AND THE ENVIRONMENT

The development of a national energy policy must, of course, be tied to a broader environmental policy. While emphasis up to this point has been on the need to meet energy requirements in order to sustain the economy, there need not be a complete trade-off between energy and the environment The already established procedures of federal controls over pollution should be maintained and extended, although the requirements set by ecologists in the late 1960s are unlikely to be met during the energy crisis. However, a long-range energy policy that reduces energy consumption is really headed in the same direction as environmentalist goals for conserving the world's resources. For instance, the eventual development of solar power would be an environmental as well as an energy gain.

Meanwhile, blatant pollution unrelated to fossil fuel problems (such as the continued poisoning of the Great Lakes with chemicals) must be halted. Reclamation costs must be paid by the polluters where possible. Where this is impossible, the federal government should carry out the task. To avoid regional industrial dislocation due to uneven enforcement of antipollution measures, it is important to establish a strong federal policy that sets minimum standards.

On the issue of nuclear energy development, Liberals, it must be admitted, are hopelessly divided at present. Some, such as the AFL-CIO leadership, believe the dangers and environmental costs have been overstated. Since the Three Mile Island accident, however, nuclear power has come under a cloud. Its direct benefits and the anticipated economic stimulus from power plant construction must be measured against the social costs of health and safety hazards. However, it should be remembered, all energy use has some adverse environmental and health effects.

Conservatives are correct in pointing out that cleaning up the environment and providing sufficient energy cannot be done without added costs. However, the costs are likely to be less painful than people think. Developing new energy sources and cleaning up the environment will create additional public and private jobs. With government expansion into the areas of energy and ecology, our economy—plagued by underemployment—can transform a crisis into economic gain.

The Radical Argument

The present trading off of environmental demands against energy needs is the logical outcome of the energy hysteria that began with the manipulated oil crisis of 1973–1974. Although Americans have become generally inclined to blame the OPEC cartel and Arab nationalism in particular for higher energy prices, it is increasingly evident that American energy companies were the prime movers in creating the initial panic over fuel shortfalls. Moreover, they have benefited handsomely as a result.

A MANIPULATED CRISIS

In the early 1970s American oil company earnings had leveled off. Even under tax arrangements with the federal government—which allowed the oil producers to deduct all OPEC-established price increases at the wellhead from their domestic taxes—after-tax profits in 1972 were just about the same as they had been four years earlier. Meanwhile, the pesky environmentalists, after the Santa Barbara oil spill, had succeeded in stalling industry plans for the Alaskan pipeline, additional offshore drilling, and new refinery and super-tanker port facilities. Fuel consumption in the United States was going up, but not fast enough by itself to produce a drastic price increase. Thus, when the Arab embargo was announced in the winter of 1973–1974, the oil companies greeted it as a blessing.

All during the winter and during most of 1974, Americans teetered between concern and panic as they queued up at gas stations to get a few dollars' worth of gasoline. The oil companies flooded the media with "save fuel" commercials that darkly alluded to no more cars, or no more jobs, or no heat in the house. Meanwhile, the government laid plans for full-fledged gasoline rationing. Americans had come face to face with an "energy crisis."

A constant theme in the corporate campaigns was that the crisis was the people's fault. (By and large Americans themselves blamed the Arabs, but it would have been tactless for the oil importing companies to point the finger at their suppliers.) Americans were told that they were energy gluttons. In point of fact they were, but not as a matter of individual choice. Without any thought to an eventual energy crisis, Americans had been sold almost every energy-wasting commodity possible. Indeed, during the peak of the "energy crisis," thoughtful television viewers must have noted some irony in a situation that juxtaposed an earnest electric company commercial instructing viewers on how to cut down on electricity and snappy jingles pushing air conditioners and other appliances.

The oil embargo and the following "energy crisis" education campaign quickly brought benefits to the oil companies. Prices of oil products went up and up, with presidential and congressional blessings. Environmentalists, some of whom may have been initially ambivalent on how to handle the energy question, were driven to the wall by the nearly universal demand to exploit new oil and other energy sources. The issue came to be understood as a choice between ecology and jobs. Meanwhile, oil price increases soon drove up the price of all fuels, and oil companies such as Exxon began referring to themselves as "energy companies," proudly reporting their growing interests in coal, nuclear energy, and even solar power.

After three years, the list of corporate gains from the energy crisis seemed limitless. Prices were up. Profits were up. Vertical integration from wellhead to gas pump had increased. The American and world market percentages of the top nine oil giants had grown. Substitute energy sources had gone up in price, and the leading oil producers were quietly gaining control of these industries. Natural gas prices, although still controlled, were also raised slightly (though not enough to suit the oil companies). The government was pledging tax advantages and subsidies to companies willing to undertake energy research. And all that silly talk about environmental priorities had been shelved.

The blunt fact is that there never was a real energy shortage. As subsequent inquiries showed, oil companies held back supplies and hid available oil at sea in tankers during the crisis of 1973–1974. When the prices of gasoline and fuel oil went up, oil suddenly and mysteriously became available. The inexorable search for profits, not Mideastern politics, had been the basis of the oil shortage.

Consumption of energy in the United States did fall slightly (by about 6 percent) between 1973 and 1975. The decline, however, cannot be credited entirely to the energy crisis. In fact if we take into account the full-fledged recession of those years, it is possible that the savings had nothing to do with conscious reduction in consumption. By 1977, at any rate, energy consumption was well above 1973 levels. Even with additional OPEC price increases, the oil giants cheerfully increased the flow of foreign oil, and American crude production sagged.

What the Arabs had been in 1973 to the oil companies, "the winter of '77" was to the natural gas combines. (It should be mentioned that most of the natural gas supply had by now fallen under the control of the oil giants; the energy program of the oil companies, after the earlier crisis, had aimed at developing a broad monopolistic control over virtually all energy sources.) As the bitter months of January and February passed, Americans were told that they were running out of gas supplies. Schools and factories closed, and, at President Carter's request, consumers turned their thermostats down to 65° Fahrenheit and lower. Congress meanwhile rushed through emergency energy legislation that laid the basis for natural gas decontrol. Charges of industry manipulation were ignored as the freeze grew more severe. There was of course no real shortage, only a short supply of what would be marketed at the existing regulated price. The object of the industry-created scarcity was to end controls and force the price upward. Just as there was no gasoline shortage at 70 cents per gallon, there would be no natural gas shortage if rates doubled. Meanwhile, the crisis managers again talked the American people into believing that higher prices were the natural, if unpleasant, result of the laws of supply and demand.

In mid-1979, gasoline shortages reappeared. Using the pretext of shortfalls supposedly resulting from the Iranian revolution and OPEC's reluctance to sell, the oil companies prepared a new assault on consumers. With the appearance of gas lines, and encouraged by the Carter administration's helpful statements that matters were bound to get worse, the oil companies sought again to create the crisis atmosphere that would justify a new round of permanent price increases. However, none of the oil companies could quite explain the supposed shortfalls in light of available evidence that showed crude imports rising and gasoline refineries working at near capacity.

These lessons should not be misunderstood. As ecologists can point out, there is indeed a real energy crisis waiting out there in the future. There may even be short-term crises in the near future as a result of further OPEC pricing actions. Thus there is a need for an energy policy—one that explores environmentally safe energy alternatives and one that attempts to deal with America's massive energy waste and disproportionate use of the world's energy supply.

NATIONALIZE, DON'T SUBSIDIZE

The first step in developing such a program must be the elimination of production-for-profit objectives in the energy field. The lessons of the past five years should show that an energy policy dominated by a few monopolistic oil companies, with the government as their accomplice and agent, is not an energy strategy but a profit strategy. At a minimum, then, the beginning of an energy policy is the nationalization of energy resources. Regulation, tax-subsidy policies, and jawboning have never worked to control the energy industries. Attempts to end monopoly abuse through breaking up the oil companies is without any special economic benefit and is probably politically more difficult than sweeping nationalization.

"Programs" such as the one enacted in 1978 not only fail to solve the energy problem, they actually worsen matters for ordinary citizens. The 1978 act continues the old theme of blaming people for the energy crisis, and it enacts "soak the consumer" programs. Natural gas is to be decontrolled but there is no check on giant corporations that will likely keep down supplies in efforts to produce a rising "market" price for gas. The subsidies and tax rebates for developing new as well as old (coal and nuclear) energy sources simply open up the public treasuries to raids by the energy giants—and these outlays will, of course, be paid for by rising personal taxes. The official public policy as laid out in the act of 1978 is, therefore, to raise the price of energy so that people can afford less; but, higher prices have always been the objective of the energy producers who correctly see this as the means to higher profits.

Energy resources—their intelligent development and fair distribution—are everyone's problem, not the special province of a few enterprises interested in profit maximization. These resources are too important to be left to the whims of capitalist control. Moreover, national control and the rational use of energy resources is also a first requirement in inaugurating an effective environmental policy. With private ownership of energy resources and under the threat of constant energy shortages, ecological concern will always be traded off for greater profits.

ISSUE 4

Monopoly Power

What Should Be Our Policy Toward Big Business?

People of the same trade seldom meet together, even for merriment and diversion, but the conversation ends in a conspiracy against the public, or in some contrivance to raise prices.

Adam Smith, 1776

Every contract, combination in the form of trust or otherwise, or conspiracy, in restraint of trade or commerce . . . is hereby declared to be illegal. . . . Every person who shall monopolize, or attempt to monopolize, or combine or conspire . . . to monopolize . . . shall be deemed guilty of a misdemeanor.

Sherman Anti-Trust Act, 1890

The problem in America is not that the top 100 corporation presidents are violating the laws, though God knows they are; the problem is they're writing the laws.

Nicholas Johnson,
Federal Communications Commissioner, 1972

THE PROBLEM

A paradoxical situation appears when we examine the structure and organization of American business enterprise. On the one hand, the official ideology of American capitalism espouses competition. Under the law, monopolies and conspiracies to monopolize have been formally illegal since the Sherman Act of 1890. Meanwhile, business enterprise in the United States has been characterized by increasing bigness. No economist, regardless of ideological preferences, denies the existence of big business. But there is wide disagreement as to whether modern corporate size and integration represent a monopoly threat to the economic and social organization of society. Technically speaking, "literal monopoly" in the United States is quite rare. According to the textbook definition of monopoly, a monopolist is the sole producer of a commodity that has no close substitutes. As "price makers," the textbooks tell us, monopolies must be regulated. The classic example usually cited is American Telephone & Telegraph (AT&T) or some other public utility.

The current debate over monopoly power, however, is not really about AT&T. Rather, it is about the monopolistic power of companies that are not literal monopolists. It is about the current tendency toward merger and combination of American business enterprises and what this tendency portends.

As Figure 4.1 illustrates, the merger activity of the past fifteen or twenty years has been considerable, easily dwarfing the more well-known merger periods of the 1890s (the era of the trust) and the 1920s (the era of the holding company). The obvious effect of such consolidation activity has been to concentrate more and more of the nation's productive capacity into fewer corporations. For instance, in 1945 the nation's 200 largest manufacturing firms owned 45 percent of all assets of U.S. industry. Today they own over 60 percent. Looking at the data somewhat differently, we find that 94 percent of all U.S. corporate assets are owned by just 12 percent of the nation's corporations.

What is the significance of this growing business concentration? To what degree is unregulated price-making power exercised by giant producers or combinations of producers? Indeed, if such power does exist widely, is it an overtly illegal effort to evade the antitrust laws or merely the result of the natural growth of the capital and technological require-

FIGURE 4.1   MAJOR MERGERS AND ACQUISITIONS, 1895–1975

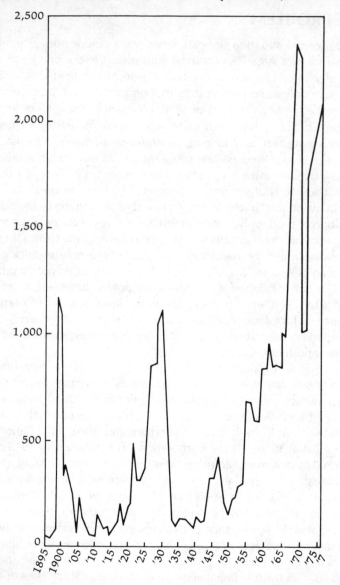

ments of modern capitalism? In either case, what are its effects on the distribution of economic and political power?

SYNOPSIS The Conservative argument asserts that there are sufficient market and legal checks to make certain that big business does not act in an exploitative way but actually improves our economic well-being. The Liberal argument accepts the fact of "bigness" but maintains that government intervention is essential to control potential monopoly exploitation. The Radical argument holds that monopoly is the logical historical development of capitalism and that there is no way to halt this tendency without abolishing the production-for-profit system.

The Conservative Argument

Public discussion of the so called "monopoly problem" in the United States is usually characterized by gross misunderstandings Foremost among these is the confusion of bigness with monopoly, and the resulting corollary that big is bad. The anti–big business attitude that emerges from these views is a serious threat to the American economic system. Far from leading to the rebirth of a competitive business society, most antimonopoly efforts erode free enterprise itself. Ironically, an attack on big business boils down to an attack on business of all kinds. More than they realize, the owners of mom and pop grocery stores and the like are themselves threatened by assaults on A&P, IBM, GM, and other business giants.

BIGNESS DOES NOT EQUAL MONOPOLY

Bigness in and of itself is not proof of monopoly power. Of course, there is no denying that concentration of markets and capital exists among manufacturing industries, but concentration does not necessarily mean collusion or domination. The share of the market held by the four auto producers ranges from General Motors' 50 percent to American Motors' 4 percent. Yet, as any car buyer knows, competition exists. This is readily apparent in competing advertising, warranties, and styling—as well as in the customary habit of haggling with any car salesperson. Moreover, there are many cases of interindustry competition among different "concentrated" industries. For instance, glass, aluminum, steel, paper, and plastic all battle each other for the food-container market. Nor should international competition be forgotten. While tariffs and shipping costs do offer some protection to American firms, the protection is not absolute—witness the 10 to 20 percent share of the auto market seized by foreign car makers. The point is simple. Big business, far from ending competition, has in fact heightened it. The solitary village blacksmith, barrel maker, or flour miller of a century ago had a far greater monopoly power over price, quality, and output than does his present-day business counterpart.

Those who worry about excessive monopoly power should consider one further point. In a market society, the great check against price gouging, by GM or by a barrel maker, is consumer demand. If prices go too high, sellers simply cannot sell their products—or enough of them to make a profit—and prices will be reduced.

If we can get beyond the silly but appealing logic of the "big is bad" argument, we might actually understand that the opposite is much more nearly correct: Big business has been good for America.

Big business has been the major vehicle of economic and technical advance in the United States. (It has done so much that people even believe totally nonsensical rumors about it—for example, that Exxon, or some other oil giant, purchased and buried the patent for an engine that gets fifty miles to a gallon of gas.) Few can deny that product progress and relatively falling prices for most consumer and producer goods during the twentieth century have been the result of expensive technological advancements; these could have resulted only from the great capital concentration and large-scale marketing strategies of big enterprise. Would those who want to abolish GM also want to abolish the assembly-line production technique with its efficiency and savings?

Recently, Liberal and Radical critics of business enterprise have directed their wrath against so-called "conglomerate mergers," combinations of companies in different lines of business.* Such attacks are threats to business growth, since conglomerate mergers presently account for about 90 percent of all combinations. This strategy is an extension of the "big is bad" argument. However, it fails to consider that conglomerate mergers may also provide consumer benefits. By strengthening inefficient and costly businesses through improved management techniques and by providing badly needed capital, prices will be lowered. Moreover, the conglomerate merger actually increases competition by resuscitating firms that would otherwise fail.

In any case, bigness is also vastly overstated. There are more than 12 million private business enterprises in the United States, including over 1.5 million corporations. Regardless of the size of the large ones, no other economy can boast that proportion of independent businesses to the whole population. The most misleading overestimation of bigness results from economists' almost exclusive focus on the manufacturing sector in monopoly discussion. Manufacturing, whatever its actual concentration, accounts for only about a fourth of our GNP

*Senate Bill 600, introduced by Senator Edward Kennedy as the Small and Independent Business Protection Act of 1979, would prohibit any merger between corporations having sales or assets of over $2 billion.

and employment. Consider, for example, the rapidly growing fast-food business, with its almost weekly competitive inventions and promotions of "Big Macs," "Super Burgers," "Wimpies," and so on. Wholesale trade, retail trade, and service sectors of the economy simply don't fit the monopoly argument.

Singling out big business is unfair and misleading. Even if business bigness were demonstrably bad, why isn't the same logic applied to big government or big labor unions? Those who cry monopoly in the business sector rarely apply that argument against the United Auto Workers or the Teamsters, nor do they see the bureaucratic state management of pricing—from hospital rooms to gasoline stations—as analogous to the imagined monopoly power of big enterprise.

GOVERNMENT CREATES MONOPOLY POWER

This discussion of the bigness issue is not meant to dodge the fact that literal monopoly does sometimes exist, but most such monopolies may be defended on technical grounds. Competing telephone companies would plainly cause a communications nightmare. This type of public utility monopoly, for the most part, is rigorously regulated. As might be expected, such regulation scarcely ever "improves" the monopoly, since profit and pricing goals are subordinated to irrational regulation decisions (see Issue 5 on the railroads). Even when technical monopolies exist, it is still preferable to allow business freedom than to impose inefficient regulation. Other government actions, such as preferential tariffs and tax legislation, also tend to generate inefficient monopoly situations, with the consumer as the ultimate loser. Government intervention is very largely responsible for whatever monopolistic inefficiency exists in the United States today.

Government, of course, is not the sole source of monopoly abuse. As Adam Smith suggested, "They do talk business at the country club." Still, while efforts at private cartelization and price conspiracy do occur, they have rarely worked—partly because of greed and partly because of our antitrust laws, which affirm the common-law doctrine that "combinations in restraint of trade" are illegal. Clearly, any truly collusive effort to rig the market must be opposed. In other words, the only rational antimonopoly policy is an anticonspiracy policy; this means ending collusion not just among businessmen whose greed outstrips their inventiveness, but also that encouraged by government among labors unions and certain favored businesses.

In following any policy, it must be remembered that bigness itself does not prove collusion or unfair price setting. It does not prove consumer exploitation. To equate bigness with monopolistic exploitation is to damn a system that produces a vast array of goods abundantly, efficiently, and cheaply.

Conservatives must not deny the existence of monopoly when it is real. Very clearly, monopoly power is unjustifiable and injurious to individuals. It prevents efficient allocation of resources. However, aside from those cases of monopoly initiated or encouraged by the government, occasional conspiratorial endeavors by individual enterprisers (and even here government tax or purchase policies often stimulate criminal activity), the "monopoly problem" is mostly a phony issue. Liberals use it as a pretext for urging massive social or governmental interference with the market, while Radicals find it convenient as an excuse for their revolutionary assault on the entire system. Both groups would use the issue in a self-serving fashion to extinguish individualism and private property rights.

The Liberal Argument

Traditional economic analysis since Adam Smith has argued that the "great regulator" for business activity is the market. Here small, competitive firms struggle against each other to sell goods and gain customers. The prices and the possibility of exploitation are always regulated by the "invisible hand" of supply and demand. While we may nit-pick over whether this type of pure competition ever existed outside of economists' minds, it certainly does not exist in the United States today. Just 2,000 businesses in all fields of the economy produce about half of our GNP; the "invisible hand" has largely been replaced by the highly visible fist of corporate power.

THE PROBLEM OF POLICY SELECTION

While most modern-day Conservatives tend to equivocate on the issue of big business, preferring not to see any monopoly problems except in the rarest of cases or only in cases where government "interferes" with the market, Liberals face the problem directly. *Business concentration does exist in the United States.* The policy issue, then, is not a matter of recognizing the obvious but of determining how to deal with it.

The most rudimentary analysis of monopoly behavior tells us that, all things being equal, monopolistic firms tend to charge higher prices and produce less than might otherwise be expected under competitive conditions. They employ fewer workers at lower wages and generally foster resource misallocation. Moreover, the greater the degree of monopoly power, the greater the consumer exploitation.

The implications of this line of economic analysis are clear. The return of competition is apparently the only way to return to economic virtue. In a policy sense, this must mean the enforcement of a vigorous antimonopoly policy, leading to the restructuring of industry into greater numbers of similar-sized units of production. Liberals are not in total agreement on this point, but most would oppose a grand "dividing up" of giant enterprises. First of all, the practical applications of a literal "break them up" policy are not politically or legally feasible. We have long ago passed the point of being able to return to some romantic eighteenth-century concept of the marketplace. This is not to say that stimulation of competition in certain industries might not be desirable or possible through the application of antitrust laws. In fact, the Justice Department must always be prepared to initiate antimonopoly legal action, but this could not be carried out on a broad scale without weakening our legal and economic structures. Second, there is no solid evidence that pure competition would be beneficial even if it could be attained without seriously wrenching the society.

What these observations mean in a practical context is that concentration in the oil industry might be approached differently from concentration in the auto industry. Domestic automobile production is limited to just four firms, with General Motors alone producing between 50 and 60 percent of the output. Charges that GM works effectively as a price leader are difficult to question. However, price leadership does not necessarily mean consumer exploitation. Nor would breaking up GM necessarily lead to social improvement. Even though GM's size has probably pushed it well beyond what is necessary for attaining efficiency from economies of scale, there is no assurance that forty or even a dozen smaller GMs could produce a product of similar price and quality, and hire the work force that the present monster does. On the other hand, the oil industry, with less actual concentration, has conspired during recent energy crises to force up the prices of gasoline and natural gas by withholding supplies.

The point is that there are different types of giant enterprises— some highly predatory and exploitative and others reasonably responsible to the public interest. Size alone is not justification for "breaking up" the auto industry. But the behavior of the oil industry is the worst kind of monopolistic activity. There are no easy "monopoly tests." Each case must be taken on its own merits.

Having rejected the rigid competitive argument, we are left to accept the reality of modern corporate concentration. However, though Liberals realize that bigness itself need not be proof of monopoly abuse, they do not subscribe to the "no monopoly" policy advanced by Conservatives. Monopoly power is not always enlightened; it may destroy business itself, as large firms act consciously or unconsciously to protect and expand their influence. Unrestrained business power may in fact subvert government to selfish ends and make the basic principles of property rights and free enterprise subject to special interest groups. Thus, the creation of a monopoly policy is essential to protect the balance of pluralistic interests in an open society. An equitable balance of labor, consumer, and capital interests must be the philosophical cornerstone of any intelligent policy toward business.

Through fair and calculated government intervention, big business can be made compatible with the social objectives of economic order, reasonable prices and high quality, and technological advancement. Government actions, depending on the situation, must go beyond mere antitrust enforcement. They may take the form of selective tax and subsidy manipulation; more extensive direct controls over pricing, hiring, and capital policies; and direct regulation of such developments as multinational business activity. Monopoly policy, however, must not be separated from general public-policy objectives directed at inflation control, maintaining full employment, and encouraging economic growth. Therefore, social control over specific business actions must be integrated with general macroeconomic policy objectives. Some people will argue that this external imposition of social objectives on the private sector is pure socialism, but they miss the point.

SOCIAL CONTROL IS NOT SOCIALISM

Pragmatic social control of big business is not the same as social ownership. First of all, corporate ownership today is widely dispersed and far removed from the day-to-day management decisions of American business. Excessive concern over *who* owns the productive property only clouds the important business and public issues at stake.

How the privately owned property is performing is the really important question. Second, even though privately owned, most large businesses are already "social institutions" with "social responsibilities." To put the point simply, GM—with its sales of almost $60 billion and its 700,000 employees—does not have the right to fail any more than it has the right to conspire against the public. To demand social responsibility is perfectly consistent with the real world structure of business and the economy, and it does not challenge private ownership in any serious way.

Businesses, moreover, are more responsive in the area of social responsibility than is generally understood. Social concern on their part is not purely altruism but good business. Flagrant monopolistic behavior invites government scrutiny and public outrage. The old era of "the public be damned" is past. Few firms, whatever their size and market power, want long and costly antitrust litigation. Even consumer boycotts and public pressure for legislative intervention are sizable threats and induce thoughtful constraint. Moreover, there is significant pressure within the business community to police itself. Monopoly abuse disrupts markets and creates economic instability; this situation, while perhaps favorable to one or a few firms, interferes with general business activity. As a result, American business wants order in the marketplace just as much as it wants government maintenance of high levels of demand for goods. Social responsibility, finally, is not an ethical question but a matter of profit and loss.

These points should not be misunderstood. The Liberal fully understands that big business may indeed be a threat in its pricing, labor, international, and other policies. The point is that big business does not have to be a threat to the economic system. It can be brought under social control.

Public policy toward big business, then, remains a matter of directing private enterprise toward social objectives that include reasonable prices, efficiency, high employment, and adequate profit return, while also taking into consideration such broad concerns as ecology, resource conservation, and the overall performance of the economy. The creation of such a policy must be the responsibility of an enlightened federal government. Government must act as an unbiased umpire, attempting always to balance the diverse economic and social interests of the nation. Such intervention need not abridge basic property rights (which is what Radicals want). But it would set social priorities above the pursuit of selfish individualistic goals (so feverishly defended by Conservatives).

The Radical Argument

To some "monopoly power" may seem to be a non-issue. Who, after all, will defend a monopolistic organization of markets? Yet, while both Conservatives and Liberals oppose monopoly power, neither group understands monopoly's place in capitalist development. Neither Conservatives nor Liberals appreciate the present-day scale and political and economic impact of monopoly organization in the United States, nor do they understand that this phenomenon has not been accidental. Thus the Radical position can be easily distinguished by its interpretation of monopoly as being the centerpiece of modern capitalism and the logical progression of capitalist development. Monopoly power is not merely *a* problem; it is, in the broadest sense, *the* problem of our time. Accordingly, this issue looms much larger for Radicals than for Conservatives or Liberals.

THE ORIGINS AND SCALE OF MONOPOLY DEVELOPMENT

Although monopolies can be traced all the way back to the great trading companies of the mercantilist era (for example, the British East India Company), modern monopoly growth in the United States dates from the closing years of the nineteenth century. Early monopoly efforts were little more than gentleman's agreements to maintain prices, divide profits, or allocate sales territories. By the close of the century, however, formal mergers and combinations were the rule. These consolidations took place under the pressure of two important developments. One was the long business decline of the 1890s, which pointed up the high level of underutilized plant and equipment (excess capacity) in American industry. Gentleman's agreements proved insufficient to prohibit the price wars that were stimulated by overproduction. The second development was vast and expensive technological expansion. The strength through size that mergers afforded gave the developing giants greater ability to control prices, technological introductions, and, most significantly, profits.

Merger activity occurred in four great waves: 1897–1900, 1924–1930, 1945–1947, and 1960–1970. During the first three periods, mergers were usually either horizontal (among producers of similar goods) or vertical (among buyers and sellers in the same production process). Most mergers in the last period were of the conglomerate type (among producers only distantly related, if at all). Early mergers led to a high level of concentration within particular industries. Later mergers produced a high degree of centralization of control in the economy. When we look at General Motors, we can see that its monopoly status involves more than what we might associate with automobile production. GM's centralization of economic power carries over into aircraft engines, a large range of household consumer products, and banking, among other things.

The dimensions of concentration and centralization are only partially apparent when we look at the record. Even so, the facts are still awesome. For instance, by 1976, 500 firms alone controlled 68 percent of American industrial sales and more than 75 percent of industrial employment and profits. In dollar volume, their sales were about $1 trillion.

Table 4.1 illustrates the immense concentration of economic power exercised by a comparative handful of giant firms. Indeed, while the United States remains a nation of many businesses (a fact usually extolled by defenders of the system as proof of the existence of competition), less than 1 percent of all corporations hold 60 percent of the nation's corporate assets. Two giants alone, GM and Exxon, reported sales equal to about 8 percent of the gross national product. Moreover, in such diverse industries as motor vehicles, aircraft, machine tools and instruments, dairy products, baking, industrial chemicals, petroleum refining, rubber, computers, cigarettes, soaps, and photographic equipment, the top four firms accounted for more than half of all output, employment, and profits.

However, beyond this data, there is other evidence of monopoly power that is often overlooked. For example, even nominal competition among the few firms at the top is reduced by the common practice of having corporate executives belong to each others' boards of directors. These interlocking relationships are further expanded by formal trade associations, common control by a few large banking houses, the old practice of price leadership, and elitist domination by a com-

Table 4.1 Control of Corporate Assets, 1971

Size (in assets)	Corporations (number in group)	Corporations (% in size group)	Assets (% owned by group)	Assets (amount owned by group)
$0–100,000	958,089	57%	1%	$33 billion
100,000–500,000	515,813	31	4	116 billion
500,000–5,000,000	177,121	10	8	226 billion
5,000,000–250,000,000	30,226	2	27	784 billion
250,000,000 and over	1,349	0.08	60	1.729 trillion
Total	1,682,598	100.00%[1]	100%	2.888 trillion

Source: U.S. Internal Revenue Service, *Statistics of Income, Corporation Income Tax Returns for 1971* (Washington, D.C.: G.P.O. 1975).

[1] Data add to more than 100% because of rounding.

paratively few wealthy families. Finally, outright collusion and conspiracies to fix prices, output, or quality are not uncommon. Certainly these practices are much more common than the occasional prosecutions under the antitrust laws indicate.

THE EFFECTS OF MONOPOLY

While Liberal policy makers worry about the political effects of monopoly and its inconvenient and awkward shifting of power balances, they tend to underestimate the enormous cost of monopoly activity to the ordinary citizen. Prices are held high in order to assure profits, so chronic inflationary pressures are a by-product of monopoly market power.

The effectiveness of giant corporations in securing profits is illustrated in Table 4.2. As the size of the firm increases, profit rates steadily advance. While Conservatives and even some Liberals will argue with some truth that larger size does produce greater profits because of economies of scale in production, the phenomenal profit rates of the few giants is mostly the result of monopolistic pricing power rather than increased efficiency. Indeed, American business leaders have tacitly admitted this fact. Then-president of American Motors Corporation George Romney testified before a Senate subcommittee on monopoly in 1958 that, in auto production, cost economies are a "negligible thing" after the production of 400,000 units per year. With

Table 4.2   Average Profit Rate by Corporate Size, 1956–1975

Size (by assets)	Profit Rate (profit before taxes divided by sales)
$0–1,000,000	3.7%
1,000,000–5,000,000	5.3
5,000,000–10,000,000	6.7
10,000,000–50,000,000	7.4
50,000,000–100,000,000	8.1
100,000,000–250,000,000	8.5
250,000,000–1,000,000,000	8.8
$1,000,000,000–and over	11.7

Source: U.S. Federal Trade Commission, Quarterly Reports of U.S. Manufacturing Corporations (Washington, D.C.: G.P.O., 1956–1975).

only American Motors still falling within this range, it is fair to conclude that the profits of such giants as GM are due more to monopoly pricing conditions than to "economies of scale." Nor should this generalization be limited to the auto industry.

Innovation, invention, and product improvement are subordinated to the protection of existing capital and technology. Without the theoretical benefits of competition or the practical restraints of social planning, the actual output of monopoly capitalism is characterized by ever greater waste. Increasingly irrational and even psychologically harmful—but nonetheless profitable—commodities glut the market. Under the steady barrage of advertising by the corporate giants, Americans are urged to squander their earnings on toothpaste and mouthwash to improve their sex lives and on appliances and automobiles to enhance their status. Advertisers play on fears consumers never knew they had. What indeed could bring greater shame and anguish than "waxy build-up" or "ring around the collar"?

Meanwhile the giant enterprises exercise their power beyond the marketplace. Education, from the public school to the university, is organized to fill the labor and consumer needs of big business at a variety of levels. Through such "charitable" foundations as Ford, Rockefeller, Carnegie, and Exxon, acceptable educational and cultural values are subsidized. Such actions, far from being examples of the "social responsibility of big business" so applauded by some Liberals, are but self-serving attempts to gain respectability for monopoly power. This fact is blatantly apparent at Exxon, for instance, whose educational foundation is organized as a sub-bureau of the public relations department.

As ITT's attempt in the early 1970s to grab the American Broadcasting Company showed, giant corporations also seek to control the media. Even when such control is not direct, it may be exercised indirectly because of the financial dependence of radio, television, newspapers, and magazines on advertising revenues from big business. When such societal controls by monopolistic enterprise are added to the exploitative economic domination of monopoly power, it is evident that almost every aspect of our lives—on the job or at leisure—is molded by the needs of giant corporations.

Nor is the influence of monopoly capitalism limited to the national boundaries of capitalist nations. In the case of the United States, its growth and expansion as an imperialist power almost exactly paralleled the centralization and concentration of capital. The same ceaseless drive to accumulate surplus and profits that led to monopoly development soon forced American entrepreneurs beyond their borders in search of markets, cheap labor, or raw materials. We shall explore the question of international monopoly power more fully in our later discussions of the growth of multinational firms; it is sufficient to point out here that the problem of monopoly power is not simply a domestic economic question. The burden of monopoly is felt around the world.

MONOPOLY IS CAPITALISM AS USUAL

It is clear that monopoly capital dominates all aspects of economic life in the United States and the nonsocialist world. As we have seen, this domination is not accidental but is the normal course of development in the capitalist system. Marx and other nineteenth-century critics of capitalism predicted that the profit obsession of business would lead first to a competitive anarchy and then to a level of concentration that would destroy business profits from above, while the proletariat rebelled from below. Business did not follow this path, however. Instead it was able to create a fairly stable, predictable, and profitable environment through combination and mutual cooperativeness. The result is the modern integrated giant firm. Big businesses have concentrated themselves so as to control resources, consumer tastes and needs, labor markets, technology, and finally, of course, the market itself.

While Marx may have erred as to the exact trajectory of capitalist development, he correctly saw that the fundamental drive of all business is to make profits. This is as true today for the urbane giants as it was for such crude Robber Barons as Rockefeller or Carnegie—only the style has changed. Nor was Marx wholly wrong in assuming that the business drive for profits would lead to cannibalistic behavior. While monopolies exploit consumers and workers, they also devour the smaller members of their own species. To support this argument, we need only recall that the recent antitrust action against IBM was initiated by the pygmies of the computer industry. Even with combined annual sales of $1 billion, these half dozen companies were still having trouble trying to compete with IBM. If this is the case in computers, what future does a mom and pop enterprise, so vigorously defended by the Conservatives, really have?

Given this grim picture of giant domination, can we construct a policy to alleviate the problem? If by a policy we mean some enlarged form of government antitrust enforcement, the answer is no. The tail does not wag the dog. As the Watergate scandal and frequent cases of "influence peddling" should show, the business of government is business.

Corporate domination of government is perhaps the most obvious example of naked monopoly power. It is hoped that this fact is becoming more widely appreciated by the mass of citizens. As Marx said, "The state is the form in which individuals of a ruling class assert their common interests." The power of business interests to dominate government dates back to the writing of the Constitution; however, it has been most obvious since the rise of the trusts and modern corporations. Business has been able to create regulatory agencies in its own interest (the Interstate Commerce Commission, for instance) and to have the antitrust laws used as antilabor devices. We have already discussed how auto makers have used and manipulated consumer protection laws, how agribusiness has created governmental farm policy, how energy companies have enlisted government to establish higher energy prices. Perhaps no recent event better illustrates the degree of integration between government and big business than the "bail out" of Chrysler Corporation. With more than $1 billion in tax moneys promised to this poorly managed giant, the "risks" of capital have now to be shouldered by ordinary citizen–taxpayers. As we shall continue to see, the manipulation of government by monopolistic business enterprise is natural to our economic organization. Neutrality is simply not possible for a government that depends on business support to elect its officials and is formally committed to the production-for-profit system. While Liberals may argue that social control and accountability is their goal, this is nonsense if the maintenance of capitalism as a system is a prior and overriding objective.

The solution to the monopoly problem does not lie within the framework of conventional economic analysis and policy. The only humane solution is socialization of the means of production. This means participation by individual workers and control by workers as a whole over such basic economic question as what goods shall be produced, how, and for whom. In terms of immediate Radical strategy, this means support for all efforts leading to greater worker control over production, profits, and wages. Worker planning, not corporate planning, is the final objective; however, such planning must be coordinated with the needs of the whole society. Simply to have existing unions replace capital in organizing production would not in itself assure the end of monopolistic practices.

One further caution might be added. Attempts at joint worker-capitalist planning should not be seen as a progressive development in correcting monopoly control. This Liberal idea will actually work to stunt real citizen control of society by coopting workers, who will see themselves as partners with capitalists in profit making. From a truly Radical perspective, it is necessary to *replace* capitalist control with worker control.

ISSUE 5

The Economics of Government Regulation
The ICC and the Railroad Problem

The committee has found among the leading representatives of the railroad interests an increasing readiness to accept the aid of Congress in working out the solution of the railroad problem which has obstinately baffled all their efforts, and not a few of the ablest railroad men of the country seem disposed to look to the intervention of Congress as promising to afford the best means of ultimately securing a more equitable and satisfactory adjustment of the relations of the transportation interests to the community than they themselves have been able to bring about.

U.S. Senate Select Committee on Interstate Commerce, 1886

The ICC is now primarily a forum at which private transportation interests settle their disputes. . . . As a passive forum the ICC has failed to provide for any useful . . . representation of the public interest.

Ralph Nader Study Group, 1970

Nationalization of all or part of this country's transportation system cannot possibly solve the financial and operating problems of the railroad industry. . . . The problems of American railroads can best be solved by a rational, private enterprise approach in concert with enlightened government assistance.

Frank E. Barnett, Union Pacific Railroad Company, 1975

THE PROBLEM

The principle of direct federal regulation of industry by independent government agencies is now over ninety years old. In fact, passage of the act creating the Interstate Commerce Commission (ICC) in 1887 predated the formal elaboration of federal antitrust policy in the Sherman Anti-Trust Act by three years. Since the creation of the ICC, fifteen other independent regulatory agencies have been established. Their concerns range from energy and the environment to financial securities, money, and banking. In addition, dozens of smaller agencies set up under specific departments of the executive branch also possess "independent regulatory" characteristics.

Probably no specific example of government regulation is a pure archetype for study. Operating problems and regulatory issues vary from industry to industry; but, given the persistent transportation problems of the nation and the longevity of the Interstate Commerce Commission, the ICC is certainly an instructive case study in the economics of regulation. The ICC is charged with regulating virtually all interstate surface movement of goods and people by commercial carriers, but our discussion will focus on railroad regulations.

Table 5.1   Volume of Intercity Freight Traffic, 1929–1975 (in millions of ton miles)

Year	Railroads	Trucks	Great Lakes	Rivers and canals	Oil pipelines	Air	Total
1929	454,800	19,689	97,322	8,661	26,900	3	607,375
1939	338,850	52,821	76,312	19,937	55,602	12	543,534
1944	746,912	58,264	118,769	31,386	132,864	71	1,088,266
1950	596,940	172,860	11,687	51,657	129,175	318	1,062,637
1960	579,130	285,483	99,468	120,785	228,626	778	1,314,270
1970	771,168	412,000	114,475	204,085	431,000	3,295	1,936,023
1974	885,700	495,000	107,451	247,431	506,000	3,910	2,215,492
1975	761,000	441,000	108,000	235,000	510,000	4,000	2,059,000

Source: Association of American Railroads, Yearbook of Railroad Facts, 1976, p. 36.

After studying the data presented in Table 5.1 and Figures 5.1 and 5.2, a number of generalizations about America's rail industry become apparent. First, and most obvious, railroads have practically ceased to

FIGURE 5.1   SHARES OF INTERCITY FREIGHT TRAFFIC BY CARRIER,
1930–1975

Source: Association of American Railroads, *Yearbook of Railroad Facts,* 1976, p. 36.

be a significant carrier of intercity passengers.* Second, the railroads'
share of the far more lucrative freight business has been in continuous
decline since the 1920s (in fact, its current share is about half that of
1929). If we add to these trends the widely publicized recent crisis of rail
operations in the northeastern United States, and the chronic shortages

---

*Even Amtrak, a government-sponsored arrangement developed in the 1960s to relieve
railroads of unwanted passenger service, has not succeeded in preventing continued decline
in passenger travel. Indeed, major airfare reductions in 1978 have led to further rail ridership
reductions and have led to proposals to drastically cut Amtrak service in 1979. Even the recent gasoline shortage has not stopped plans to abandon many Amtrak routes.

FIGURE 5.2   SHARES OF COMMERCIAL INTERCITY PASSENGER
MOVEMENT BY CARRIER, 1930–1975

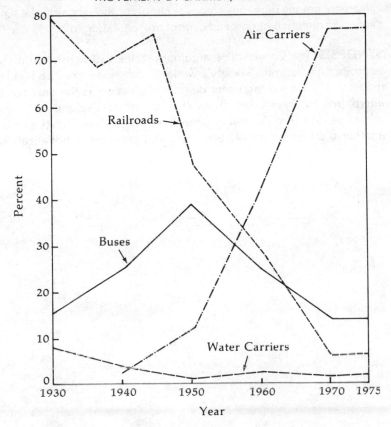

of rolling stock and new investment that plague practically all railroads, it is easy to get the impression that railroads are an industry on the brink of ruin.

Ruin or not, railroads remain far more important than most Americans realize. Although their traffic shares have fallen, they move more freight today than during the boom years of gasolineless World War II. Important industries and entire lines of commodities are dependent upon railroads for transportation to markets. Therefore the future of the railroad industry and the proper role of government toward that industry are pertinent problems.* As we shall see, however, there is wide disagreement among our representative schools of thought as to the significance and direction of past and current rail regulation trends.

SYNOPSIS The Conservative argument states that regulation is counterproductive, harming society's welfare and weakening the regulated industry. The Liberal argument defends regulation as the only possible alternative to the market chaos that industries like railroads would otherwise face. The Radical argument sees regulatory efforts as merely another prop for monopoly privileges and proposes nationalization of all public transportation.

*As the energy crisis deepens, the importance of the railroads to the national transportation network should grow. Approximately three times as fuel efficient as trucks in moving freight, railroads should enjoy a growing fuel cost advantage. In fact, a combination of rising fuel prices and creeping deregulation produced a sharp upturn in railroad earnings in 1979, practically doubling profits from 1978 levels. Whether or not this signifies a permanent change in rail fortunes remains to be seen. See *Forbes*, January 7, 1980, pp. 161–167.

The Conservative Argument

The Conservative position on the ICC, railroads, and regulation in general is based on two sturdy and now familiar principles. First, regulation—or any interference with the market—tends to create resource misallocation, inefficiency, and, ultimately, greater costs to the community. Second, left alone, the market is capable of more rational decisions about the success or survival of a firm or industry than is the voting public or its representatives and bureaucrats.

THE FAILURE OF REGULATION

The creation of federal and state regulatory agencies under the guise of "improving" the performance of the market has had precisely the opposite effect. By making pricing and resource allocation matters of committee decision, all the natural checks on inefficiency are eliminated. The "right" price and the proper allocation of goods, labor, and capital are now merely matters of "administration." But administration, regardless of how noble its motives or how efficient its marshaling of evidence, is at best hit and miss.

Probably the best known example of regulatory failure has been the ICC. As our oldest regulatory agency, it has the longest list of failures and is a good example of all the debilitating effects that age brings to commission activity. The original intent of the ICC was to bring order to the chaotic and excessively competitive rate-making practices of the railroads. Its goal was to protect the public from railroad price collusion and to protect the railroads from one another. By the mid-1930s, ICC power extended to all surface commercial transportation in the country. Specific ICC controls covered rate setting, merger, financial issues, abandonment, and service discontinuance as well as carrier layoffs of labor. There was virtually nothing that a rail carrier or any other carrier regulated by the Interstate Commerce Commission could do without first obtaining commission approval.

How well has the ICC performed its regulatory task? The proof of the pudding is the eating. Today most of the American railroad industry is in serious trouble. Most of the roads in the Northeast are in bankruptcy or have become part of the federal rescue effort known as Conrail Corporation. Passengers are left to the tender mercies of the government's Amtrak, which operates what is left of a once-splendid intercity passenger network. Across the nation, railroad earnings on both capital and sales remain, as they have been through most of this century, extremely low. Capital is not attracted, although it is badly needed.

Though still the primary mover of commodities, railroads have steadily lost ground to trucks, air freight, and water transport alternatives. Under an ICC mandate to operate in the "public interest," railroads have been required to offer services and charge rates that continue to erode their capital position and their ability to compete with other forms of transportation. The physical deterioration of tracks and equipment is hard to appreciate because it is so staggering. In much of the Northeast, on tracks where fast freights cruised at 50 to 60 miles an hour a half century ago, average speeds have been reduced to 20 to 25 miles an hour, and even these speeds may be dangerous.

The ICC is not the sole cause for railroad deterioration, of course. The government's decision to subsidize truck, air, and water transportation by building and maintaining their "roadbeds" (highways, airports, and canals) gave these transport alternatives an unfair advantage over the heavily taxed railroads. Certainly the railroads would profit from more equitable subsidies and taxes. But the ICC has made a bad problem worse.

In misguided efforts to "maintain competition among different modes," the ICC long followed the strategy of "umbrella rate making," a practice of setting a rate high enough to allow less efficient modes of transport to earn a profit on specific service. This provided a special handicap to railroads which lost traffic to other modes simply because they were not allowed to set lower rates (prices) and utilize their greater efficiency in certain goods movement. In protecting trucks and water carriers, the rails saw the ICC direct business away from them. Meanwhile, shippers and consumers absorbed higher than needed transport charges in their purchases.

Similar anticompetitive outcomes have resulted from the ICC's long-standing opposition to rail mergers. This has led to costly "balkanization." The 400 line haul railroads have not been able to combine to increase freight exchange and coordination and to strengthen their financial structures. By denying the industry access to these economies of scale, service has remained expensive and inefficient. At the same time the ICC also prohibited intermodal mergers. Railroads were not allowed to consolidate with trucks and other carriers to improve their overall efficiency.

Meanwhile in search of the will-o'-the-wisp "public interest," the ICC also acted to raise transport costs and reduce rail efficiency by maintaining redundant routes and little used spurs. Permission for abandonments of low density or loss-producing operations were difficult to obtain from the commission, and railroads were compelled to pour millions of dollars into expensive routes that generated only a few dollars in traffic.

By prohibiting railroads from setting their rates freely, denying them the right to develop joint rail-truck transportation companies, and demanding that they continue to operate costly and inefficient services and schedules, the ICC has rendered the railroads' competitive situation virtually hopeless. ICC decisions on rates, abandonments, and mergers are presented as proof of the agency's commitment to the public interest. In point of fact, conditions are so bad that its actions harm, rather than protect, the nation's welfare.

THE MARKET ALTERNATIVE

What might have happened if railroads, buses, airplanes, and trucks had never been regulated? Certainly the overbuilt American railroad network of the 1900s would have contracted. There never was a good economic reason for a quadruple-tracked main line between New York and Chicago, and many other roads were laid without any economic justification at all. On the other hand, buses, trucks, and private autos would not have offered such a competitive threat to railroads if they had not been subsidized at the same time that railroads were being heavily taxed. Before the collapse of the Penn-Central in the early 1970s, the president of the railroad ruefully reported to Congress that, parallel to and within sight of the main line through New York's Hudson Valley, there were two state highways, one interstate highway, and a state canal system; overhead was a federally subsidized air corridor. Profit making was indeed tough for a private railroad under such circumstances.

We might speculate that, left to the dictates of a free market, a national transportation mix might have emerged that would have al-

transport mode to develop its inherent strengths. Instead
icial competition that pitted trucks and railroads against
but provided no way of determining their relative efficiency, each form of transportation could have exploited its own advantages, dropping out of markets where it had none. The present
transportation crisis would never have developed if the market had
been allowed to determine pricing and operational advantage.

REGULATION CREATES BUSINESS DEPENDENCE

One last characteristic of regulatory agencies that should be
noted is the special relationship between business and its regulators.
After a time, all regulated industries come to be reliant on the commissions that regulate them—and in the worst possible ways. Liberals and
Radicals argue that commissions become dominated by the industries
they are supposed to regulate, but this is simplistic. Since almost all
highly regulated industries show rather poor earning records, the
alleged domination doesn't seem to benefit these industries very much.
Reliance on regulation, however, is another matter.

Business can become accustomed to living in a regulated environment. Like junkies on heroin, railroads may hate the ICC, but they
have come to believe they need it. In the 1930s, they used the ICC to
regulate their trucking competitors. In the 1950s and 1960s, they used
the ICC as a weapon against troublesome state regulatory commissions. In the 1970s railroads enlisted ICC support to obtain government aid in the form of loans and, later, Conrail and Amtrak. Given
the economic problems of the railroads, these were small gains indeed.
But they reflected a management outlook that had adapted to regulated life. Accepting this condition, railroads had long ago lost the will
or capacity to be innovative. Their capital improvement record would
probably be poor whatever their actual capital position. Regulation,
therefore, not only makes ordinary business actions inefficient, but
also creates a business psychology that is inefficient and passive.
Regulation frustrates and finally destroys the entrepreneurial motive.

A NEW DIRECTION?

The long battle against regulative inefficiency seems recently to
be gaining important converts. In 1976 Congress finally passed the

Railroad Revitalization and Regulatory Reform Act. With its creation of Conrail (to operate the six bankrupt railroads of the Northeast on about 17,000 miles of track) and its provisions for enlarged federal financing for railroads, the act still evades a pure market solution to rail problems. Nevertheless, it reduced the regulatory powers of the ICC. The act specifically adopts price flexibility in dealing with the railroads although the ICC is still the final arbiter on rates. The ICC is now directed to take a more passive role. Without getting into particulars, the return of greater rate-making freedom to the railroads, plus encouragement for merger and easing of restrictions on abandonment, promise a new era for the industry. While the rail network will certainly contract (and it should) and the number of line haul companies will decline, competition will actually be increased as railroads grow stronger and can effectively challenge the other subsidized modes of transportation. Operating costs will fall, and these savings should lead to reduced rates paid by the public.

Taking into consideration that the Railroad Revitalization Act of 1976 was only a beginning and looking at other regulatory developments in transportation, Conservatives are heartened. For instance, the actions of the Civil Aeronautics Board in late 1978 to reduce its regulation over airline routes and let the industry fly on a "first-come, first served basis" to many U.S. cities is noteworthy. It ends the old practice of granting virtual monopoly power (with fixed rates) to carriers over certain routes. That approach was inefficient to the airlines and costly to the public. Now the air industry *must compete*, and air service will improve. Fares will fall as the market takes the place of public regulation. Meanwhile, similar extensive deregulation plans are being considered for truckers, buses, and of course, the rail industry itself. Who says that it's impossible to roll back all that federal bureaucracy and get back to market basics?

The Liberal Argument

Regulatory agencies are the logical outcome of the need to improve market conditions in certain industries. Direct regulation is not essential to all market conditions. But in certain cases—mainly where natural monopolies tend to develop or should be encouraged—regulation by government agencies can maximize the benefits to both the consumer and the affected industry. Antitrust action, as we have noted earlier, is employed in cases of conspiracy to attain a socially undesirable monopoly advantage in the market, but direct regulation is a ratification of monopoly power. In exchange for this recognized monopoly position, a firm submits itself to close political and economic supervision.

THE "RULES" OF REGULATION

Under regulation, business firms are guaranteed certain rights. For example, their property rights are legally protected, and confiscation is not a serious possibility. They are entitled to receive "reasonable prices" and a "fair rate of return" on their capital. In the specific geographical area in which it operates, a regulated firm is given partial or total protection from competition. A firm can challenge in the courts any regulating decision made by the relevant commission.

Regulated firms also have certain obligations. Their prices and profits must not be excessive. Prices should be established so as to offer the greatest possible service without compelling a company to forfeit its capital through continuous losses. Moreover, the regulated firm must meet all demand at the prices established. Any change in the quantity or quality of service (in the case of the railroads, this means especially the abandonment of service) must be approved in advance by the regulatory agency. The final decision in such cases as railroad petitions for abandonment of track or service must balance two conflicting objectives: the firm's operational benefits and the public interest. Finally, all regulated industries must be committed to high levels of performance with the highest possible standards of safety to the public. The key to regulation philosophy which has developed through nine decades of experience and sixteen independent agencies is this: a balance of public and private (corporate) interests.

The American experience with regulatory agencies is long enough, especially in the case of railroads and the ICC, so that we can judge how well they work. Admittedly, the evidence is mixed. Regulation has not always provided a fair balance between carriers and the public. But the record is not altogether bad. An accurate judgment of the worth of regulation might best be reached by asking what would have happened in its absence. In terms of railroads and the ICC, how might commercial transportation have developed without regulation? Does the Conservative argument for a purely "market solution" have much basis in fact?

RAILROADS AND THE ICC

Railroads were America's first big business. By the late 1880s, more than 150,000 miles of main-line trackage had been built. Railroads reported their current book value of investment at about $8 billion. (To understand the significance of this investment, we should note that GNP in 1890 has been estimated at about $13 billion.) The 750,000 railroad workers represented more than 5 percent of the nation's nonfarm employment. Millions more were indirectly employed by the railroads in steel, machine tool, rolling stock, and related industries. Added to this, the commercial interaction facilitated by railroads had stimulated investment and created jobs all across the nation that had not existed before the railroads came to town.

For all this apparent vitality, railroads were in trouble. Most had been built in advance of traffic demand. Many were purely speculative roads, laid down by promoters with an eye to quick profits from construction and from securities sales. Railroads, especially in the Northeast and Midwest, paralleled and duplicated routes. In almost every case, they were overcapitalized. Debt payments and dividend expectations simply outstripped the corporations' real earning power. To summarize, the industry was suffering from excess capacity and excessive capitalization. Big as it was, the economic foundation of the railroads was laid on shifting sands.

Periodically, bloody rate wars would break out among the giants as each tried to gain a larger share of the restricted transportation market. As a result, there were frequent bankruptcies and breakdowns in service. Because of their critical central place in the economy, as railroads went, so went the nation. Every major financial panic and recession after the Civil War—in 1873, 1884, and 1893—started with railroad bankruptcies. Attempts at private rate-fixing and cartels, even before their unconstitutionality was established by the Sherman Act, almost always failed. Even so, these expedients harmed farmers and other shippers. This, then, was the situation when the ICC was created in 1887. The free-market operation of the rail industry could no longer be tolerated. This view was widely held by bankers, farmers, shippers, and railroad management.

Space does not permit a detailed description of the gradual elaboration of ICC authority. It is sufficient to say that the initial limited powers of the commission over rate-setting were enlarged to cover virtually all operations of railroads operating in interstate commerce. Eventually all commercial surface transport enterprises came under ICC jurisdiction. The accretions of power in every case were responses to the failure of competitive market operations in the transport industry.

With regard to the railroads, the ICC has basically been preoccupied with the industry's chronic excess capacity problems, since virtually all rail problems are traceable to this difficulty. During the 1920s, even before trucks offered serious competition, the ICC tried to encourage the merger of American railroads into a limited number of systems (four or five systems for the entire Northeast, for instance). The railroads successfully fought this plan, and consolidation came only in the wake of financial collapse in the 1950s and 1960s. Meanwhile, the ICC permitted a 20 percent reduction in main-line trackage from the peak of 254,000 miles in 1916. It allowed railroads to end expensive less-than-carload shipment and permitted the virtual elimination of passenger service. As truck competition grew, the commission attempted to price the services of this rival so as to hold up railroad revenues and assure adequate returns. While not all ICC actions were rapid or supportive enough to suit rail management, it cannot be said that the ICC was indifferent to railroad needs. Moreover, in all its actions the commission considered the public interest—a factor in which the railroads had no natural interest.

In many cases ICC actions were inadequate. In the high-density traffic of the Northeast, no rating policy or abandonment policy could save the Penn-Central. Burdened by a merciless debt structure, challenged on all sides by state-subsidized truck competition, and plagued by plain bad management, the road collapsed in 1970.

Despite the current problems of the railroad industry, it is not fair to single out the ICC as a major cause of railroad crisis. Nor is it correct to conclude by implication that government regulatory commissions are failures. The ICC was not responsible for the rail industry's excess capacity or excessive capitalization. Neither was it responsible for the growth of truck competition or the proliferation of the private passenger car. The fact that it could not untie the Gordian knot—setting fair rates for various transit modes, one heavily subsidized and one heavily taxed by government—is hardly proof of failure. Transportation rates in the United States have remained low, and virtually any shipper in the country has easy access to some form of transportation. This is a distinct benefit to the public, one that would not have been assured if railroad bankruptcies and abandonments had followed the dictates of free-market decision making.

RECENT TRENDS RECONSIDERED

Despite its difficulties, regulation remains the only viable solution to the railroad problem. If there are troubles with regulation, it is because we have moved too slowly to develop a national transportation policy. The ICC executes but does not make national transportation decisions. Rather than providing proof that government regulatory agencies do not work, it shows that public regulation does work if all the issues are understood. The ICC has balanced as best it could the public interest in cheap and easy transportation with private goals of obtaining profits. Even in the depths of the 1974 recession, railroads reported net earnings of $770 million (the highest since 1966).

While Conservatives may see the recent "4R Act" (Railroad Revitalization and Regulatory Reform Act of 1976) as a new direction, they fail to grasp its real significance—an attempt to develop a more rationally planned national transportation network. Far from abandoning railroads to the unregulated whims of the market, the "4R Act" was a large step in developing a national transportation plan. The chaos in the Northeast, largely the result of past market failures, was replaced by Conrail, a government-organized merger of the six bankrupt roads. However, in this reorganization the principle of private ownership was retained, for Conrail was eventually to become, after a necessary period of government subsidy and reorganization, a private for-profit rail operation. Certainly the market could not have facilitated such a maintenance of private ownership in the rail industry.

In addition, the "4R Act" provided funds for the capital improvement of railroads, expanded the power of the Interstate Commerce Commission over intrastate rates, ended discriminatory taxation by separate states on rail property, and provided for the reorganization and streamlining of ICC decision making. The trend created by the Railroad Revitalization and Regulatory Reform Act points to a period of improved regulation, not the end of regulation.

Critics of the regulatory system who proclaim the market to be a better determinant of price and quantity might well be right in saying that an unregulated transport system would earn more profits. What then would happen to the public interest? Who would protect the public against monopoly power?

The Radical Argument

Public regulatory commissions are organized in modern monopoly capitalism to ratify the existence of monopoly. Not only that, but such commissions—regardless of the intention of reformers who championed their development—work primarily on behalf of the industries they regulate. The creation of the ICC, its development in the Progressive Era (1900–1920), and events of the past fifty years do not support the Liberal claim that "public interest" is a major element in regulatory action.

THE ICC AS A CREATURE OF INDUSTRY

Progressive Era legislation and regulatory enactments, rather than being simple-minded efforts to "compromise" the differences of parties on either side of a particular market (as the then-current political rhetoric maintained), were really efforts to bring order to highly disrupted and overly competitive markets. But "order" was achieved on terms that supported the principle of private property and corporate profit-seeking, terms that replaced competition with official recognition of limited monopolistic power and the principle of cartelization.

The ICC from its very beginning was an attempt to create an official cartel in rail transportation. This policy was steadily enlarged and elaborated upon by the industry. The development of the ICC was not a haphazard abandonment of high principles, but rather the unfolding of a planned and rational policy. (It was rational at least in the sense that it consistently pursued clear ends, even though they might ultimately result in economic and social loss to the nation.)

Although many economic interests favored the creation of a federal railroad regulating agency in the late 1880s, one of the most influential groups consisted of railroad leaders themselves. The closing decades of the nineteenth century had witnessed costly rate wars and other competitive difficulties, resulting largely from the enormous excess capacity built into the industry. These conflicts could not be dealt with through private efforts at cartelization, partly because these efforts usually collapsed of their own enforcement weaknesses and partly because other economic groups challenged such blatant attempts to build monopoly power. The railroads therefore turned to the federal government and official sanction of cartel creation. Progress toward this end began with passage of the Commerce Act of 1887; over the next twenty years, in the ICC and in Congress, railroads obtained important recognition as a cartel. Indeed, the Elkins Act (1903) which ended the hated competitive practice of paying rebates to certain shippers, was written in the legal offices of the Pennsylvania Railroad. The Hepburn Act (1906), which enlarged the ICC's power, supposedly at the expense of the rail monopolies, had considerable management endorsement.

"Community of interest" (informal domination of all rail operations in a region by a few large roads) and other plans formally to integrate rail properties for the purpose of obtaining greater monopoly power were frustrated for a time, but railroads emerged from World War I, after their ignominious operational collapse and more than two years of government control, with the Esch-Cummins Act of 1920. This law, as interpreted by the ICC and the courts, firmly established the principle of railroad cartelization. The old competitive situation within the industry existed no longer, and the rail network was reduced to a limited number of essentially noncompetitive systems. Most state regulatory powers over finance and operations were abolished. The old ambition of industry pooling and rate bureaus was given nourishment during the Depression. During the disastrous 1930's, the government, at Franklin Roosevelt's insistence, extended the courtesy of officially recognizing as the industry-wide policy-making body the Association of American Railroads, a powerful lobbyist and a tool for encouraging collusion within the industry. At the behest of rail leaders, the government moved in 1935 to control competition from the hated trucks and buses by placing them under ICC regulatory control. Finally, with the passage of the Transportation Act of 1940, the federal government officially declared an end to any pretense of maintaining "costly competition" either between railroads or among competing transport modes.

None of these regulative and legislative successes by the railroads, however, could insulate the industry from competition and from structural and demand dislocations that persistently wreaked havoc with railroad balance sheets through the 1950s and 1960s. The decline was not halted even by the hastily drawn Transportation Act of 1958, which took away the last effective regulatory power of the states over passenger trains, or the ICC's growing willingness to approve virtually any kind of merger or abandonment. The railroads had succeeded in getting themselves established as a protected cartel. Though they were not totally free to undertake whatever was in their interest, the official commitment to maintaining railroads as a privately owned industry meant that railroad legislation and regulation was loaded in their favor. The industry had to be kept going—on its own terms. For the society, this translated into the reduction of rail service and the steady deterioration of what remained.

Nor has the recent and much heralded emergency railroad legislation presented a new policy direction. As Conservatives accurately proclaimed, this act was largely written on the industry's own terms. In the name of increasing competition, the legislation was intended to stimulate merger, abandonment, and greater freedom by carriers in price setting. Meanwhile the ICC was retooled to give "public interest" blessing to new private efforts at profit maximization.

In many respects the emergency legislation efforts to deal with the rail crisis in the Northeast corridor reveal the actual content, past and present, of our transportation and regulatory policy. Under the 1976 Regulatory Act, the six bankrupt northeastern railroads were organized into Conrail. Two points are noteworthy in this development. First, Conrail, although federally organized, was to become a private production-for-profit corporation after it had been reconditioned by a massive infusion of government funds and by ruthless reduction in its trackage. Second, Conrail was devised to rescue the funds of the bankrupt railroads' investors. Although the initial government estimate of the scrap value of the bankrupt roads was set at $621 million, the owners claimed their deteriorated rolling stock and rusting rails to be worth at least $7 billion. Under pressure from banks, insurance companies, and other holders of railroad securities, Conrail was initially granted $2.1 billion in federal funds to acquire the nearly worthless financial paper of these roads. As of this writing, individual stockholder and bondholder suits promise to vastly increase this figure. The prospects of monetary gain from Conrail was evident to the investors in the bankrupt lines, many of whom spoke glowingly of government ownership. There was little talk of such actions being "socialistic," but John Kenneth Galbraith has correctly called it "socialism for the rich."

A DIFFERENT ALTERNATIVE

Whether or not this scenario for ICC-Railroad and government-railroad collaboration is accepted, we are still left with the "railroad problem." The alternatives to the nation's present railroad dilemma are limited to four: (1) a completely free and competitive transportation system in which it is assumed that private resource allocation will produce both the desired efficiency and social benefits; (2) vigorous public regulation of all or some privately owned and operated transportation facilities, with the assumption that somehow the public goal of maximum service can be squared with corporate expectations of a "fair return" (this alternative could include the "service at cost" or "cost plus" ideas now being widely discussed in the industry itself); (3) an intermediate position between the first two; and (4) nationalization.

Except for a small but influential band of free-market advocates, there will be few supporters of the first solution. Whatever the logic of a simple free-enterprise, profit-directed determination of resource use, it is simply not practical, whether one considers a single industry like public transportation or society as a whole—where such a free-enterprise system would ultimately be necessary in order for economic freedom in any of its sectors to exist. To most Liberals, the only realistic choices are solutions 2 or 3—some balance between private ownership decision making and public interest criteria. This, of course, is the stuff that dreams are made of: a little social planning here, some private ownership gratification there—the best of two possible worlds. But the double-headed policy of pursuing a transportation program that is simultaneously profit-oriented and in the public interest is an irreconcilable paradox.

The only way to serve the public better is to reduce private decision making. Ultimately nonmarket allocative decisions must be made, unless we abandon altogether any pretense at social planning. When that is done, the principle of private ownership and decision making is bit by bit reduced to little more than a meaningless and socially dangerous fetish.

If competition is an impossibility and a mixture of public-private responsibility is indeed as unworkable as the past eighty years of ICC experience would indicate, reopening the public ownership question is now essential. This is not just a matter of digging back into history and dusting off some old "nationalize the railroads" arguments. Social ownership and operation of the railroads is no longer a sufficient solution to the railroad dilemma, for increasingly there is no "railroad problem" but rather a "transportation problem." Social control of the railroads at a time of direct and liberal subsidy to privately operated trucks, buses, and commercial aircraft would be a monstrous folly. It would not arrest the collapse of the railroads except by an extravagantly inefficient use of resources, and the public interest would be no better served. Such important social issues as air and noise pollution, crowded cities, and the surrender of more open space to the inexorable advance of concrete and asphalt would be as far from human control as they now seem to be.

The railroad problem cannot be dealt with apart from all public transportation (and, probably, individual auto usage as well). Public transportation, whether viewed narrowly as a question of resource allocation or as a larger variable in the future economic and social development of the United States, can no longer be treated as if it were just another business, like the corner grocery or even U. S. Steel. The slogan for those who truly seek a radical change in transportation policies must not be limited to a merely unpopular "nationalize the railroads," but should be expanded to a more revolutionary "nationalize all public transportation." If we can admit that idea into our discussion long enough, perhaps the fancies and myths we harbor about attempts to balance private and public interest may be revealed and understood for what they are.

Social ownership—not alleged "social control" of private property—is the lesson to be learned from the experience of the railroads and the Interstate Commerce Commission. Nor need the lesson be limited in application merely to the "railroad problem."

ISSUE 6

The Multinational Firm
How Sovereign an Empire
for International Business?

Imperialism . . . [is] parasitic or decaying capitalism. . . . On the whole capitalism is growing far more rapidly than before. But this growth is not only becoming more uneven in general; its unevenness also manifests itself, in particular, in the decay of countries which are richest in capital.

V. I. Lenin, 1917

American factories are making more than the American people can use; American soil is producing more than they can consume. Fate has written our policy for us; the trade of the world must and shall be ours.

Senator Albert Beveridge, 1897

As sympathetic as I am to labor's viewpoint in the matter of employment, I sincerely believe they are whipping the wrong horse in attacking multinational corporations.

N. R. Danielian, President,
International Economic Policy Association, 1971

Multinational corporations indulging in unbridled pursuit of corporate profit pose a direct threat to the economic health of the United States.

I. W. Abel, President
United Steelworkers, AFL-CIO, 1975

THE PROBLEM

Up to this point, we have examined American economic problems from a distinctly parochial perspective, acknowledging the existence of the rest of the world only incidentally. Clearly the American economic system does not exist in a vacuum. Each year we buy and sell more than $145 billion worth of commodities in world markets. We are crucially dependent on foreign sources of raw materials that range from petroleum to coffee. In turn much of the world depends on our exported technology. Business and financial changes in one country have quick and pronounced ripple effects in all others. In an economic sense, the planet has shrunk considerably.

Certainly the most controversial economic development in this internationalization of world production and consumption has been the multinational corporation (MNC). While an international focus on business and financial affairs is scarcely new, the MNCs have forged a new era in international trade and development. At the same time they have produced profound changes in the structure and organization of all domestic economies. More than at any other time in our history, our own domestic economic well-being depends upon economic actions of American business beyond our shores.

In the simplest terms, a multinational corporation is an enterprise based in one country but carrying on production, extraction, research, and sales operations in many other nations. In general, MNCs are highly integrated and diversified. Their large size and economies of scale in production are enhanced by their ability to shift capital assets and production according to profit objectives. The old constraints of geography and nationalism are minimized. Whereas national firms had to trade across national barriers and compete with foreign enterprise, the MNC can enjoy multiple national personalities in its day-to-day operations.

Sometimes the MNC can take the form of a single company such as Pepsico with a comparatively limited product line. Pepsico still ranks near the top 100 of American manufacturing firms. It manufactures Pepsi-Cola in 114 foreign countries in over 500 plants, two-thirds of which are foreign enterprises. More frequently the MNC takes the form of a giant international conglomerate such as Ford or General Motors. Ford, for instance, is much more than the Ford Motor Company. It is a combination of over sixty subsidiary companies, two-thirds of which are located overseas. Ford's activities range from autos to radios to machine tools.

As we shall see in the following discussion, there is little agreement among the three groups of economists about the meaning of multinational corporations. Their economic effects on host and parent nations are hotly debated. So is the question of whether their economic power results in the actual corporate creation of American foreign policy. About the only area of agreement is that the MNCs are big. Just how big is staggering. By 1977 the combined gross earnings of the world's four largest multinationals (General Motors, Exxon, Texaco, and Ford) was exceeded by the gross national products of only seven nations in the world. The GNP of only about fifteen nations exceeded GM's total sales. The immediate and long-run significance of such corporate concentration of capital and economic strength cannot be minimized.

SYNOPSIS The Conservative argument contends that the multinational corporation is not new but is a continuation of business efforts to seek profits, and improves standards of living everywhere. The Liberal argument maintains that MNCs have gained unjustifiable economic power that now poses a threat to American workers and consumers. The Radical argument perceives the international expansion of business as simply a recent form of the capitalist desire to maximize profits whatever the cost to parent or host country; in it success lies the failure of the capitalist system.

The Conservative Argument

The recent singling out of multinational enterprises for abuse and possibly punitive legislation is unjustified and singularly dangerous for the national economy. While it is difficult to specify all the roots of the persecution of multinationals, one basic misunderstanding is obvious: their opponents erroneously believe that multinational business is a unique and recent phenomenon of capitalist development.* Accordingly multinational enterprise is set up as the special whipping boy for a wide range of contemporary domestic and international problems that have nothing to do with international business development.

NOT A NEW IDEA AT ALL

In point of fact, multinational business dates from the very beginning of capitalist enterprise, with the founding of the great joint stock companies in the early seventeenth century. The Dutch East India Company and the British East India Company were, after all, enterprises formed in and based in one country, but organized to carry on their economic activities in several nations or areas. In the United States during the middle and late nineteenth century, several manufacturers opened overseas plants and sales offices, among them Samuel Colt (firearms), the Singer Sewing Machine Company, and International Harvester (farm equipment). At the same time, American banking, transportation, and extractive industries also established profitable overseas operations and sources of investment. A measure of this internationalization of American businesses can be seen in the fact that direct overseas American investment had grown to $1.6 billion by 1908. (Incidentally, this was equal to about 5 percent of our GNP, almost the same proportion as our current $100 billion in overseas direct investment.)

*Another misunderstanding of multinational development is perceiving them as a uniquely American phenomenon. Although many U.S. firms are involved in MNC operations and practically all large firms have become MNCs, about two-thirds of the world's multinationals are not American owned companies. Indeed, as the thoughtful consumer must know, the British, Japanese, German, and other non-American based multinationals offer significant competition to American producers in domestic markets.

In view of this background, there is no foundation to the Radical and Liberal charge that the multinational is a unique and recent development demanding "special" attention. The inference of these attacks—that the multinational is a threat to domestic or international economic harmony—is even more obviously incorrect.

MNCS BOOST THE DOMESTIC ECONOMY

The international search for profits by American enterprise, particularly overseas manufacturing growth since World War II, has benefited the domestic economy. Higher overseas profits have strengthened the domestic operations of business enterprises. This has meant more stable business conditions, more jobs, and higher wages for American workers. The continued internationalization of business has led to steady improvement in the American standard of living.

A frequent refrain of MNC critics is that U.S. corporations have emphasized overseas investment at the expense of domestic spending on plant and equipment. Supposedly, this has led to the stagnation of business in the United States and the loss of domestic jobs. However, the evidence does not support this claim as Figure 6.1 shows. Repatriated earnings from overseas U.S. investment have been consistently greater than capital outflows. In the very good year of 1974 (in terms of international business), repatriated earnings of almost $18 billion was more than twice the investment outflow.

As to the charge that overseas investment has "substituted" for national investment, a recent *Business International* study has shown that overseas activity actually stimulates domestic spending. In 1972 all U.S. manufacturers increased their national spending on plant and equipment by 108 percent over the previous year. However, businesses participating in multinational activities increased their American plant and equipment holdings by 141 percent. Indeed, such factual evidence is not surprising since multinational activity has significantly stimulated those American companies participating in overseas operations. And growth is the chief determinant of business investment.

The frequent argument that overseas United States investment has lowered American employment is far off target. Those who take this view usually assume that all or most foreign employees of American firms would have been American workers if businesses had located their operations here. What they forget is that most overseas

FIGURE 6.1   U.S. DIRECT INVESTMENT FLOWS

Source: International Economic Report of the President, March 1976, p. 85.

production is aimed exclusively at overseas markets. American businesses would have lost these markets to foreigners had they not invested in foreign enterprise. The comparatively high price of American labor and the general inflation pressures of the past decade simply would not have permitted exclusively American production to meet foreign prices. Thus 100 percent American production would not have stimulated employment in the United States at all. On the other hand, the overseas expansion of American investment did create markets for American-made goods and components within MNC overseas operations. Despite the high price of American labor, which has caused the export of many jobs, the U.S. Tariff Commission estimates that a half million domestic manufacturing jobs were created between 1966 and 1970 by MNC operations.

Multinational development has also improved the American balance of payments situation. Without the revitalization of American industry and trade through multinational activity, all United States business would have suffered. High-priced American exports would have been unable to find foreign markets, and low-priced foreign goods would have glutted ours. Moreover, on their own accounts, multinationals based in the United States export much more than they import. In 1971 multinationals were adding $17 billion to our balance of payments—two-thirds from exports and one-third from investment income. Another $1.5 billion came from royalties on American multinational technology. Without these contributions, our balance of trade position would be much worse than it was and is. MNCs actually have mitigated the international trade crisis caused by domestic American inflation over the past decade.

With regard to the charge that multinational growth has strengthened monopoly power, the Conservative position holds to an entirely different conclusion. MNCs are indeed giant enterprises, but size and economies of scale are essential in effective international competition. If the United States government had pursued a drastic antitrust policy toward MNCs for purely domestic regulatory purposes, it would have hampered their overseas effectiveness. This in turn would have had adverse effects on profits and employment while producing no real economic or social benefits.

Looking at MNCs as we have, we can see how disastrous a policy of narrow economic nationalism would have been. If the advice of union leaders and some Liberal economists had been heeded, the domestic effects would have been (1) worsened employment conditions, (2) a considerable weakening of American business vis-à-vis the rest of the world, and (3) generally higher prices for the American consumer. In short, the failure of American business to invest overseas would have greatly increased our domestic economic problems of unemployment and inflation.

THE GAINS FOR INTERNATIONAL TRADE

What about the international effect of multinationals? The usual Radical protest is to shout "Imperialism!" If this appellation means that American businesses invest overseas to make a profit, the charge is correct. That's the name of the game. However, if the term means the heartless exploitation of what is popularly called the Third World, it is false. Today 68 percent of all direct United States investment is in developed nations. Not counting the oil producing nations' bloated share of our imports, the developing nations account for only 19 percent of our import volume. The relative imbalance between the developed and developing nations is today just about reversed from what it was fifty years ago. We have actually moved in quite a different direction from Lenin's interpretation of imperialism.

Yet even if we were to consider the small part of our trade and investment that is directed to the Third World, the Marxist scenario would not be applicable. In most Third World nations, multinational activities have to do with extracting minerals and other raw materials. These Third World nations have nothing else to trade, no other basis for their economies. To be sure, MNCs do seek cheap raw materials, but they also create jobs, savings, and indigenous industry that would not otherwise exist. They enable poor countries to buy the machines and technology they could not purchase if their resources stayed in the ground. Per capita income has consistently climbed in practically all Third World nations where MNCs have been active. The old practice of colonialist rape of resources and people has been replaced by a mutually beneficial trade relationship.

The internationalization and global reach of business has been a long and steady development. Given free rein, it will ultimately aid efficient global resource allocation and raise living standards. These are benefits to be obtained by all economies—developed or developing— that are not possible behind the gates of narrow economic nationalism and trade restraints. The Conservatives' international objectives, like their domestic objectives, are free trade and development. The MNC is an important device for bringing this about.

We should not, however, be deceived into believing that the ideal of "free development" of international business and trade is immediately at hand. Government interventionism still exists. Foreign governments subsidize their multinationals with cash payments and social programs for workers. In the United States, favorable tax laws have been created to help American businesses offset these foreign subsidies. But international tariffs and exchange rate rigidities interfere with the free development of business and trade. To the Conservative, all of this is anathema. Ending all artificial restrictions in international trade and business development is a necessary goal, although it will not be reached quickly.

The Liberal Argument

The Conservative contention that multinational corporations are merely a logical development in a long history of international capitalism, while literally true, understates the significance of their operations today. We need to understand exactly how large the multinationals are and how they have transformed capitalist economies. First of all, more than half of America's 500 largest corporations have extensive manufacturing interests outside the United States. Many large corporations (for example, Exxon, ITT, IBM, and National Cash Register) have more than half their assets overseas and earn half or more of their profits from overseas operations. From this and other available evidence, it is obvious that the MNC phenomenon is no inconsequential change in the manner of doing business.

Although MNCs and their defenders have labored to put a good face to their development, their arguments rest upon an "either-or" kind of analysis. *Either* MNCs should have developed as they have and should be allowed to do the same in the future *or* domestic economic conditions would be worse than they are at present. Such analysis rarely considers an alternative scenario in which business investment might have been national rather than multinational. As a result all MNC activity is blindly defended as good for business and hence good for America.

From the multinationals' point of view, the overseas export of capital and production operations has been marvelously successful. Freedom from higher American labor costs (actually, freedom to hire miserably paid foreign labor), evasion of overseas tariffs, and flight from domestic taxes have meant considerable profit gains. This flight of corporations and capital, however, has cost the American economy dearly.

SURVEYING THE COSTS

One of the more important long-run costs of the multinational transfer of operations has been to increase industrial obsolescence in the United States. By 1975 about one out of every five dollars of domestically generated capital investment was going overseas. As a result, net American capital investment was falling behind real GNP growth. This means that American plants have been getting older and American production techniques have been slipping behind overseas technologies. The American worker, long the world's most productive, is increasingly attacked in the Conservative and business press as American output per man hour has become the slowest growing in the industrial world. The usual explanation is laziness or too much union control over output. The real cause, however, is that workers have poorer equipment and technology. Meanwhile, the old anxiety about machines displacing labor is becoming a reality—except that it is overseas automation (by American firms) that is causing domestic job displacement. One study found that between 1966 and 1970 productive jobs overseas grew about fifteen times faster than similar domestic jobs, and overall overseas employment by MNCs grew five times faster than MNC employment in the United States.

Conservatives argue that foreign job gains were not American losses because foreign business would have created the overseas employment if GM, GE, Ford, and others had not. This could be true only if foreign-based producers had a competitive advantage over United States multinationals and could have protected their markets from American-made goods. This clearly was not and is not the case. American industry expanded overseas where virtually no local competition existed. The result was at least 1 million jobs lost to American workers between 1966 and 1973.

The shift to overseas production has had a very adverse effect on American wages. Threatened with corporate flight, labor is losing its competitive balance with capital in key industries. As a result, real wages in the United States have been held down and the real standard of living of Americans has been lowered.

It is true that corporations did enhance their short-run profits by abandoning (relatively or absolutely) American labor, hiring cheap foreign labor, and using expensive but highly productive new technologies. The long-run gains are less obvious. Inflation and wage increases overseas are far greater than in the United States. Of the industrial nations, only Japan is reporting higher GNP growth rates. The illusion of quick profits to be gained by running away is fading, but the damage has been done. In the United States unemployment is high and technology is quite backward after a decade in which workers paid for the overseas flight of American companies. No auto worker could have missed the irony of Ford's initial advertising program for its Pinto—"the American answer to foreign competition." On the assembly line they knew that the Pinto's engines came from Germany and England, and its standard transmissions from France and Italy. As one worker quipped, "If the car was any more American, we wouldn't be working at all."

Another long-run cost of the MNC flight has been the heightening of economic concentration and monopoly profit making. The profitable MNCs eagerly swallowed up domestic and foreign competition in efforts to diversify and integrate their operations. Contrary to the Conservative view that the MNC is an example of greater international competition, it represents the growth of potentially dangerous monopoly power. Ford and GM, as giant multinationals, are more independent and insulated from the market in their pricing and output policies than purely "national" American Motors. Invariably, MNC profit rates are higher than those of national firms operating in the same fields, but MNC efficiency has not benefited consumers. In fact, as we have already seen in the case of the oil cartels, multinational integration can lead to horrendous exploitation of the consumer.

The American consumer has already been victimized by huge government tax and subsidy supports for the MNCs. The most important of these is the "foreign tax credit." Under this arrangement all foreign taxes on MNC operations may be credited against the company's corporate income tax liability. This amounts to a tax subsidy for doing business overseas. There are other benefits as well: deferring all taxes on overseas income not returned to the United States, 50 percent deferral of taxes for exporting firms, low cost Export-Import Bank loans, and government insurance against foreign expropriation. Clearly American taxpayers substantially bankroll the very MNC tendencies that threaten their jobs and incomes.

Overseas expansion by American corporations has also harmed our international trade situation. The MNCs defense of their overseas investments as operations strengthening American balance of payments largely rests on the evidence that repatriated income from foreign earnings vastly exceeds annual investment outflows. While this may be essentially true, it misses an important point. The overseas operations of U.S. business have reduced exports of manufactured goods from within the United States to foreign markets. At the same time, the United States must import ever larger amounts of manufactured goods made overseas. Manufacturing shares of our imports have grown from 40 to 65 percent of our imports in two decades. Meanwhile, our export economy has shifted from a manufacturing to an agricultural foundation, a balance sheet of a nation in decline. Looking only at the cash flows of investment out and repatriated income in, MNCs do give the appearance of improving our trade balance. However, the deeper structural effect on exports and imports of shifting manufacturing overseas more than offsets these gains.

To summarize, the long-run tendencies of multinational development cannot be tolerated. MNCs have devastated the American industrial base, eroded productivity, created domestic unemployment, lowered wages, increased tax deficits, and worsened our international trade position. These national costs are too great to justify the short-run profit gains for the MNCs, and they demand greater public regulation of multinational operations.

CONTROLLING MNCS

Economic regulation of multinationals must take place on two fronts. We must end the existing economic advantages that stimulate overseas capital movement. And we must create specific regulatory machinery to monitor overseas business operations.

On the first front, we must put an end to all preferential tax treatment for MNCs. Foreign tax deferral and the foreign tax credit must be repealed. Government loans and insurance should be sharply curtailed. Like tax breaks, these act as federal subsidies to overseas movement. They create profits that would not be possible under normal business conditions, and they are paid for by the American people. As a labor leader observed, maintaining the present tax arrangements for the MNCs is rather like forcing the condemned to tip the executioner.

On the second front—that of specific regulation—a number of actions are necessary. First, all overseas direct investment might be studied and approved by one or more government agencies, perhaps the

Departments of Labor and Commerce. Each proposed overseas movement of capital and operations should be evaluated against its effect on domestic jobs, wages, investment, and production. When the overseas expansion would cause a clear hardship for Americans, it must be prohibited or modified. Second, exporting advanced technology to existing and new overseas operations should also be regulated. Such technology transfers, although enhancing the trade position of MNCs, reduce America's competitive advantage.

Another area where multinational behavior should be regulated is the political realm, a matter not discussed before. The overseas operations of American corporations are not just matters of economics, as the Conservatives suggest. ITT's attempts to manipulate the overthrow of the Chilean government of Salvador Allende in the early 1970s, the Lockheed Corporation's notorious bribery of Japanese officials, the corporate-military ties with the South Korean government, and the deep involvement of American MNCs in Iran, while undertaken in the business spirit of making a profit, have had serious foreign policy effects. In the Iranian case, the degree of MNC penetration, particularly in the area of oil production and military sales, doubtless contributed to the official American blindness toward the repressive character and domestic unpopularity of the Shah's regime, to the Shah's eventual downfall, and to protracted political turmoil in that nation. The result was a major diplomatic defeat for the United States. Present multinational involvement in South Africa, Saudi Arabia, and throughout South America will certainly create additional foreign policy crises in the future.

When MNCs enlist the support of American public officials, directly or indirectly, to obtain business advantages or interfere in overseas elections, they are assuming foreign policy roles without being responsible to elected officials or to the American people. There is absolutely no reason to believe that short-run profit objectives coincide with long-run foreign policy goals of the United States. The Constitution cannot be subordinated to corporate balance sheets.

The threat of uncontrolled multinational activity is real and the effects not hard to understand. They will not bring the "heaven on earth" goal of free trade, but will lead instead to national bankruptcy. This is not speculation but a lesson from the history books. Beginning in the early years of this century, Great Britain shipped vast amounts of capital overseas while operating domestic enterprises in increasingly inefficient fashion. The ultimate collapse of Britain's tottering domestic economy after the 1950s was the price paid for foreign profits earned earlier.

While Liberals support the production-for-profit system, it is clear that profit making is not an absolute consideration. National economic order and political stability are higher objectives. The Liberal position is positively opposed to the philosophy of such industrialists as the chairman of Dow Chemical; his personal "dream" of multinational development was to buy a deserted island where he could locate his company's international headquarters, "beholden to no nation and no society." The cost to the American people of that kind of "dream," if realized, cannot be permitted.

The Radical Argument

The multinational corporation is the latest expression of capitalist imperialism. As Conservatives argue, capitalism has from its very beginning been international in character. The maturation of a worldwide extension of the capitalist production-for-profit system has seen many stages: the mercantilist and slave-trading epoch of the eighteenth century, colonial expropriation of the noncapitalist world in the nineteenth century, and international cartelization by business and finance in the first half of this century.

THE LOGICAL OUTCOME OF THE SYSTEM

The internationalization of capital is the logical outcome of a system wholly dependent on perpetual expansion for existence. Capitalist enterprise can never tire in its search for profits and its effort to assert advantage over rivals. As any business leader knows, when a business stagnates, its collapse is imminent. Each capitalist enterprise is driven by the search for new products, new sources of supply, new markets, new technologies, and new techniques of doing business. In the drive to grow rather than die, one market is not enough, one nation is not enough, and ultimately one world is not enough. The growth imperative at first creates sharp competition among capitalists, but this gives way to monopoly behavior as a few large firms become dominant. As we have noted earlier, this was the experience of American capitalism at the beginning of this century. The recent expansion of the multinational corporation is merely the international expression of monopoly capital's need to move beyond national markets to fulfill growth requirements.

Seen from this Radical perspective, multinational activities are merely a modern elaboration of old capitalist strategies and tactics. MNCs are only a new vehicle in the historical capitalist tendency toward imperialism and the domination of the entire world. However, the assertion that there is nothing theoretically new in the development of MNCs should not be understood to mean that multinational development does not change world economic and social conditions. While the profit-maximizing dynamic of capitalism is a constant, it expresses itself in different sets of contradictions in people's lives.

The principal irony in the era of the MNC is that while a few giant international corporations grow fatter, the individual economies of both capitalist nations and developing nations grow poorer. It is simply not true that what is good for General Motors is good for America. Nor is it good for Germany or Japan or Nigeria.

DETERIORATION AT HOME

The increasing shift of American capital to overseas production, beginning in the mid-1950s, accelerated the already evident trend of a growing labor surplus in the American economy. Almost exactly when American firms expanded overseas, unemployment began to rise and real wages began to stagnate. Only the war economy of the Vietnam era masked the seriousness of this exporting of employment.

The newest and best American technology rushed overseas to fill the new European markets for electronics, machine tools, and consumer goods. Cheap foreign skilled labor attracted other investment to the Far East, where goods were produced for sale in the United States. The effect of both moves was virtually to halt the growth of skilled jobs in the United States. At the same time, labor-intensive firms discovered the unskilled labor markets of Korea, Taiwan, and the Philippines, where workers were paid the equivalent of twenty cents an hour. This discovery had adverse effects on unskilled American labor. Only the domestic growth of low-wage jobs in the service sector and the expansion of government war and social spending mitigated the dramatic export of employment. It does not demand mastery of *Capital* to realize that an economy based on McDonald's drive-ins, war, and government bureaucracies is in deep trouble.

The reported profits of MNCs (which are certainly much lower than their real profits) expanded precisely as the well-being of most Americans declined. Income inequality was increased, government fiscal problems worsened, and labor's bargaining power diminished. The MNC export of domestic capital (past American labor) was producing a tremendous economic contraction in America. And, by the mid-1970s, Americans everywhere were being urged to lower their expectations as workers and consumers. Corporations, however, were not lowering their profit targets. From an American point of view, the multinational corporation was an effective new tool of capitalist exploitation at home.

DETERIORATION OVERSEAS

America's losses, however, were not necessarily everybody else's gains. In Europe and Japan, where most of the new MNC direct investment went, there was a brief economic boom. Labor was relatively scarce in the new capital-intensive, high-technology industries. Compensation per hour doubled and tripled in many countries between 1960 and 1975. There was much talk of prosperity, but two factors tended to blunt these advances. First, even with wage gains, most foreign workers, skilled or unskilled, were still relatively impoverished by (dwindling) American standards. Second, the domination of foreign economies by American capital sparked political reactions from foreign governments. When one adds to this the sudden rise to power of the OPEC cartel, it is apparent that European and Japanese gains from American MNC expansion were slight indeed. By 1977, in fact, Japan was the only industrial nation to report a real growth of GNP greater than that of the United States. Meanwhile, as industrialization has increased everywhere in the capitalist world, so does the specter of trade wars among developed nations, trying to improve or protect their markets. Far from realizing the Conservative dream of free trade, multinational development has actually stimulated economic protectionism.

Of course, the most devastating effect of multinational growth has been in the Third World. Although a comparatively small part of

American direct investment has gone to the poor nations, it has been critical to both the MNCs and to Third World countries.

Most Third World investment is earmarked for the extraction of raw materials. The rest produces profitable but socially useless consumer goods for sale to the population. Neither type of investment creates a usefully employed economy or broadens the technological base of the host country. This type of MNC activity is the worst kind of parasitism. Subsistence wages to unskilled labor draw off a nation's resources cheaply without any regard for its long-range development. "Coca Colonialization" meanwhile absorbs the nation's scant savings in useless consumer goods. "Progress" is a soft drink machine at the exit gate of a Bolivian tin mine or a cheap radio in a Brazilian shanty.

To protect their investments and perpetuate the perversion of the domestic economy and society to MNC needs, overseas operations must constantly interfere in local domestic politics to maintain friendly repressive regimes. Always in the background there is the might of American military power and economic sanctions that can be employed against recalcitrant nationalists. United States multinationals know full well that they can manipulate overseas American military and economic strategy to suit their needs.

THE FUTURE

Remedial efforts proposed by Liberals to "control" American multinationals, although well intended, show an incomplete grasp of the situation. First of all, such programs are purely "American" efforts at control. They fail to see MNC development as a world capitalist phenomenon. Probably excessive restrictions on American MNC operations, or at least those operations that can actually be reached by regulation, would cause more domestic harm than good. They might actually stimulate job and capital outflows. Second, Liberals presume naively that the present government can "control" the multinational corporation. In point of fact, MNCs make our foreign policy. Any effort to change this situation will be much more socially wrenching than Liberals understand.

What then does the future hold from a Radical viewpoint? As we have repeatedly pointed out, capitalism is racked by contradictions. Its very successes are its failures. The multinational firm, as the latest development in the world organization of capitalist production, also generates the greatest international contradictions. Precisely as it now succeeds in the world, its future failure is assured.

The MNC has eliminated much of the anarchy of capitalist production. By control of international production, distribution, and consumption, many ordinary business risks are avoided. In terms of its own balance sheets, MNC costs, revenues, and profits are more rationally controlled. Balance for the firm, however, does not mean balance in the world. Costs and gains fall unevenly on people and nations around the globe. Very few, if any, nations can be at ease with the MNCs. National political needs—for example, higher employment and improved living standards—can always be subverted by the profit needs of a corporation when it shifts assets or operations elsewhere. Indeed, MNCs make these moves to exploit the uneven development within and among nations. Contrary to the argument of Conservative apologists, free trade among equals is not the objective. Freedom to exploit economic inequality is.

It is probable that continued MNC integration and "success" will set off decisively unsettling political repercussions in the world. The failure of MNCs to produce balance and growth in the developed economies may trigger trade wars across national borders and anti-capitalist sentiment within them. In the Third World, the clearly exploitative nature of the MNC actually stimulates nationalism and the possibilities of expropriation. The search for private profit, even under an integrated international form of social production, fails simply because it is private and individualistic in its objectives.

As the editors of *Monthly Review* have argued, MNCs and nations must in the long run be in opposition to each other. Each by its own interests opposes the other. The possible outcomes: "World Empire or World Revolution." However, international corporate empires have no permanent constituency and, except in the cases where they can totally dominate governments, they have no armies or navies.

Corporate leaders are themselves aware of the world-wide crises they face. In fact, the Rockefeller-sponsored Trilateral Commission (made up of key industry and government leaders from Europe, Japan, and the United States) has studied the economic future of the MNCs and developed economies as part of its overall strategy of planning for strengthening the capitalist world economy. It concluded that lowered living standards in the industrialized countries are unavoidable in the future. At a meeting in Tokyo in 1975, Trilateral Commission members listened earnestly to a working paper that called for greater repression and abridgement of civil liberties in industrial countries. This was thought to be the necessary response to mass worker restiveness. Farfetched? Only to those who fail to grasp the true meaning of capitalism.

Ultimately, world-wide reaction against the multinational corporation is the only assurance of its elimination. A domestic American Radical strategy would be limited to a program similar to the one proposed by Liberals—but with one big difference. Radicals know full well that truly to reform the MNC is in reality to end it, but only on an international scale. Purely national controls would have no useful purpose if Ford, GM, and the rest could move their base of operations to Brazil or Argentina.

For Radicals, the multinational corporation teaches the final lesson on the nature of capitalism. It must be opposed by everyone everywhere. One person's struggle is everyone's struggle.

ISSUE 7

Labor Problems

Are the Unions Too Powerful?

We, the members of the National Association of Manufacturers of the United States of America . . . do hereby declare
the following principles. . . . (1) that fair dealing is the fundamental and basic principle on which relations between em-
ployes and employers should rest. . . . (6) Employers must be
unmolested and unhampered in the management of their
business, in determining the amount and quality of their product, and in the use of any methods or systems of pay which
are just and equitable.
Statement of Principles, N.A.M., 1903

In the profit sharing scheme, we're trying to find a rational
means by which free labor and free management, sitting at the
bargaining table, can attempt to work out in their relationship
practical means by which you can equate the competing
equities—in workers, stockholders, and consumers.
Walter Reuther, United Auto Workers, CIO, 1958

TIME TABLE OF THE HOLYOKE MILLS
(to take effect on or after Jan. 3d, 1853)

Morning Bells . . . first bell at 4:40 A.M.
    yard gates open at ringing of bells for ten minutes
Breakfast Bells . . . ring out at 7 A.M.; ring in at 7:30 A.M.
Dinner Bells . . . ring out at 12:30 P.M.; ring in at 1 P.M.
Evening Bells . . . ring out at 6:30 P.M.*
*excepting on Saturdays when the sun sets previous to ⸮:30.
    At such times ring out at sunset. (in all cases the first
    stroke of the bell is considered as the marking time)

Posted Hours of a Massachusetts Mill, 1853

THE PROBLEM

Of the total civilian labor force of over 100 million, only about 22 percent, or 20 million Americans, are members of labor unions. As Figure 7.1 shows, organized labor's share of workers has been steadily declining since the 1950s, nevertheless, union power is still formidable. The AFL-CIO, which claims about 80 percent of all union members, remains a major bloc in the political coalition that makes up the Democratic party. Thus the lobby representing organized labor in Congress and at the White House is vital in determining government policy toward unionism and other social policies affecting labor. Welfare, social security, job programs, and minimum-wage laws all bear the imprint of organized labor.

Although the labor union movement can be traced back to colonial times, the development of unions as a political and economic force is comparatively new. As recently as forty years ago, there were fewer than 5 million union members in the nation. The sudden growth of union membership and political influence during the last four decades has raised serious questions of just how powerful unions should be and in whose interest they really operate. The problem is not simply a matter of periodic labor-capital struggles (or warfare, as some would call it). The present and future problem, as many see it, is the long-run balance of power between unions and other sectors of the economy. To what degree is the power of organized labor consistent with the general economic welfare of the whole society?

SYNOPSIS The Conservative argument presents unions as true monopolists, which exact higher wages at the cost of higher prices to consumers, reduction of business profits, and interference with the labor market. The Liberal argument maintains that unions are a necessary balance to corporate power and that they have improved the general well-being of all workers. The Radical argument, while agreeing that the union movement has aided workers, holds that it has not played a sufficiently active political role.

FIGURE 7.1   UNION MEMBERSHIP, 1900–1975

Source: From U.S. Bureau of the Census, Historical Statistics of the United States, 1976, p. 389, and the Bureau of Labor Statistics.

The Conservative Argument

While union members represent only a small proportion of all American workers, unions have inordinate power. Concentrated in critical industries and trades, they are able to use extraordinary leverage in obtaining wage gains and other benefits. To a very considerable extent, their power is simple blackmail. If government or business fails to agree to union demands, the result can be devastating strikes in key industries, with spill-over effects involving the entire economy. A protracted labor struggle in the steel industry, for instance, can throw millions of other Americans out of work and create a national recession. A truckers' strike can keep food off thousands of tables. With such economic strength, it is not surprising that union political power has been growing even though membership has been more or less stabilized for the past decade.

Liberal dogma tells us that the growth of union power has been beneficial to all Americans. Does this argument stand the test of the most obvious economic analysis? How have unions produced more and more for everybody with nobody the loser? The answer is that they haven't. Union progress has had a very high price tag for the American people.

WHO PAYS THE BILL?

First and foremost, unions adversely affect the price and total output of goods and services. Gains in wages and fringe benefits, won through union pressure, add to the costs of any firm's output. The only options for a business are to absorb the costs through lower profits or pass them on in the form of higher prices. The first alternative reduces a firm's competitive strength and lessens its ability to acquire capital and make needed investment. The second alternative penalizes consumers by forcing them to pay prices that are higher than necessary. High prices, of course, tend to stimulate higher prices, since everyone has to run a bit faster to catch up.

It is not that unions don't know about the effects of unreasonable wage gains. They don't care. I. W. Abel, former head of the United Steelworkers, was asked in 1977 whether he felt that his union's current contract demands for a guaranteed life income might not be a heavy burden for the steel industry and, ultimately, the consumer. With the unionist's typical indifference to the cost of union victories, Abel replied, "We're not concerned with that side of the question. We must look out for our members."

Even more burdensome than the direct wage costs of unionism are union efforts to usurp ownership and management powers. Unions force on firms contracts that interfere with efficient labor hiring and use (railroad full-crew, or "featherbedding," arrangements are an example) and that often specify maximum daily or hourly output. The result is industrial inefficiency and reduced productivity. Such violations of employers' rights to their own capital and property and their freedom to hire and fire also add to production costs and finally to consumer prices.

Furthermore, the excessive power of labor unions disrupts the operation of supply and demand in the labor market. Since unionized industries must pay higher wages, they lower their demand for labor as they shift toward greater, and cheaper, capital use. Moreover, as individuals are forced out of, or prevented from entering, jobs "protected" by unions, they drive down wage rates in other areas. With a greater supply of available labor, all things being equal, wages are lowered in nonunion jobs. The overall effect of these shifts has been an increased imbalance in national income distribution. The gulf between the labor union elite and the disadvantaged bottom grows; union gains have to come from someplace, and they come mostly from other workers, especially the poorest workers.

Another undesirable effect of unionism is the aggressive advocacy of "union shop" or "agency shop" conditions for employment. Under this arrangement, a company-recognized union can compel union membership (union shop) or at least dues payment (agency shop) as a requirement for employment. Such specifications obviously deny individual workers the free choice of joining or rejecting a union. Perhaps of equal importance, this forced dues collection vastly increases a union's economic (read "strike-making") power. To halt this trend, Conservatives have fought hard in recent years for "right to work" laws which would end enforced union membership and union appropriation of part of each worker's pay.

Aside from these direct effects on the marketplace, others— equally undesirable—result from union efforts to develop so-called progressive legislation. A couple of examples should suffice. First, let's take union support of a national minimum wage. Superficially, this support is justified as an attempt to improve the lot of the nonunion worker. In fact, unions favor the minimum wage concept because it lays an ever-rising legal floor on which they can build ever-higher union-wage ceilings. The actual result is not to help the poor but to increase union wages and lower the average nonunion worker's income. This happens because hikes in the minimum wage destroy jobs, especially marginal jobs; if an employer must pay more than a worker creates in value, he will lay off the worker.

A second example of unions and legislation was their practice, a decade or so ago, of supporting social legislation to "protect" female workers. Protection in fact became discrimination, as laws and union contracts denied women access to certain jobs and kept them locked in low-paying "female" occupations. Feminists who charge business with sex discrimination should start looking in the right places—among the labor unions and social-rights advocates of several decades past.

One further example of excessive union influence is their use of "union-made" power. By forcing industries to purchase from and sell to unionized firms only, and by pressuring fellow unionists to buy only union-made products, industrial unions can effectively lower the demand for the goods of certain nonunion firms. While this practice is a direct interference with property rights and should be opposed as such, it also creates inefficiency, destroys jobs, and causes needlessly high prices.

The unions' monopolistic efforts have a suicidal tendency. They have hurt their own members precisely as they "succeeded." Higher wages, for instance, have certainly accelerated the substitution of capital for labor. The proof is that, despite the continued growth of output in union industries, employment gains in these areas have been slight. Moreover (as noted in Issue 6 on multinationals), union wage gains have led to the export of American jobs. Competition from lower-paid workers overseas has often been the price of labor's domestic victories.

Doubters may ask: Why should Conservatives single out union monopoly but overlook business monopoly? The answer is simple; union monopoly is legal (exempted from antitrust laws), while business monopoly has been a crime since passage of the Sherman Anti-Trust Act. As we have argued before, government is largely responsible for monopoly creation, and government-created monopoly power is the worst kind of monopoly. Government-sanctioned labor monopoly has political as well as economic power. Situated as it is at the center of the Democratic party, the nation's majority party, labor unionism is able to entrench itself deeper and deeper politically.

THE SPECIAL PROBLEM OF PUBLIC SECTOR UNIONISM

The policial clout of the unions in recent years has been enhanced by the rapid growth of public sector unionism. During the past fifteen years, precisely as public sector employment was undergoing rapid growth, public sector union membership increased by over 500 percent. Today, one of every five American unionists is employed in the public sector, raising especially troublesome questions. First of all, public sector unionism leads to unionist activity directly in opposition to the interest and welfare of the society at large. Strikes by police officers, firefighters, and teachers have become common, and the monopoly power of public sector unions over these critical functions has led to the extortion of unjustifiably high wage increases and expensive fringe benefits (for example, pensions). Given society's dependence on the public sector, union activity in this area has produced greater relative gains for union members than has private sector unionism. These gains are, of course, considerable tax costs to the ordinary citizen.

A second problem is that the unionizing of public employees creates a special interest group committed to ever expanding state bureaucracy. For instance, the 1 million members of AFSCME (American Federation of Federal, State, County and Municipal Employees) have a vested interest in protecting and expanding public sector expenditures and areas of public intervention in the economy. The reason is obvious enough. Their jobs depend upon it. Thus, public unions can exert, through the strength of their numbers and their placement in the economy, enormous political leverage in subverting the market system. At the same time, their "gains" represent a heavy cost to the taxpayer.

DEALING WITH THE UNIONS

A Conservative program for dealing with the union problem could be reduced to the slogan "Don't outlaw the unions, outlaw their power." Workers, like everyone else, should have the right of free association. Much can be said in favor of fraternal workplace or skill organizations. Indeed, these groups should have the democratic right to lobby for their ideas and programs. However, union strength should be curtailed by a three-pronged attack on their monopoly power.

First, unions' special exemption from antitrust laws should be terminated. Second, compulsory unionism should be ended; "right to work" protection should be given all workers, whatever their feeling about joining a union. No worker should be compelled, as is now the case in many states, to join a union as a prerequisite to getting and holding a job. Third, the right to strike should be defined and limited to specific lawful ends. While workers should have the right to withhold their labor, they should not be able to do this if (1) the national welfare is endangered; (2) the purpose is purely political; (3) the union has made no effort to negotiate—in other words, no wildcat strikes; or (4) there is violence.

Such a program would go a long way toward restoring the balance of power between unions and management. With some exceptions, organized labor has marched down a one-way street for the past forty years.

With regard to the problem of public sector unionism—its extortionist tactics and political lobbying power—there is really only one solution. As a condition of their employment public employees should be prohibited from joining unions. This is not inconsistent nor does it violate a Conservative commitment to freedom and free association. It merely recognizes that government, its scale and operation, should be under the democratic control of the entire population. Public sector unions in effect deny the general public their rights of review and control over government processes. As such they are a monopoly, or special interest infringement, on both the economic and political processes of a free society.

The Liberal Argument

The Liberal position with regard to the place of unions in the economy is very simple: Unions are necessary in order for labor to have an equitable balance with management in establishing wages, hours, and conditions of work. Without a balance of power in bargaining, one side soon dominates the other and the very essence of a pluralist democratic capitalism is endangered. From the Liberal standpoint, commitment to governmental intervention to redress imbalances is essential, for history shows that working out labor-management issues in a "free market" leads to chaos.

THE FAILURE OF FREE-LABOR BARGAINING

Contrary to the fantasies of its Conservative defenders, a free labor market is not free at all, but controlled by the purchasers of labor. To attack unions as disrupters of the economy may be defensible within free-market logic, but it shows no understanding of economic conditions in the real world. Without the protection of unions, workers have always been price-takers, forced by the necessity of survival to accept whatever wage rate is offered. To be sure, as the free-market advocate may point out, a worker is free to turn down a wage he considers inadequate. However, this is somewhat like saying that a man has the choice of death by poison or execution by a firing squad. Freedom he has, but his choices are equally dismal.

Perhaps in an idyllic Adam Smith world of many buyers and sellers, no one of whom had excessive economic or political power, the society might depend reasonably on the "laws of the market." At any rate, this was not the actual condition as industrial capitalism began to emerge in the last century. The few who hired had excessive power over those who worked, and unionism was a natural, humane, and necessary development. Any other view simply ignores American history.

Necessary as it was, unionism did not emerge without a long struggle. Efforts to unionize in the late nineteenth century were opposed in the courts, which upheld entrepreneurs' property rights and treated unions either as criminal conspiracies or, after the Sherman Act of 1890, as monopolistic efforts to restrain trade. Management ruthlessly attempted to weed out union organizers and members. Under threat of being discharged or blacklisted, workers were compelled to sign yellow-dog contracts—promises never to join or support a union. When these efforts at intimidation were not sufficient, management simply staged lockouts—closing down, so that laborers, without savings or strike funds, were driven back to work by the reality of starvation. When all else failed and it was faced with a full-fledged strike, management could hire strikebreakers and finally, use police and bullets.

These struggles between management and labor were creating irreversible class divisions and bloody social disorder. Haymarket, Homestead, Pullman, and Ludlow (classic labor struggles, 1880–1910) were names synonymous with industrial warfare and harbingers of what might happen on a grander scale unless labor-capital relations were improved. Largely under the pressure of Liberals, first in the Progressive Era and then during the New Deal period, a new strategy for dealing with labor-business conflicts evolved. In its simplest form, the strategy had two parts. One was legalizing and protecting the rights of workers to organize; the other was establishing the principle of collective bargaining between labor and management, in order to determine wages and work conditions in all unionized businesses. With the passage of the Wagner Act in 1935, labor received its "Magna Carta." This law forbade employer interference with workers' rights to organize unions, outlawed company unions, prohibited discriminatory anti-union action by employers, compelled employers to bargain in "good faith," and established a National Labor Relations Board to oversee labor-management affairs. Unions finally had arrived, and membership grew from 4 million in 1935 to 18 million in the next twenty years. Collective bargaining had replaced industrial violence as the basis for industry-worker relations.

It is doubtful today that many businesses would like to return to the wild "free market" era of labor relations. Collective bargaining is as much a part of business as it is of labor. As business has grown larger and more complex, uncertainties of all kinds are less desirable. Collective bargaining and long-term labor contracts have tended to stabilize labor situations, to business's distinct pleasure. Nevertheless, criticism of unions continues. Here we must deal with several of the more inaccurate and obnoxious arguments.

CORRECTING THE EVIDENCE

Many critics of unions argue that they have caused economic inefficiency and suffering in our society. The record does not bear this out at all. Before the union movement succeeded in forcing higher wages, improved working conditions, and greater concern for the rights of labor, suffering was the common plight of *all* workers. The history books are replete with examples of the abominable working conditions during the early industrial period in England, the United

States, and all developing capitalist economies. Even in the more "enlightened" modern period, union political pressures are virtually the only check to assure safe working conditions and adequate rates of pay for all workers.

Meanwhile, union-sponsored social programs in the areas of improved education, compensation for illness or disability, and security against unemployment and old age have become accepted facts of life. Without union political agitation in these areas, state and federal action would simply not have happened.

What about the charge that unions cause inefficiency, higher prices, and even joblessness? There is no hard evidence. Although American labor struggles date back to colonial times, the great advances made by unions have come in this century, mostly in the last forty years. During this period, the United States has become the preeminent industrial power in the world. The standard of living for all Americans has continually advanced. To argue that union gains have been won at a cost to other members of society is not true. As union wages and benefits have increased, they have pulled up those of nonunion workers. While unemployment and unfair income distribution remain serious problems, the modern union era—that is, 1941 to the present—has actually seen a doubling of the income share (percentage of national income) of the lowest fifth of the population. Such evidence disputes the Conservative logic that the poor pay for unionism.

With regard to the Conservative charge that union shops and agency shops deny some workers their rights and their wages by compelling them to pay union dues, Liberals view this as a smokescreen. "Right to work" laws aimed at ending this long-established practice are in reality efforts at union busting. Required union dues are designed to prevent "free riders," workers who enjoy union-gained wage and job benefits but wouldn't otherwise pay to support union expenses. Most important though, they wouldn't have these benefits and their salaries would be much lower if the comparatively small contributions to the union were not paid. It is not the worker's free choice which "right to work" advocates have in mind but the employer's. By dividing the workers against each other on the issue of union dues, worker solidarity—the first requisite for effective unionism—is destroyed. Breaking the union is the next step.

Another spurious argument used against unions is that they are the basic cause of our present rising prices through cost-push inflation. There is valid reason to believe that wage increases have occasionally been inflationary in the past—for example, in the 1950s and 1960s, when industry sometimes came to the bargaining table willing to give up more than unions were asking for. However, average real wages have fallen during most of the 1970s. Under the Carter administration's voluntary wage guidelines, labor was asked to hold the line at 7 percent annual increases, while inflation rates grew at more than 10 percent. Meanwhile, corporate profits soared, averaging more than 25 percent for 1978. Such evidence does not support the charge made by some "cost-push" critics of inflation that wage increases are the initial and causal factor in upward spiraling prices.

A LIBERAL STRATEGY

Liberals' historical commitment to the cause of the union movement and concern for the rights of workers should, of course, not be uncritical. Labor's right to strike should be supported from mindless Conservative assault; without the right to withhold their labor, workers have lost not only a democratic freedom but their most effective weapon in negotiating. But the right to strike is not absolute, to be guaranteed in all situations. Society at large has rights, too. It has the right to military and police protection; it has the right to be spared the physical harm that might result from certain strikes. The consistent Liberal must look for the greater social good in such situations and not be inflexibly committed to absolute principles.

The right to organize in the public sector poses a special problem in balancing employee rights with those of the community. Since the 1940s, government employment has been growing faster than any other sector of the economy, and over the past ten years union efforts in attracting new members in the public sector have been quite successful. Most Liberals would support this growth of public sector unionism, but not without qualifications. Indeed, do firefighters, police officers, sanitation workers, and teachers have the right to strike in the same sense that auto workers do? The predominant answer among Liberals would probably be *no!*—on the grounds that such strikes often do vast and irreparable damage to the general society. However, this does not mean public sector unionism should be abolished. In New York and some other states, public unionism is legally defined as a two-way street. Employees are required to be members of a bargaining agency (union) of their choice but at the same time they are prohibited from striking.

While some will argue this amounts to putting discriminatory limits on public sector unions, they miss the point. The objective of such legal requirements is to produce collective bargaining between the public employer and public employee without the larger society suffering from strikes against the general welfare. Employee rights are protected through compulsory bargaining or arbitration without necessary recourse to strikes. To be sure public employee strikes do occur in states like New York but not with the frequency and severity found in states which do not recognize both the employees' rights to organize to protect their interest and the society's rights to essential public services.

There may be other types of excessive union power or misuse of power, ranging from political coercion to corruption of both union and public officials. Such evils should not be overlooked simply because they are union matters. However, the Taft-Hartley Act (1947) and the Landrum-Griffin Act (1959) provide for considerable scrutiny of and control over abuses of union power. Overall, alleged abuses by organized labor can be handled without altering our commitment of the past forty years to labor-management balance.

The Radical Argument

Without much doubt unions have brought workers protection and advantages that could not have been obtained in the "free market." By organizing together, many workers have obtained job security, higher wages, better working conditions, and a host of fringe benefits (paid vacations, retirement and health plans, and the like). These would not have been possible if they had stood, hat in hand, waiting for their capitalist employers to humanize work conditions and better their incomes.

THE FAILURES OF AMERICAN UNIONISM

There are, however, basic defects in the American system of trade unionism. First of all, with the exception of the Industrial Workers of the World (known as Wobblies) in the early twentieth century and a few communist and socialist unions of the 1930s and 1940s, American unionism has usually lacked a radical political direction. In fact, political organization or agitation of any kind has never been important in the big unions. While one thinks of the AFL-CIO and the Democratic party as almost synonymous, the union's support for this traditional party is not political activism in any radical sense. To Samuel Gompers of the AFL, the founding father of modern unionism, labor struggles were motivated basically by bread-and-butter issues. Gompers, who was interested only in organizing along craft lines, believed that unions should avoid political involvement and support the social order of capitalist society. Neither the broadening of the union movement to industry-wide organizing under the CIO in the 1930s nor the AFL-CIO merger in 1955 changed this outlook. In World War I, in the New Deal of the 1930s, and in World War II, establishment unionism was handsomely rewarded by both government and business as they came to appreciate the politically nonmilitant nature of American unions. Contrary to the views of Conservatives and some Liberals, American corporate leaders came to see unions as more beneficial than detrimental. As industry, especially heavy industry, became more technically complex and economically concentrated, unions served as useful organizers of the labor supply. They provided stability in hiring and employment that more than compensated for the enforced recognition of unions and the legalization of such labor tactics as the strike, the boycott, and exclusive jurisdiction.

This is not to say that all businesses agreed with unions all the time. Some remained implacable and willing to resort to violence to destroy "bolshevik" unionism. The Republic Steel Massacre on Memorial Day 1937 is a bitter example of this type of thinking* However, such business attitudes are pretty much past history, as is labor militancy. Today, few businesses oppose unions in principle. And most unions support the capitalist system in practice. Union leaders worked with the FBI and CIA in the 1950s to purge radicals from their ranks and to help eliminate radical elements in the unions of friendly foreign nations. Most union leadership vigorously supported the Viet-

---

*Ten strikers were killed outside Chicago's Republic Steel plant on Memorial Day 1937. They were peacefully demonstrating for recognition of their union when they were fired upon and beaten by city and plant police. No police were convicted but a number of strikers went to jail for disturbing the peace.

nam War and continues to support a strong military-foreign policy for the United States. In times of domestic economic crisis, union leaders have shown a willingness to collaborate with business to hold down wages and prices, as when President Nixon introduced wage-price controls in the early 1970s. The point is that in our time, the corporate attack on unions has been mostly rhetoric; practice indicates mutual acceptance and collaboration.

Although the growth of public sector unionism is often viewed with alarm by believers in the traditional economic and political faith, it too has proved to be a blank cartridge among the weapons of working class struggle in the United States. Very much as private sector unions serve to organize and discipline workers in private industry, public sector unions serve the same function in government employment. The level of militancy among public sector workers has never proved to be very strong. During the 1950s and 1960s the general growth of the economy permitted public employee wages to rise very swiftly, in many cases faster than in the private sector. While union membership grew, it did not reflect a growing revolutionary consciousness among its members—who were, after all, doing quite well by past standards. Presently, in the wake of California's Proposition 13 and the growing fiscal crises of all governments, public sector wage gains have slowed even below the inflation rate. However, this contraction has not produced militancy but rather passive acceptance, since many public employees frankly fear making waves as the prospect of government sector retrenchment grows. While public employment remains extremely vulnerable during this contractionary stage in American capitalism, it should be expected that unions in this sector will react no differently than other unions. They will try to protect their more senior members, even collaborating with management efforts at payroll and employment reductions if this must be the price.

RADICALS DISAGREE ON TACTICS

On labor's side, the growth of the collaboration between unions and management has been facilitated by the domination of a distant, elderly, and bureaucratic leadership. The "professional" leaders and managers of the unions have usually found themselves more at home speaking with their management counterparts than with their own members. Not infrequently, they have negotiated sweetheart contracts that sold out their members very cheaply; the "no-strike" steel agreement of 1973 is an example.

Up to this point, most Radicals would agree. Labor unions have been more of a conservative than a radical force in American history, and current labor leadership is hopelessly detached from the real interests and needs of workers. But what does this mean for the future and for developing a Radical program toward labor unions?

The working class must finally be the political vehicle for radical social change. Without working-class support and, ultimately, working-class leadership, a radical reordering of society remains only the dream of intellectuals. Labor unions are a critical institution in approaching the working class. But should unions be opposed on the basis of past evidence, or should they be utilized? Radicals are divided on this question, and the division must be explained.

The antiunion position, which sometimes sounds surprisingly similar to Conservative logic, holds that unions are elitist, both at the top and among their members. Union membership is comparatively small (and even smaller than official figures indicate if we recognize that many unionists are inactive). Thus the old socialist idea of seeing the unions as a means to reach most workers is wrong today. Moreover, because of their wage and job security advantage over other workers, union members are the least politically developed of American workers. In fact, many of their wage gains have come as the result of relative wage losses (through inflation) and greater job insecurity for nonunion labor. Union workers are at the top of the hierarchy of American labor, and they would have little to gain from a Radical program aimed at greater worker control of jobs and a fairer distribution of income. Arguing from these premises, some Radicals see unions as an enemy, an element that increases internal working-class warfare and division. They argue, however, that the heyday of powerful unions is over; more and more of the work force now occupies less secure and less remunerative jobs. Unions thus become unnecessary and even insignificant as labor organizes directly against capital.

The other, and preponderant, Radical view argues that labor unions are essential in developing working-class consciousness against the system. To be sure, unionism is not a substitute for militant worker efforts to seize control of the means of production. However, if the present conservative leadership of unions is replaced, there is a real possibility that unions could become a progressive force toward this end. The present struggles of the rank and file against union bosses, as seen in the recent steelworker and mineworker cases, is a genuine effort to make the unions democratic. Moreover, the rank and file are increasingly militant and willing to challenge rights of management that the union leadership take for granted. Increasingly workers will move beyond mere bread-and-butter issues to deal with such questions as labor control over the introduction and use of capital equipment and labor's sharing directly in corporate earnings. Such progressive ideas and increased militancy, the prounion argument holds, will carry over into nonunion labor.

While this division among Radicals on the position of unions should not be underestimated, it is only a tactical disagreement. Organization of the working class into a radical force is still a common objective. Quite as Conservatives have stated, the Radical objective *is* to replace capitalist control with that of labor. The final goal is the social ownership of the means of production and worker determination of output. That means the bringing together of workers, union and nonunion, in a common struggle and the support of all efforts to enlarge worker power, whether through existing union offices or other types of organization. Given the past history of collaboration between union bureaucracy and capitalist management, Radicals are united in their opposition to allowing elite labor leaders to act as political brokers for either their own union members or the working class as a whole. Thus, the Radical position is to go beyond the "union question" as it is posed by either Conservatives or Liberals. Radicals may seriously differ in evaluating the progressive possibilities of the existing union structure, but they agree on the necessity of organizing labor against capital in whatever ways possible.

Thus, if the real question before us is, "Are the workers too powerful?" the Radical must answer *no*. Worker power must be encouraged, either through the structure of formal unions or by other means.

ISSUE 8

Taxes and Welfare
What's Happening To
The Income Gap?

Like all other contracts, wages should be left to the fair and free competition of the market, and should never be controlled by the interference of the legislature.

The clear and direct tendency of the poor laws is in direct opposition to those obvious principles: it is not as the legislature benevolently intended, to amend the condition of the poor, but to deteriorate the condition of both poor and rich; instead of making the poor rich, they are calculated to make the rich poor.

David Ricardo, 1821

It is not to die, or even to die of hunger, that makes a man wretched; many men have died; all men must die. . . . But it is to live miserable we know not why; to work sore and yet gain nothing; to be heart-worn, weary yet isolated, unrelated, girt in with a cold, universal Laissez Faire.

Thomas Carlyle, 1853

. . . a very substantial portion of poverty and unemployment is chronic, beyond the control of individuals or the influence of rising aggregate demand.

The President's Commission on
Income Maintenance Programs, 1969

THE PROBLEM

Taxation and transfer payments to individuals operate from different sides of the government balance sheet, but both must be considered together when we look at the question of income equality in the United States. Both affect, adversely or favorably, different income groups, and so should have some impact on the national distribution of income. We have discussed taxes and transfers in general ways in a number of preceding topics; now we turn to a look at their specific structure and discrete effects.

The existence of an income gap is certainly not a new problem in the United States; indeed, some would argue that such a gap is not a problem at all, but is desirable. However, over the past fifteen years—especially since the initiation of President Johnson's War on Poverty—Americans have been made greatly aware of the existing maldistribution of income. The issue has become a permanent fixture in campaign debates. Ironically, however, the distribution of earned income in the United States has changed very little over time. As Table 8.1 shows, before-tax and before-transfer income is distributed just about the same as it was thirty years ago.

Table 8.1   Shares of Earned Income by Families (in percentages)

Income Level	1975	1969	1964	1960	1956	1950	1947
Poorest fifth	5.4%	5.6%	5.2%	4.9%	5.0%	4.5%	5.0%
Second fifth	11.8	12.3	12.0	12.0	12.4	12.0	11.8
Third fifth	17.6	17.6	17.7	17.6	17.8	17.4	17.0
Fourth fifth	24.1	23.4	24.0	23.6	23.7	23.5	23.1
Richest fifth	41.1	41.0	41.1	42.0	41.2	42.6	43.0

Source: Roger A. Herriot and Herman P. Miller, "The Taxes We Pay," Conference Board Record, May 1971, p. 40, and U.S. Bureau of the Census, Statistical Abstract, 1976, p. 406.

While income shares have not changed, income has absolutely risen for all. Today about half as many Americans fall into the official category of poverty (currently more than $7,500 per family) as did in the early 1960s (poverty level then was $4,000 per family).

Of course, the before-tax, before-transfer distribution of income is misleading. As noted earlier, there has been a general increase in total taxation and social welfare transfers since World War II. The dominant economic wisdom tells us that the combined effect of taxing and transferring has been to reduce much of this maldistribution. Table 8.2 indicates the impact of taxes and transfers on different income groups.

Table 8.2 **Estimated Effective Tax Rates by Income Levels (taxes as a percentage of income)**

(1) Family income	(2) Federal taxes	(3) State and local taxes	(4) All taxes, or (2) + (3)	(5) Government transfer payments	(6) Net taxes, or (4) – (5)
Under $2,000	22.7%	27.2%	50.0%	106.5%	–56.5%
2,000–4,000	18.7	15.7	34.6	48.5	–13.9
4,000–6,000	19.0	12.1	31.0	19.6	11.4
6,000–8,000	19.4	10.7	30.1	8.6	21.5
8,000–10,000	19.1	10.1	29.2	5.5	23.7
10,000–15,000	19.9	9.9	29.8	3.9	25.9
15,000–25,000	20.7	9.4	30.0	3.0	27.0
25,000–50,000	25.0	7.8	32.8	2.1	30.7
50,000 and over	38.4	6.7	45.0	0.4	44.7
Total tax on all income	21.7%	9.9%	31.6%	6.9%	24.6%

Source: Roger A. Herriot and Herman P. Miller, "The Taxes We Pay," *Conference Board Record*, May 1971, p. 40.

The combined effect of taxes and transfers, according to these data, would appear to suggest that income inequality is reduced. Critics of this view might interpret the data in different ways. Some might point out that taxes remain higher for the poor than for everyone else except the very well-to-do. Others might note that the real magnitude of government transfers to the poor is very small, so that even if their welfare gains exceed their taxes, they still remain poor. Still others, looking at the last column would argue that our taxes and transfers system is too progressive. Citizens, politicians—and economists—are divided on the policy implications of data like these.

SYNOPSIS The Conservative argument holds that income inequality is natural and that efforts to change it through taxes and transfers will diminish the entire society's well-being. According to the Liberal argument, a more equalitarian distribution of income is humane and will improve general economic performance. The Radical argument contends that income inequality is normal and even needed in capitalism, but at the same time undermines the system.

The Conservative Argument

A unifying feature of all centralist (Liberal and Radical) programs for the past hundred years has been the call for egalitarianism in income. The "Robin Hood" illusion is the very beginning of any collectivist's social dream—and the basis for serious errors of economic and social thinking.

A JUST SYSTEM OF REWARDS

Distribution of income should be governed by the simple and equitable principle that all members of a society should receive according to what they, or whatever they own, are able to produce. The abilities, tastes, and occupational interests of individuals vary. People value work and leisure differently. Some individuals are willing to forgo an assured lower income in favor of taking a risk and possibly earning more. Enforced equality of income utterly fails to consider these possibilities. It presumes that greater social satisfaction is attained by income parity than by letting people make their own valuations of what money means to them.

Consider, for instance, a man who is quite content to live on $100 a week. From his point of view, his needs are satisfied, and he has achieved the right balance between leisure and work. To transfer to him one quarter of the wages of a worker who makes $200 a week will hardly increase his welfare or happiness. At the same time it subtracts much satisfaction from the man or woman who is willing to work hard enough to earn the $200 wage. If we could now add up the relative satisfactions of the two workers, it would be lower after redistribution than before. In other words, proof is lacking that a more equal income distribution actually maximizes community satisfaction.

At another level, egalitarianism leads to more serious troubles. Enforcing equal distribution of income penalizes the industrious and inventive, and subsidizes those with less initiative. If the industrious fail to obtain rewards for their talents and work, they will naturally slacken their efforts. As a result, the total product of the society is lessened. In the subsequent egalitarian redistribution, everyone gets less than before. Just how far the detrimental effects of income equalization can go in destroying a society is evident in Great Britain. There, subsidy for nonproduction and confiscation of earned income have lowered national output and put the nation at a disadvantage in world trade. The best minds and the nation's capital have fled to other countries. At home there is a shabby equality and mediocrity.

While the discussion above has been mostly with regard to individual labor, it also applies to individuals' command over capital and wealth. Appropriating the wealth of one to support another denies the individual's right to property and will lead to inefficiency and economic contraction in the whole society. (Whether the wealth is inherited or has been earned by the individual is irrelevant). This is not just an economic matter. Seizures of wages and property are violations of freedom. It is not a big step from telling people what their income will be to telling them what work to do or what ideas to think.

Of course we must move from the realm of abstract theory justifying income inequality and protecting property rights into the real world. There, taxes must be collected to carry on the business of government (even if that business is excessive). And, to help those who are not able to take care of themselves, transfer payments are necessary. However, taxes and transfers must express the principles just summarized.

TOWARD A FAIR TAX STRUCTURE

The federal tax system, which collects more than two-thirds of all our taxes, is characterized by two serious errors: (1) the graduated personal income tax, and (2) the belief that corporate taxes are painless.

The graduated income tax is wrong philosophically as a confiscation of wealth and a violation of freedom. It is also wrong in practice, for different reasons. Rather than having the intended "Robin Hood" effect, it has encouraged legal tax evasion by creating numerous tax loopholes: tax-free status for state and municipal bonds, capital gains privileges, unfair "effective" rates (lower for single taxpayers), expense accounts, and so on. Thus for many taxpayers the actual rates are much lower than the published rates on their incomes. Since not everyone enjoys the same loophole privileges, tax collection is uneven and unfair. Make no mistake, true Conservatives are not heartened to learn that several hundred millionaires legally avoid tax payments every year. Quite apart from these inequities, our tax structure encourages individuals to take actions that may save taxes but are economically foolish. They may decide to buy tax-free municipal bonds rather than corporate bonds. Thus, urban debt is traded off against corporate expansion.

The political custom of hitting corporations with high taxes goes back to the days of Franklin Roosevelt. After all, corporations don't vote, so higher corporate profits taxes are politically painless. This is very shortsighted. There is no such thing as a painless tax. The question is only where the pain appears. Corporate taxes affect costs and profits. They may put firms out of business (railroads, for example) by denying them capital. They encourage capital to leave the country. They also stimulate uneconomic decision making through what we might call a loss-producing psychology. (If corporate taxes are about 50 percent, then each dollar of losses actually costs only 50 cents.) Most important, though, corporate taxes raise the cost of doing business; consumers either pay higher prices or buy fewer goods.

The only intelligent solution is a simple, no loophole, proportional income tax. This flat rate without deductions and exemptions would probably lower taxes for most taxpayers. (Some economists have estimated that a rate as low as 18 percent on all personal income would be sufficient.) Such a system would be fair in that those who pay more would do so in proportion to their income and the benefits they receive from government. It would be democratic in that special interests could not have their way with Congress or the Internal Revenue Service. The only possible "bad" effect would be the growth of unemployment when thousands of parasitic tax lawyers lose their source of income.

THE WELFARE PROBLEM

While taxes are one way of equalizing income, a second and more disruptive method for doing so is the welfare system. Broadly speaking, welfare includes a wide variety of subsidies paid to individuals to offset low incomes. These include direct support transfers (as in the Aid to Families with Dependent Children program), public housing, minimum-wage laws, unemployment insurance, Medicaid, and Social Security.

Table 8.3 reveals the extent of cash and in-kind welfare programs administered at the federal level. Eighteen separately maintained social insurance and public assistance programs disbursed more than $185 billion in 1977.

With additional state and local contributions, the total was in excess of $325 billion. Looking at the data somewhat differently, the American welfare system equals about 17 percent of the nation's gross national product (GNP). More astounding than these aggregates, though, is the marginal growth in welfare spending. In still depressionary 1940, it accounted for just 6 percent, and in 1965, during the "giveaway" years of President Johnson's War on Poverty, it amounted to only 14 percent of the GNP. The rate of growth in welfare programs and spending is particularly dangerous since it means that ever greater tax sacrifices must be demanded of working citizens. For many workers, after-tax income is less than welfare grants paid to nonworkers.

Apart from their cost, however, have the welfare programs and other efforts to assist low-income Americans attained their goals?

Whatever their intentions, most of these programs fail to do what they promise. Indeed, they often do more harm than good. Aid to Families with Dependent Children (AFDC), given only to mothers and children in the absence of a working father, has broken up families. Public housing programs, which involve tearing down old neighborhoods and building new housing complexes, have actually caused a shortage of low-income rentals and forced up rents. Minimum-wage laws, rather than assuring a desired wage, have destroyed marginal jobs. Unemployment insurance induces people not to work. Medicaid has forced up health costs. Virtually all cash-granting welfare programs encourage fraud, and as a result our welfare system is not only excessively expensive, but it acts to encourage criminality. The list of tragedies resulting from well-intended social tinkering is endless. And on top of all that, we are burdened with a vast bureaucracy at all levels of government to administer these programs.

Beyond their more obvious defects, welfare efforts are particularly lamentable because they create a strong disincentive to work and discourage people from improving themselves. People have to be poor in order to qualify for welfare protection, and they have to stay poor to keep getting it. Thus our welfare system has created a vast and per-

Table 8.3   Government Income Maintenance Programs, Fiscal Year 1977

Program	Date enacted	Form of aid	Source of funds	Benefit payments (billions $)	Beneficiaries (millions)
Social Insurance:					
Old age and survivors insurance	1935	Cash	Federal	71.3	28.5
Medicare	1965	In-kind	Federal	20.8	25.4[1]
Unemployment insurance	1935	Cash	Federal-State	14.3	9.8
Disability insurance	1956	Cash	Federal	11.1	4.7
Workmen's compensation	1908	Cash	Federal-State	6.7	2.6
Veterans' compensation	1917	Cash	Federal	5.7	3.5
Railroad retirement	1937	Cash	Federal	3.8	1.0
Black lung	1969	Cash	Federal	1.0	.5
Public assistance:					
Medicaid	1965	In-kind	Federal-State	15.3	21.6
Aid to families with dependent children	1935	Cash	Federal-State	9.8	11.2
Supplemental security income	1972	Cash	Federal-State	6.2	4.3
Food stamp program	1964	In-kind	Federal	5.0	17.1
Child nutrition	1946	In-kind	Federal	3.5	28.0
Veterans' pensions	1933	Cash	Federal	3.1	3.4
Housing assistance	1937	In-kind	Federal	3.0	7.1
Basic opportunity grants	1972	Cash	Federal	1.4	2.0
General assistance		Cash	State	1.3	.9
Earned income tax credit	1975[2]	Cash	Federal	1.3	6.3

Source: Economic Report of the President, 1978, p. 222.   [1]Eligible to receive benefits as of July 1, 1977.   [2]Varies by state.

manent subculture of the disadvantaged. Meanwhile, the rest of the society must pay support costs.

The ideal solution would be to end such a system of transfers, but realistically we must face the fact that some people are indeed unable to care for themselves or will be the victims of lags and "stickiness" in the economy. We shall have to pay some welfare support. That support, however, should not reduce the incentives to work or self-improvement, and it should be administered as simply as possible.

As with proportional, no-exemptions income tax, welfare payments should follow simple and unalterable rules. First, we should determine a minimum subsistence level of income for a family, and assure it through a negative income tax payment. Additional private income may be added to this figure until the direct payment plus the private earnings raise total income to levels of legal taxability. At this point, the recipient becomes just another taxpayer. These transfer arrangements, however, should be tied to a "workfare" system for all able-bodied recipients. The obligation to be ready and willing to accept work is a fair one. At a minimum, this would probably require registration at employment offices and active job searching. Obviously there are a number of possible ways to set up a negative income tax program, but Conservatives should support those that encourage work incentives, lead to dismantling most present subsidy efforts, demand the least administrative overhead, and are subject to rules and not discretion.

The Conservative, while recognizing the adverse effects of taxes and transfers, also understands the need for them. However, taxing and transferring efforts must be based on economic reason and not the collectivist obsession with creating greater income equality. The market distributes income. When politicians do, economic order is lost.

The Liberal Argument

As Conservatives have correctly pointed out, the tax and transfer efforts to close the income gap in the United States have largely failed. However, the failure is not a matter of having created the "collectivist" income equality that Conservatives oppose. The problem is that taxes and welfare have not reversed the chronic tendency toward income inequality. While there has not been much change in the shares of total income going to different proportions of the population, the dollar gap between the bottom and the top has been increasing. This is not the result of the market recognizing hard work and rewarding it (as the Conservatives argue). Rather it reflects a fundamental inequality of opportunity.

This inequality has left America with a vast subculture of poverty. The dimensions and distribution of this poverty may be seen in the following data:

More than 12 percent of the total population lives in poverty.

Black poverty is four times greater than white poverty, with more than 30 percent of all nonwhites living in poverty.

Poverty hits the old and the young very hard: about a fifth of those over sixty-five live in poverty, and about 40 percent of all those classified as poor are under the age of eighteen.

Poverty affects working Americans: more than two-fifths of those classed as poor come from households in which the head was reported as employed over the year, a fourth from families whose head worked the entire year.

Poverty and poor education are closely related, with more than half of all the poor reporting less than nine years of education.

Families headed by women have a high incidence of poverty: about a third of all female-headed families are poor, and, at the same time, female-head-of-household poverty describes more than a third of all the poor.

Poverty is self-perpetuating; the highest correlation between poverty and any other attribute is that the poor themselves come from poverty-stricken backgrounds.

THE ADVANTAGE OF EQUALITY

Poverty, then, is the result of inadequate education, poor health, racism, sexism, and a lagging economy. An individual does not surmount these obstacles through his own personality. Poverty, of course, breeds more poverty, just as wealth takes care of its own. To believe that the existing shares of income reflect people's ability is naive. To fail to see that income disparity is the root of social decay and political instability is simple blindness. At bottom, the question of a more equitable distribution of income will not stand or fall on such microeconomic questions as "Is total happiness maximized?" A more equal (although certainly not perfectly equal) distribution is needed for humane purposes and to hold society together.

In terms of a macroeconomic analysis of the problem, modern economic theory shows us that a more equal distribution of income tends to improve general economic conditions. With income spread among larger numbers of people, a nation's propensity to consume will rise. This increase in total demand for goods creates jobs and stimulates economic expansion. On the other hand, income inequality leads to excessive savings and a slowdown in economic activity. The exaggerated Conservative concern for protecting work incentives through income disparities has exactly the opposite impact: it abolishes jobs.

THE GOAL: PROGRESSIVE TAXATION

Ever since the adoption of the progressive income tax in 1912, the United States has been committed to the principle of a more equal distribution of real income. The goal is not a perfectly equal distribution, since that would affect work and saving incentives. Liberals have never encouraged confiscatory taxes on upper incomes. They do believe that, in recognition of the ability to pay and real benefits received, the well-to-do should pay proportionately more as their income rises. The tax system in practice has been another matter.

The progressive intent of our federal income tax structure has been offset by loopholes that permit wholesale legal tax evasion. Almost all the beneficiaries of these loopholes are businesses and wealthy individuals. As Conservatives correctly point out, the tax laws permit the well-to-do to pay lower effective rates than the middle and lower classes. At the state and local level, regressive taxation is common. These units of government rely heavily on sales taxes and property taxes, which fall proportionately more heavily on those with lower incomes. In sum, the existing tax structure fails to reach those individual and corporate tax bases able to pay more, and puts the burden on people in the middle and at the bottom of the income scale. In many cases our taxes actually cause greater real income inequality.

Liberals want thorough tax reform to restore the principle of progressive taxation. Special loopholes for the privileged should be closed. Liberals do not advocate taxation without discretionary exemptions, however. Taxing is integral to fiscal policy, and tax incentives may be needed from time to time to encourage or discourage certain spending decisions by business and individuals. For instance, limited exemptions or deductions to home builders can be used to stimulate the construction industry in times of economic contraction. The no-discretion approach of most Conservatives is too arbitrary and limits flexibility in fiscal and monetary policy. Whatever discretionary changes are made, however, should sustain the principle of progressive taxation.

FEDERALIZING WELFARE

The popular, essentially Conservative, attack upon the nation's welfare program as being extravagant is far off the mark when the facts are examined. As Table 8.4 indicates, welfare assistance has not boosted recipients into income levels comparable to very many working families in the United States. Median family income is still more than twice that of the almost legendary New York City welfare family and about three times as great as the poverty line definition which the Departments of Labor and HEW use as their welfare guideline.

The present American welfare system is a patchwork of different

Table 8.4   Comparison of Public Assistance and Other Income Levels, Family of Four, 1976

Item	Level (dollars)
Median four-person family income	17,315
Bureau of Labor Statistics low-income budget	10,040
New York City family with AFDC, food stamps, medicaid	8,302
Illinois family with AFDC, food stamps, medicaid	6,412
Family earning full-time minimum wage, plus food stamps and earned income tax credit	5,958
Official poverty line	5,815
Texas family with AFDC, food stamps, medicaid	4,174
Mississippi family with AFDC, food stamps, medicaid	2,914
Two-parent family with food stamps only (all states)	1,992

Source: Economic Report of the President, 1978, p. 226.

Note. Data relate generally to mid-1976.

programs with different levels of administration. As any recipient knows, it is a tangle of inconsistency and red tape. There is a wide disparity in benefits within welfare programs, at least those sponsored locally or jointly between state and local governments. In the case of AFDC, (Aid to Families with Dependent Children) which is a joint federal-state-local program, monthly payments to the 11 million recipients in 1975 varied from a high of $120 in Massachusetts to a low of $14 in Mississippi. Existing federal formulas have penalized states with the highest welfare benefits. Thus Massachusetts payed 50 percent of its welfare burden in 1975 while Mississippi payed only 22 percent. The object may be to discourage welfare growth, but the effect is to create welfare inequity. It also creates tax inequity, since some states must contribute more than others for each recipient. Critics who question the "generosity" of Massachusetts toward its poor miss the point. Welfare recipients in Massachusetts still average less than the poverty line income (excluding medical aid). In thirty states, recipients receive less than two-thirds of the poverty level income.

The first step in improving the welfare system is to place it totally under federal jurisdiction. A nation-wide minimum must be established, and must be paid for federally, not locally, so as to equalize the cost burden.

There has been much talk in recent years about a federally guaranteed annual income (GAI) or negative income tax (NIT). These methods of providing a national social minimum deserve policy attention, and even Conservatives like Milton Friedman have advanced some support for the idea. However, the basic problem with GAI and NIT proposals is how to determine and administer a minimum which helps only the genuinely poor and which does not at the same time destroy work incentives. While the GAI or NIT problem may be resolved and one of these cash payment solutions may be adopted in the future, the federalizing and redesigning of existing programs is a more plausible current solution.

When this course is urged, opponents of welfare usually howl about the cost of the system. However, there is considerable misinformation about the actual amounts of our welfare outlays. At the federal level, only about $50 billion of our social insurance and assistance spending requires a "needs" or income test on the part of the recipient. In other words, only about a quarter of our so-called welfare bill is directed specifically to the poor, with the remainder available to Americans of all income levels—primarily for social security payments (which are in large part paid for by the individuals themselves) and medical insurance for the elderly. Our true "welfare" bill for the poor is equal to only about 3 percent of the GNP and is slightly more than one-third of what is spent on national defense.

Let us assume that the nation adopted a minimum guarantee of two-thirds of the poverty level income for the 25 million Americans who live below it and that the federal government took over the present state and local welfare contributions up to that level. Such a proposal has been studied by the Committee for Economic Development, a prestigious policy group of business leaders. Applying their estimates of additional costs to the present situation would amount to about a $25 billion increase in the federal budget. While not modest, this would be a small outlay in a federal budget of over $500 billion. Moreover, such a guaranteed income approach would reduce the need for the present multiplicity of federal programs and effect savings by shrinking the overblown federal welfare bureaucracy. It would also reduce state and municipal welfare costs although local government units would of course be free to add to their welfare minimum if they saw fit.

While reasonable minimum welfare payments are necessary (and should be higher than those now administered under our present patchwork programs), welfare is not the real solution to eliminating poverty or income inequality. Welfare programs designed merely to pacify the poor create a permanent poor. A useful federal program aimed at greater income equalization must attack the roots of the problem. This means that welfare efforts must be related to educational and job-creating programs. Racism and sexism must be attacked directly by law. Welfare efforts should encourage work and stimulate jobs. However, they should rely on the carrot, not the stick. The Conservatives' plan for virtually starving people into work, coupled as it is with their belief in the merit of income inequality, is a return to an earlier, barbaric capitalism.

Of course, the capacity of any society simultaneously to end poverty and ameliorate income disparities depends on its own economic vitality. Regardless of efforts to improve our taxing and welfare systems, little can be done unless the economy is expanding.

THE CARTER PROPOSAL

At this writing the Carter administration's program for reforming the welfare system is still a matter of congressional debate. Without taking up the specifics of the program, it may be characterized as a "welfare-workfare" proposal. On the welfare side, it is aimed at assuring standard minimum benefits to all Americans unable to work. At the same time, it stresses work rather than welfare as a cure to poverty. For example, the original Carter proposal called for the creation of public service jobs and an end to all welfare qualifications that deter the poor from seeking employment.

Perhaps the most striking element of the initial Carter plan was to "scrap and completely overhaul the current public assistance programs, combining them into a simplified, uniform, integrated system of cash assistance." Under this proposal, "AFDC, SSI and Food Stamps will be abolished." In place of the old programs, Carter proposed a type of GAI. Although complicated, his proposal can be generally appreciated in the following case: A family of four would be guaranteed two-thirds of the poverty line income (this would have been as much as $4,200 if paid in 1978). These cash benefits would be reduced fifty cents on each dollar gainfully earned by the recipients until their income reached $8,400. Thus a uniform minimum would be assured, but welfare recipients would still be encouraged to work.

From a Liberal position, such a program, at least in theory, could be a step forward. The creation of uniform federal guidelines for welfare aid would be a vast improvement over the present system, with its great state-to-state inequities. The emphasis on work rather than a submissive welfare existence is laudable. The creation of a public jobs program is especially desirable. *However*, the Carter proposal is simply too small a box to stuff the poverty problem in.

The initial Carter price tag for his welfare reform proposal in 1977 was only about $4 billion more than was already in the budget for fiscal 1978. No serious observer of the problem of joblessness and income inequality in America believed that real improvements for the poor could be purchased that cheaply. To make matters worse, the growing inflationary pressures in the economy after 1977 demanded that the administration hold the line on all spending—but especially social spending. President Carter's 1980 budget reflected this pressure. Total welfare outlays remained about the same as in the previous year which, given inflation, meant a reduction. The public sector jobs aspect of his earlier proposal was greatly reduced. The overall welfare revision plan of 1977, although still mentioned in his budget message, was now targeted for a safely distant 1983 or later.

The Radical Argument

In terms of understanding the role of taxes and welfare in capitalist society, both Conservatives and Liberals are correct on two different points. First, as Conservatives argue, the combined income effects of our tax and transfer policies must not destroy work incentives. Second, as Liberals argue, tax and welfare policies are also intended to ameliorate the most glaring inequalities in income, or at least hide them. In American capitalism, maldistribution of income is essential to support the work ethic, but too big a gap erodes the credibility of American political and economic institutions. Thus taxes and transfers walk a tightrope, maintaining yet hiding the income gap.

TAXES: A TRANSFER FROM THE POOR
TO THE RICH

Our national tax system does not close the income gap, but, in fact, tends to widen it. Although Table 8.2 understates how regressive our tax structure really is, it does indicate that all taxes are regressive through the $15,000 range and only mildly progressive until the highest income level is reached. While the well-known tax loopholes of the rich allow legal evasion, we tend to forget the heavily regressive effect of certain taxes on the poor.

Take property taxes for instance. These account for about two-thirds of collections by local governments. A Senate study in 1973 determined that property taxes, whether paid by individual homeowners or by tenants in their monthly rents, averaged about 4.9 percent of family income. However, the rate was 16.9 percent for those earning less than $2,000. For those earning over $25,000, the rate was a mere 2.9 percent.

Sales taxes, the other important source of state and local revenue, are also regressive. As these taxes have been extended to cover necessities, they fall more and more heavily on those with little discretionary income. Obviously the taxes on a wealthy man's electricity are much less of a burden for him than are electricity taxes for a low-income worker, regardless of the number of rooms in the wealthy man's estate.

The result in absolute terms is that lower-income and middle-income groups pay for most city and state governmental expenditures. They receive fewer of the social benefits. The poor have less police and fire protection, poorer roads and schools, and inadequate sanitation services. Thus a serious effort to develop a fair—let alone progressive—income redistribution must start at the level of local tax inequality.

The passage of California's Proposition 13 on June 6, 1978, left no doubt that taxpayers at the local level were prepared to rebel against the real and supposed oppressions of the property tax. The revolt, however, was not much of a victory for the ordinary citizen. After years of agitation by certain business groups, real estate lobbies, and many middle-income taxpayers who chafed under rising property taxes, Californians passed by referendum a measure that set local property taxes at a maximum of 1 percent of assessed valuation. Furthermore, a 2 percent per year ceiling was placed on assessed value increases. To be sure, Proposition 13 had the initial effect of lower taxes. However, of the $7 billion in tax relief that was gained, only $2.3 billion went to home owners. The rest went to landlords and owners of business property. Moreover, local governments, with their income radically reduced, trimmed vital services—fire, police, sanitation, and education. At the same time, highly regressive user fees and taxes were adopted to maintain many needed government operations. Although all of the burden of Proposition 13 has not yet been felt by Californians (and other voters around the nation who followed this lead), it is obvious that this kind of "tax reform" only aggravates the inequalities in our tax structure.

At the federal level, although politicians constantly promise to close the loopholes that benefit the rich, they are unlikely to do so. For one thing, loopholes are the result of political power and lobbying—something that is not likely to end very soon. Not only that, but many are seen as economically necessary. For instance, the mortgage and property tax credits of middle- and upper-income taxpayers serve as a stimulus to the construction industry. Business investment tax credits are intended to encourage business expansion. Therefore the discretionary use of tax policies for fiscal manipulation will always create loopholes that benefit the few greatly and the masses slightly.

Equalization of income through taxation cannot be a serious objective in a capitalist system so long as the powerful control government. Under capitalism the tax structure will remain merely another device to transfer income and wealth ("surplus" in Marxist terms) from the poor to the rich.

THE REAL BENEFICIARIES OF WELFARE

The primary function of welfare measures is not humanitarianism but legitimation. The problems of the poor are a social threat. This has been especially obvious in the recent history of black Americans. Although the deteriorating condition of the ghettos was well known before the urban riots of 1964 and 1965, there was no expansion of welfare programs or benefits. Only in the wake of the riots were AFDC payments tripled and other welfare programs enlarged. Life did not improve as a result of this welfarism, but, by the early 1970s, the combination of massive police armament, drugs, and internal political change had brought a calm to the ghetto. Precisely at this time, President Nixon initiated his "benign neglect" policy of closing down the urban welfare apparatus. The pretext was the need for governmental economy; the basic reason was that such legitimation transfers were no longer politically essential.

The welfare system is as much an economic benefit to the well-to-do as it is to the needy. Welfare dollars buy the goods of corporate America. They assure doctors, dentists, and drug companies of payment (usually excessive) for health services. Poor people, in fact, get a very small amount of the public dole. In 1976, for example, state and local public assistance payments in the United States came to about $7.5 billion. This was less than half the amount paid in subsidies to large farmers, doctors and hospitals, universities, shipping concerns, airlines, banks, and construction companies. There is little concern that the recipients of these "corporate welfare" transfers might be losing their incentive because of "living off the dole." As someone aptly observed: "In America, we have free enterprise for the poor and welfare for the wealthy."

A NOTE ON WHO IS POOR

Both Liberals and Conservatives tend to explain income inequality, particularly poverty, in terms of some specific characteristics of poor individuals over which they presumably have some control. To Conservatives, poverty—except in the case of "madmen and children," to use Friedman's phrase—is a matter of an individual's failure to take advantage of employment opportunities. Essentially Conservatives view poverty as the fault of the poor, the result of their laziness or indifference. Liberals have a better understanding that structural and institutional aspects of the economy can thrust people into poverty regardless of their commitment to the work ethic. These factors include lack of training and education, changes in technology, and the location of specific industries. The Liberal response is to "help" individuals through more job training, income transfers, social counseling, and education so that they can survive or, better, get back into the productive labor force. Neither Conservatives nor Liberals understand that attention must be focused on the causes of poverty, not its casualties.

Contrary to general impressions, very few of America's poor are poor because they don't work. At least two-thirds of the families with income below the poverty line have one or more members working at a job of some sort. Of the remaining poor, most are in that category because of some disablement. In 1976, for instance, fully one-sixth of American workers reported disablement lasting more than six months. The Conservative argument that poverty is the result of laziness is not proved.

Poverty is a function of the capitalist system: it forces many workers to labor at jobs that are not adequately recompensed; its general tendency, as we discussed in regard to unemployment, is to make labor itself increasingly irrelevant. In other words, marginal income from marginal jobs is more and more characteristic of labor in the United State—another expression of capitalism's overall tendency to create a labor surplus.

Marginal income and poverty, however, do not fall randomly on the population. Few owners of capital are poor. Poverty in the United States is almost exclusively the privilege of those who have nothing to sell but their labor. More particularly, all studies of poverty indicate the presence of discrimination—racism and sexism. Perhaps to the surprise of those who have observed the "official" efforts of the past decade to end formal discrimination, the available data suggest we have made little headway on this front. Even before the recession of 1974–1975 widened the gap between whites and blacks, it was apparent that blacks had made few gains (see Table 8.5).

Table 8.5   Median Income of White and Black Families and Ratio of Black to White Income, 1967–1974

	1967	1970	1971	1972	1973	1974
White Family	$8,234	$10,236	$10,672	$11,549	$12,595	$13,356
Black Family	4,875	6,279	6,440	6,864	7,269	7,808
Ratio Black to White	.59	.61	.60	.59	.58	.58

Source: *Social and Economic Status of the Black Population, 1974*, Current Population Reports, SSP-23, No. 54, U.S. Department of Commerce (July 1975), p. 33.

For women the case is very much the same. By 1974, the United States Department of Labor reported, median income for all American women stood at 56 percent of male earnings, down from 63 percent in 1955.

A common argument offered in discussions of "solutions" to the poverty problem is that poverty is the result of inadequate skills. While it is true that those with the least education tend to be the poorest (and also that the poorest get the worst education), the payout of education for non-white and female Americans is not proven by the evidence. Tables 8.6 and 8.7 summarize data from detailed studies of black male-white male and male-female earnings by level of education in the late 1960s, when poverty attracted far greater public attention than it now does.

Less complete recent studies, after almost a decade of "equal opportunity" and "affirmative action" indicate the same general trend, that educational attainment does not close the income gap for non-whites and women. By 1977 only at the very top (sixteen years of education or more) had these groups made some slight gains. Rather than proving that education raises income, this more accurately reflects "tokenism"—a little room at the top to placate civil rights and women's movement pressures.

On the basis of this information, it is difficult to put much faith in the Liberal line that educating the poor will change their income situa-

Table 8.6   Median Income for all Males—by Race and Education, 1969

Years of Schooling	Black Male	White Male	Ratio
Less than 8	$3,000	$3,600	.82
8	4,300	5,500	.79
High School, 1–3	5,200	7,300	.71
High School, 4	6,100	8,600	.71
College, 1–3	7,100	9,600	.74
College, 4 or more	8,600	12,400	.69

Source: U.S. Department of Commerce, Bureau of the Census, *Current Population Reports*, Series P-60, No. 75, p. 105.

Table 8.7   Median Income of Men and Women (25 years old with full-time jobs) by Education, 1969

Years of Schooling	Male	Female	Ratio
Less than 8	$5,300	$3,300	.62
8	6,600	3,600	.55
High School, 1–3	7,300	3,900	.53
High School, 4	8,300	4,800	.58
College, 1–3	9,300	5,500	.59
College, 4 or more	11,800	6,700	.57
College, 5 or more	12,800	8,300	.64
Total	8,100	4,700	.58

Source: U.S. Department of Commerce, Bureau of the Census, *Current Population Reports*, Series P-60, No. 66, p. 98.

tion. The solution to poverty is income and better jobs, not education. The United States has the most educated poor in the world. If we understand this, we can see that the plight of those at the bottom of the ladder is not personal but systemic. The system's response to inequality is not to eradicate it but to make it tolerable—to mask the racial and sex discrimination and the social-class distinctions between workers and capitalists.

A RADICAL PROGRAM TO END INEQUALITY

It is obvious that the combined effect of our tax and transfer system is to maintain income inequality. It serves the system well. The welfare poor act as a potential labor pool to be tapped as needed and to be used as a check on excessive labor demands by those who work.

With large numbers of people held in a "poverty reserve," unions cannot push too strongly against capital's power. Inequality also serves the purpose of disciplining labor. Maintaining the bottom layers of society at bare subsistence levels does provide a work "incentive." Given the oppressive and alienating nature of most work in America, wages and the hope for better wages are practically the only device to keep labor in the market and keep it producing. Inequality also serves an important social purpose of dividing the working class. The over-taxed and underpaid worker frequently turns against the welfare- supported nonworker. Nonworkers often hate themselves and those above them who have comparatively slight income advantages. The source of income inequality is thus ignored.

From a Radical view, income equalization is crucial. In terms of short-run socialist reforms, this must mean a total renovation of the tax structure—elimination of taxes on incomes below a certain level, along with the guarantee of a *reasonable* minimum income for everyone, working or not. The elimination of tax loopholes, adoption of high and steeply progressive taxes on all income, and virtually con-fiscatory taxes on accumulated wealth would be essential. At the same time, the extent and content of social welfare programs should be altered to fit human needs.

All of these steps, even though they fall short of actual long-run social ownership of capital, would be unacceptable to defenders of the capitalist system. However, the system's failure, indeed its inability, to achieve some measure of income equalization—along with the chronic problems of unemployment, inflation, and fiscal crisis—erodes popular acceptance of existing inequities. Thus it is likely that general pressure for tax reform and more humane welfare programs will grow. The realization that inequality in income and wealth is not legitimate will very probably signal the beginning of the end of the production-for-profit system. At any rate, it is in the area of income inequality that the contradictions of modern American capitalism are most obvious.

PART 3

PROBLEMS OF AGGREGATE ECONOMIC POLICY

Part 3 focuses upon issues that are primarily *macroeconomic* in origin. In other words, our attention will be directed to issues affecting the economy as a whole and to variables affecting its aggregate economic performance. Specifically, we shall examine such problem areas as business cycle behavior, stabilization policy, inflation, unemployment, government finance, international trade and money policy, and centralized economic planning. Part 2 examined problems of specific economic units—households, firms, industries, labor groups, and the like. As one economist has described the difference between micro and macro, the former examines the trees while the latter studies the forest.

ISSUE 9

The Macroeconomy Examined
Are We Depression-proof?

We have nothing to fear but fear itself.

Franklin Roosevelt, 1933

We do have a great many safeguards that make another crash and depression unlikely, but we could have another 1929. I remain unconvinced that human behavior has changed a great deal.

William McChesney Martin,
Former Chairman of the Federal Reserve, 1979

The danger today is that we could become so concerned about inflation that we could bring on another depression.

Arthur Okun, 1979

The only thing the depression gave us was the curse of Keynesian economics.

Frederick Von Hayek, 1979

In world market crisis, the contradictions and antagonisms of bourgeois production break through to the surface. But instead of investigating the nature of the . . . catastrophe, the apologists content themselves with denying the catastrophe itself.

Karl Marx, 1867

THE PROBLEM

Although the Great Depression is no longer part of "recent American history" and is remembered only dimly by a comparative handful of Americans, its impact remains very great among economic thinkers. The years from the stock market crash of 1929 to the beginning of World War II were a crucial watershed for modern economic policy. Depression, the specter of depression, and most important, the ability to avoid any future depressions have since held the attention of macroeconomic policy makers.

The domination of modern economic thought by events and developments now nearly a half-century old is understandable when the severity of this "Great Rupture" in American history is examined. Between 1929 and 1933 the gross national product (the nation's annual output of goods and services) was sliced almost in half. Unemployment, which had averaged about 13 percent in 1929, soared to 24.9 percent by 1933. Unemployment for 1933 totaled 13 million men and women, but this figure was deceiving since several times that amount, perhaps 65 percent of the labor force, suffered some unemployment or could obtain only part-time work. On the business side, before-tax corporate profits fell from a record $11 billion in 1929 to an operating loss of $1.2 billion four years later, and industrial production declined by more than 45 percent.

Although 1933 was the bottom of the Depression, it was not the end. Contrary to some popular impressions that Franklin Roosevelt's New Deal brought an end to the crisis, the Depression held on another half-dozen years. By 1939, as war clouds gathered over Europe and America began to gear up its industry and mobilize for defense, unemployment still stood at 17 percent, with 9.5 million citizens out of work, and the current value of national output (GNP) was still 10 percent below that of 1929.

Historians have documented the wrenching effect of the Depression on institutions and values. However great the changes in modes of American thought and behavior, none were more profound than those in economic thinking and practice. Before Black Tuesday's stock market collapse (October 29, 1929) and the crisis that followed, conventional economic wisdom unashamedly espoused the virtues of laissez faire. The economy was to operate freely. Although this meant the periodic toleration of bad times as business activity occasionally slowed, these downturns were offset by succeeding periods of expansion and prosperity. Left by itself, economic analysis held, the economy would right itself and, over time, move upward to new, higher levels of output, employment, and real income.

But recovery was not spontaneous in the Great Depression, and for good or ill the orthodox belief in the self-regulatory business cycle fell from favor. Ruminating on the worldwide depression in England, John Maynard Keynes concluded it was time to clear the intellectual stage of all the old furniture of economic orthodoxy. In 1936, his *General Theory of Employment, Interest, and Money* proclaimed that capitalist economic institutions were not self-balancing mechanisms but instead tended toward chronic stagnation. This situation demanded action by governments through fiscal and monetary policy to forestall collapse. Not given to modesty, Keynes correctly warned his readers that his ideas would change the way people thought about modern capitalist economies.

The acceptance of Keynesian ideas was not immediate but it grew steadily. Within a decade and a half of publication, the *General Theory* had conquered the classrooms. Within two and a half decades it conquered public policy. By the early 1960s ordinary newspaper readers needed some knowledge of such concepts as "full-employment budgets," "the multiplier effect," and "fine tuning" to understand the economic news from Washington.

If all these terms and new economic concepts seemed confusing and sometimes contradictory to plain "commonsense" economics, that was all right. By the mid 1960s the economy was booming and depression concerns had, at least temporarily, disappeared.

The daydreams of permanent prosperity, however, were quickly dashed in the 1970s. With the recessions of 1970 and 1974–1975, the specter of chronic crisis had returned, but this time in the form of a two-headed monster—unemployment amid a lagging economy *along with* constantly rising prices. Paul Samuelson dubbed this creature "stagflation." It had a name but public authorities, with all their economic tools, seemed incapable of dealing with it. Then, to make matters worse, the nation was hit with an energy shortage.

To be sure, the economic and historical context had changed, but once again Americans, including no small number of economists, began to worry out loud about the possibilities of chronic economic stagnation. Nervous backward glances at the 1930s became more common. Had we really made our economy depression-proof?

SYNOPSIS The Conservative position maintains that depression and protracted economic stagnation are not central to capitalist economic systems and that the business cycle downturn after 1929 was worsened, not moderated, by government intervention in the economy. Liberals argue that only through vigorous and active countercyclical policies by government can the economy's natural propensity toward recession and depression be controlled. To Radicals, crisis and depression are quite natural to production-for-profit systems, and while crises may be delayed by governmental actions, they cannot be eliminated in the long run.

The Conservative Argument

The Great Depression continues to dominate the popular imagination. It exercises considerable influence on the thinking of most economists. However, such worries, rather than reflecting the real significance of events, attest to the persuasiveness of myth over reality. To put matters directly, most of what is believed about the causes of the Depression is wrong. More important, the body of economic policy developed to make us depression-proof is dangerously irrelevant, constructed to deal with a problem that never existed. Alas, the cumbersome structure of government intervention in the economy through countercyclical fiscal and monetary policy and the consequent chilling economic effect of bloated government budgets and deficits have been unnecessary. Indeed, government intervention is more of a threat to stability than a bulwark.

ON MISREADING THE SIGNIFICANCE AND CAUSES OF THE GREAT DEPRESSION

Contrary to popular economic beliefs, the initial business downturn in 1929–1930 was not in itself a unique event. As most economists know but sometimes overlook, the general economic performance of the United States, both before the Great Depression and after (even with the tools of the new economists), has followed a cyclical course. Indeed, the expansion-contraction rhythm of economic affairs had fascinated many students of business cycles long before the depression of the 1930s. As Figure 9.1 shows, business contractions had appeared at about eight- to twelve-year intervals, each eventually succeeded by a counteracting stage of growth and prosperity. Economists offered a variety of explanations for such cyclical behavior, including new inventions, changes in investment or consumer behavior, and even sunspot activity. But before the 1930s, few, except perhaps the Marxists committed to the destruction of the system, held that business contraction could become a permanent state of affairs. Just as surely as the business cycle turned downward, it would sooner or later turn upward.

This, however, did not happen in 1929–1930, and to obtain a clearer understanding of modern day economic tendencies we must ask why.

FIGURE 9.1   A CENTURY OF BUSINESS FLUCTUATIONS

Source: AmeriTrust Company. Adapted with changes.

For about four decades now, the interpretation set out by Keynes and his followers has been dominant. According to Keynes, the depression of the 1930s was not merely a periodic movement within the business cycle. Instead, it was a problem of chronic "stagnation," a situation in which the economy could no longer maintain high levels of employment and output because of the inadequacy of business investment. In short, depression had become a permanent state of affairs.

Such a situation, according to Keynes, demanded firm action. First, the economy would have to be managed by government since Treasury and monetary authorities could no longer count on the natural bottoming out of the depression. Second, government would have to act to "stimulate demand"—to increase consumer spending and business investment. Third, this demand stimulation would probably have to come from enlarged state expenditures, purposely unbalanced budgets and deficit spending for public goods, and transfer payments to business and individuals.

Thus began the "modern" period of economic thought. The epoch of laissez faire was to be closed, with government replacing private accumulation and private instincts as the driving force of the economic system. Never mind the past spectacular performance of the private and open economy in building the nation. Never mind the implied assaults upon individual economic freedom and choice which were the underpinnings of political freedom in the United States. Lord Keynes and his followers had determined that these were now outmoded beliefs and that only through massive government intervention in the economy could survival be assured.

For good or ill, new interpretations of economic events and new programs to deal with these events, whether real or imagined, were

Year

unleashed. Regardless of how Conservatives feel about this new analysis, they cannot deny its impact. Quite certainly Keynes had produced a theoretical and practical revolution.

A BETTER INTERPRETATION

Ordinarily the best test for a hypothesis that interprets a set of events is to ask whether the hypothesis adequately explains the situation and is the best explanation possible. Applying this rule to the Keynesian critique, we find it wanting.

First, there is no evidence to support the idea that the Great Depression was, at its beginning in 1929, exceptional or that it differed markedly from past business downturns. Therefore, there is nothing to support the Keynesian belief that depression had become a permanent and congenital economic condition by the 1930s. What we do know, however, is that the depressed business conditions were worsened by the money-policy actions of the Federal Reserve Board, the government authority charged with maintenance of the nation's money and banking system.

Lowering interest rates had always served to bring forth new investment and stimulate recovery in past downturns. However, reacting to the speculative bull market, the Fed had pursued a tight money policy even when it was apparent in early 1929 that a business downturn was forming. With high interest rates discouraging new business borrowing and reducing the stock of money (the money supply), business investment and consumer buying sagged even before the stock market collapsed. This was the Fed's first mistake. Its second came in December 1930 when the Bank of the United States in New York City closed its doors. Although it was an ordinary commercial bank, many people believed it to be an official government bank and panic set in. Depositors in New York City and elsewhere rushed to withdraw their savings. Bank after bank faced liquidity crises. Unable to meet depositors' demands, banks began to fall like a line of dominoes. Meanwhile the Fed, created in 1914 for just such an emergency, failed to take any action to improve bank liquidity. In fact, its next action was simply disastrous. In September 1931, as international financial problems spread worldwide and more and more gold was drained from the United States, the Fed raised interest rates in an attempt to stop the overseas flow of gold. Banks, now unable to borrow from the Fed (because of the high interest rates), had no recourse but to fold. Fourteen hundred closed their doors in three months, and the nation's money supply (consisting largely of demand deposits) fell by 12 percent. Meanwhile, on the business side, high interest rates discouraged new investment, and consumer spending fell as the money supply contracted. An ordinary depression had been transformed into an unprecedented financial crisis and, in turn, a near-complete prostration of business.

The foregoing analysis differs sharply from the Keynesian stagnationist approach. While the Keynesians are partially correct that the Depression did finally become a matter of insufficient aggregate demand, that happened only after and as a result of the failure of the Federal Reserve System. Rather than the economy manifesting some sinister and fatal stagnationist flaw, the evidence suggests that the Great Depression was largely accidental. That being the case, there is no proven analytical foundation for the Keynesian prescription that only through massive government intervention can a free enterprise economy be kept afloat. Ironically, when we focus on the critical failures of monetary policy between 1929 and 1933, we find the reverse of the Keynesian analysis to be true: that government actions (through the Fed) in fact caused the Great Depression.

The worsening and deepening of the Depression after 1933 was also the result of government activity. Liberal defenders of Franklin Roosevelt like to depict the New Deal as an experimental and pragmatic program to "prime" the economy. Not yet convinced by the Keynesian arguments, FDR is usually presented as doing too little with countercyclical policy to get things going (until the government spending boom of World War II). This interpretation of the New Deal period of the Great Depression is guilty of a serious error of omission.

FDR's antidepression strategy, Keynesian or not, was antibusiness and antibanker. The president's public addresses identified these groups as both the cause of the Depression and the reason why his own policies had not turned the economic tide. His attempts to increase regulatory agency power, to insert government in the pricing mechanism, to reform the banking community, and especially to reform the Supreme Court when it threw out key pieces of his interventionist legislation created considerable business uncertainty. Within such a charged political atmosphere, business expectations, key to the undertaking of new investment and critical to recovery, remained essentially negative. Thus, the interventionist policies of the New Deal tended to deepen and broaden the already critical business depression.

ARE WE REALLY DEPRESSION PROOF?

While the Depression has long since passed, its debris is still with us. The victory of the Keynesian analysis has led to the building of even more elaborate theories to justify the enlargement of the government sector. The size of federal spending has grown, and the extent of fiscal and monetary manipulation of current business activity has been enlarged. For decades, beginning students of economics have been taught as if it were received religious truth that deficits do not matter, that the growth of the public sector is healthy, and that the macro performance of the economy can be insulated from depression and "fine tuned" to produce desired levels of output, employment, and price stability both instantaneously and in the long-run.

In point of fact, most of these developments have had a destabilizing influence. As we shall see in the following issues on fiscal policy, inflation, and unemployment, the enlargement of the government sector has distorted the economy. It has interfered with the market and private economic decision making. The growth of government spending and deficits, far from having a stabilizing impact, has generated a permanent inflationary tendency in the economy. This in turn has led to international crisis for the American dollar and destabilization of international trade and finance. Meanwhile, the quixotic stop-and-go policy shifts of the monetary authorities have created considerable investment instability at home resulting in growing unemployment.

Turning to the original question of whether or not another Great Depression is possible, the Conservative position, although similar to the Liberal Keynesian position in giving a negative response, should be seen in light of its own assumptions. First, a massive depression is not the natural outcome of a free enterprise economy. Second, the elaborate policy tools developed to insulate the economy from depression are both unjustified and inherently dangerous. Third, the fact that we have not experienced a serious depression since the 1930s should not be accepted as proof that Keynesian macro policy has worked. Rather, it might just as easily prove that the private economy is basically durable and adaptable—even with Keynesian roadblocks thrown in its way.

Thus, we can conclude that another Great Depression is not inevitable unless, of course, we continue to rely upon mistaken interpretations and cures in the formation of public policy. The "cures" we learned from the last depression are a far greater menace to future stability than anything else on the horizon.

The Liberal Argument

Although the recent popularizing of a reconditioned laissez-faire economics and the public mood of antigovernment conservatism have tended to obscure matters, it is just as true today as it was in the 1930s that mature capitalist economic systems tend to stagnate. That was the case in the Great Depression, and that scenario, with some modifications produced by the present energy crisis and the current price inflation, could be repeated again. Indeed, it will be repeated if we forget the lessons of the Depression and the economic analysis of J. M. Keynes and his followers. The development of a severe economic downturn is unnecessary, however, for modern economic policy makers now have both the theoretical tools and the policy weapons to insulate the economy from depression.

THE COLLAPSE OF ORTHODOX
IDEAS IN THE 1930S

The prevailing economic view in 1929 was that the economy was a "natural," self-adjusting mechanism. Wages, interest, and rents were paid to individuals according to the value of their contributions to national output. Such payments were, over time, equitable and just rewards for work and risk. The general mode of economic activity was pure competition. Interferences in the economy, whether by government, labor unions, or collusive business practice, were condemned. The "economy" was thus described and analyzed theoretically in terms of an open laissez-faire system. To be sure, periodic downturns in the national economy were possible just as periodic stickiness in wages, savings, and business investment were possible. However, the focus was on the long haul, and, over time, such deviations were thought to be self-correcting.

Within this general economic structure, economists of the traditional order based their analysis of the national economy on a four-cornered foundation. First, there would be no long-run overproduction of goods (or to look at it from the other side, no long-run underconsumption). This was true because payments to the producers, labor, business, and so forth, were always equal to the value of the goods produced. As the nineteenth-century French economist Jean Baptiste Say had put it, "supply creates its own demand." This is the essence of Say's law.

Second, and following from the first point, there could be, again in the long run, no such thing as involuntary unemployment. With flexible wages and prices, there would always be sufficient work at any given wage level to employ all those willing to work at that wage. Individuals who chose not to work at a particular wage (supposedly because they valued leisure more) were not "unemployed" at all.

Third, through free and flexible interest rates, private savings would be just enough to meet the investment (or borrowing) needs of businesses. If business sought greater investment, then interest rates would rise, people would now choose to save more, and funds would become available for business expansion. This, in turn, would create jobs, raise wages, and stimulate balanced economic growth.

Fourth, the level of prices in the society were determined by the rate of growth of the money supply. An increase in money would stimulate spending and demand for goods, which would raise market prices. A decrease in money would lower prices.

To the orthodox, these theories offered policy solutions to the periodic downturns in the economy. If business output exceeded consumer demand, wait! Prices would fall to clear the market of goods. Wages would fall, and the number of workers seeking employment would be reduced until an equilibrium wage was reached. Interest rates would fall, and individuals would shift savings to consumption.

With lower interest rates and increasing consumption, business would again invest. Public policy within such a self-balancing economic order could be described quite easily: Do nothing!

As the international economy continued to inch downward after 1929, John Maynard Keynes began to rethink the orthodox analysis and reach his own conclusion on the evidence at hand. First of all, he observed that the automaticity of Say's law was unfounded. Indeed, it was possible for overproduction or underconsumption to develop if individuals hold money rather than save it (lend it to borrowers). Second, wages were not, in the real world, freely flexible. Business could and did keep prices up and laid off workers while awaiting the sale of inventories. The alternatives available to workers were not lower wages or leisure but simply increased unemployment. Third, lowered interest rates did not induce business investment at a time of overproduction. Business, with goods on hand, would be unlikely to produce more goods even if the cost of borrowing were near zero.

Thus, in the Keynesian analysis, the "short-run" business fluctuations of the economy could become very long indeed. The self-correcting nature of the economy was an incorrect premise. And, squaring with the real evidence that continued to build after the early 1930s, it was possible to have a continuing low level of output that left large numbers of workers and factories idle. Indeed, it was not only possible, it was quite natural in an unregulated economic system.

THE KEYNESIAN SOLUTION

Keynes's objective in his *General Theory* was to lay out the path to a high-employment economy. His approach emphasized aggregate rather than microeconomic aspects, as orthodox analysts did. First, aggregate levels of employment depended upon the total demand for goods, including consumer purchase of goods and business investment as well as government spending. Second, the primary culprit in the cyclical downturn of an economy was the activity of investors, since it is through changes in investment outlays that changes in total demand for goods and services are affected most directly. Consumer spending was a fairly constant function of total income, with consumer outlays rising and falling directly as national income fluctuated. Government spending was small, and, in depression conditions, tended to get smaller as governments tried to live within the orthodox doctrine of annually balanced budgets.

Keynes's approach led to the position that only through artificially induced higher levels of aggregate demand would it be possible to attain full employment and full utilization of plants and equipment. The course was clear: business investment had to be stimulated or government spending had to be inflated, or more likely some combination of both had to be tried. The combined effects of expansionary fiscal policy (enlarged government spending and/or tax cuts usually accompanied by a budget deficit) and expansionary monetary policy (lower interest rates and easier money) were to produce enlarged aggregate demand and diminished unemployment.

Keynes's economic theories did not, however, concentrate solely on depression economics. As his adherents soon learned, the reversing of policy direction could work equally well against inflation. In the face of rising prices and full employment, the expansion spigot could be turned off through higher taxes and reduced spending while the monetary authorities acted to tighten credit.

THE VICTORY OF THE NEW ECONOMICS

Although Keynes quickly gained academic adherents for his ideas, he made little headway in Washington during the Depression. For all his alleged fiscal profligacy, Franklin Roosevelt, with his "pump priming" and "ABC" government agencies, never grasped the Keynesian analysis and never embraced massive federal spending until he was forced to—during World War II.

There was enormous federal spending during the war (with government spending in 1944 nearly twice the GNP of 1933), and this produced a rapid growth of demand that was restrained only by rationing and price controls. Simultaneously there was an equally rapid growth in the federal debt. When the war ended, many economists still feared the economy would drop back into depression. Instead, the stored-up wartime demand became the engine for a long postwar boom. Even before the inadvertent Keynesianism of World War II proved to be effective, however, the United States had rung down the curtain on the laissez-faire era. On February 20, 1946, President Truman signed Public Law 340, better known as the Employment Act of 1946. The act committed the federal government to the triple objective of providing high levels of employment, maintaining stable prices, and encouraging economic growth. The groundwork had been laid for countercyclical fiscal and monetary policy.

The lessons of World War II fiscal expansion and the license for government fiscal and monetary intervention in the economy granted by the Employment Act of 1946 opened American economic thinking to the New Economics. Although Presidents Truman and Eisenhower showed only passing interest in the new doctrines and the new possibilities for public policy, the university economists were quickly won over.

With the election of John Kennedy in 1960, Keynesian theory became policy. Coming to office during the third Eisenhower recession (1960–1961), Kennedy introduced a fiscally experimental program. With an investment tax credit worth $2.5 billion to business in 1962 and the proposal for an $11 billion general tax cut in 1963, the Kennedy program offered sound Keynesian medicine. Lyndon Johnson continued and elaborated upon the Kennedy theme. For almost eight years the economy moved forward, and Americans learned (although they were soon to forget) that economic crisis, periodic or congenital, need not be the nature of the economy.

IS THE KEYNESIAN ANALYSIS STILL RELEVANT?

Since the late 1960s the "new economics" has suffered badly in the press and at the hands of a resurgent laissez-faire element within the profession. Nor have Liberals been altogether confident about their Keynesian roots. The stubborn stagflation, two recessions (in 1970 and 1974–1975), and a growing energy crisis have cooled the enthusiasm of many who saw the economy as completely under control in the mid-1960s. Displaying a propensity "to throw out the baby with the bath water," many economists, politicians, and ordinary citizens have incorrectly identified the Keynesian contribution as a primary cause of current macroeconomic problems. We shall return to this matter in the next issue on fiscal policy, but it is necessary to point out here that this is an unfair and inaccurate assessment of the contribution of the New Economics. It must be remembered that during the last two years of the 1960s and for most of the 1970s, Keynesian policy makers were effectively "out of office" in Washington. During this time fiscal and monetary policy devices and objectives were subordinated to political opportunism and political needs or simply handled in a stupid fashion.

Indeed, to identify the new modes of economic thought that developed in response to the Great Depression as the origin of current economic ills is a dangerous tendency. Such developments as the growing popularity of a "balanced budget" amendment (which would limit federal expenditures constitutionally to the amount of revenues collected) would effectively "destroy" antidepressionary fiscal policy. Budget limitations would make it impossible to use deficit spending as a device to enlarge aggregate demand. The nation would be returned to the vulnerability that existed in 1929, but this time it would be law rather than obsolete ideas that would inhibit countercyclical public policy. With the threat of economic stagnation heightened by the growing energy crisis, this disarming of our economic policy-making ability might prove fatal.*

Although the structure of the American economy has changed considerably since the 1930s, nothing has happened to make an essentially private, capitalistic economy more insulated from economic collapse. There is no better reason today than there was in October 1929 to believe that, left completely to itself, our economy would "naturally" avoid depression. Indeed, only the size of the public sector (which accounts for about one-third of our GNP) and the impact of government policy in stimulating economic activity and aggregate demand hold back chronic economic stagnation. We should not forget that the growth of government in the aggregate economy has occurred largely in the absence of private sector growth. To maintain the opposite— that the private sector has been retarded by the growth of government budgets, government debt, and an active public policy—is to forget the great lesson of the 1930s.

*As of this writing, the balanced budget advocates promise to make the constitutional requirement for ending federal deficits a major issue in the 1980 presidential election. Whether they will be successful remains to be seen. Voters are becoming increasingly disturbed by nagging inflation and consistently rising tax bills. However, as the AFL-CIO has pointed out, a legal requirement to balance the federal budget may increase rather than lessen these problems: "The emotional urge for a balanced budget is to keep taxes down . . . [but] if at some future time the president and congress are not allowed to borrow they will have to raise taxes to make ends meet" (AFL-CIO American Federationist, April 1979). However, the simple logic of this argument is often lost in the growing popularity of taxpayers' revolts. For further discussion of this problem, especially at the state and local levels, see Issue 14.

As we shall see in the succeeding sections on stabilization policy, unemployment, and inflation, the tools of Keynesian economics— along with new policies to deal with energy, chronic unemployment, and price increases—are the only means to ensure economic stability. Is another Great Depression possible, then? Only, it would seem, if we forget the past.

The Radical Argument

For both Conservatives and Liberals, albeit for different reasons, the imminent or future collapse of the American economy is not an inevitable event. Their views, of course, are not very startling. That defenders of varieties of capitalism believe the system has a future should be expected. However, the evidence, if looked at closely, points to a different conclusion. Contrary to the cheery Conservative view that free enterprise economies suffer only periodic and inconsequential business downturns, it is apparent from a historical as well as a recent perspective that crisis is part of the nature of production-for-profit economies. The Liberal contention that the countercyclical use of fiscal and monetary policy can insulate us from depression enormously understates the systemic roots of economic crisis and fails to comprehend the costs and effects of the tools of countercyclical policy.

Crisis is the ordinary tendency of the capitalist economy. It is not accidental, nor can it be eliminated permanently by remedial means. Short-term breakdowns in the capitalist system may occur sporadically, but ultimately the economic and social contradictions of capitalism will overwhelm the system.

THE CHRONIC TENDENCY TOWARD CRISIS

Economic crisis and instability are not peculiar to capitalist societies alone. However, with the dawn and maturity of capitalism, crisis (or what we presently might call depression) took on a new dimension. In precapitalist societies economic contraction largely resulted from wars, plagues, crop failures, or other natural disasters. The granaries were empty, people starved, and there were shortages of goods of all kinds. Crisis was associated with underproduction. Paradoxically, in the capitalist era of crisis this situation has been reversed. Capitalist contraction usually appears after an era of growth in the productive forces of a society. With excess goods on hand and no market, producers reduce current output, unemployment rises, and wages and prices fall. In short, capitalist crises usually occur when the granaries are full.

To be sure, the periodic panics and depressions that strike capitalism usually have been followed by recoveries. For many years, before the appearance of Keynes's work, the periodicity of boom and bust (especially boom) was sufficient to describe economic contractions as "mere disturbances" that would go away and therefore did not merit very serious analytical study. No effort was made to see stagnation as fundamental to the capitalist order. Nor has this view changed much among modern Conservative economists. Keynesian Liberals, meanwhile, have accepted the fact that overproduction generally leads to depressions in modern capitalism, but they hold that the tendency is easily manageable through the tools of modern public policy.

From the Radical perspective, however, economic crises are both fundamental to capitalism and beyond the capitalists' capacity to resolve. As capitalist economies grow and mature, crises become even more frequent and progressively deeper, each succeeded by less satisfactory recovery.

The crises are inherent in the capitalist system of production. In their perpetual search for expanded profits, capitalists must create surplus value—that is, they forever attempt to maximize the difference between the higher price for which goods sell and the lower price of the labor involved in production. To acquire greater profits, the capitalist must enlarge surplus value through the introduction of greater amounts of capital equipment, through the direct exploitation of labor, or by some combination. The object is to produce greater output per unit of wage labor that is paid. As capitalists endeavor to produce more and more at greater profit, the capacity of the workers (consumers) to purchase this output declines. Although the people may "need" the goods, they do not have the "effective demand" to obtain them. Overproduction and underconsumption create periodic gluts of goods, which in turn cause crises wherein production ceases, capital is destroyed or left idle, and human beings starve.

As capitalism progresses, its productive capacity constantly enlarges. The possible depths and duration of production-consumption crises are heightened, and the ultimate end of the system is brought that much closer. Nineteenth-century Marxists observed the growing incidence of capitalist crises and predicted early collapse as profits fell, unemployment grew, real wages declined, and the system became discredited before the masses.

In point of fact, all this has not happened, but that is not proof that the underlying Radical analysis was wrong. Rather it must be adjusted to take into account certain events.

First, the capitalists' persistent need for markets to dispose of their surplus production and to realize surplus value and profits was partially attained through overseas exploitation—imperialism. One case might illustrate the point. In the latter half of the nineteenth century, the depressed British textiles industry experienced a significant boom after the British colonial rulers of India systematically destroyed the Indian weaving industry. British machines, and even British workers, went back to work precisely as Indians were forced from old occupations and compelled to buy imported British textiles.

Second, capitalist enterprise, which Marx had depicted as largely competitive, began to respond to the periodic crises by developing monopolistic characteristics. Industries became more integrated and dominated by a few firms. Possessing the power to set and control prices, output, and quality, monopoly capitalism was able to avoid the internecine struggles that had wiped out enterprise in the earlier competitive era.

Third, the growth of the state in the economy provided additional insulation from crisis. The state could foster or sanction monopoly behavior, mitigate the effects of labor exploitation and unemployment, and act directly to absorb the surplus production through government purchases (especially during war) and transfer payments.

THE COLLAPSE OF 1929

The expansion of overseas markets and sources of cheap labor and resources, the increasingly monopolistic behavior of business enterprise, and the enlargement of government protective actions held back the breaking of the dike before 1929. It did not, however, stop serious leaks.

In the case of the United States, seven major business cycles can be identified between the panic of 1893 and the beginning of World War I. Each downturn lasted longer and became more pronounced.

As the United States entered World War I and a wartime business boom, unemployment stood at about ten percent. The "roaring twenties" were not much better. Probably the worst depression in U.S. history to that point occurred in 1921–1922, and throughout most of the decade unemployment was higher than 4 percent. Meanwhile, real wages moved upward only slightly. Only the phenomenal expansion of consumer debt buoyed the economy. For those who wished to see the evidence or could at least understand it, it was apparent that the dike would soon collapse.

The crisis after 1929 was a near-classic example of Marx's overproduction-underconsumption scenario. Moreover, it precipitated a general international collapse. The mature capitalist economies had exhausted markets for their goods. Overseas, the underdeveloped economies had little capacity to absorb output. At home, warehouses bulged since consumers lacked effective demand. As the first signs of crisis appeared, the banking and financial system, which itself rested upon the capitalists' ability to realize their surplus, tottered and collapsed: first the Wall Street crash, then New York bank failures, then European bank failures. Full-scale industrial contraction followed.

THE OLD ECONOMICS IN A NEW PACKAGE

The Keynesian response to the deepening Depression was to accept the essential outline of the older Marxist critique of capitalism: Overproduction and crisis were endemic to the system. However, the Keynesians neatly evaded the Marxian conclusion. According to their analysis, insufficient business and consumer demand could either be manipulated by fiscal and monetary policy or supplemented by government spending so as to raise the level of aggregate demand. In Marxian terms, government now became the vehicle to "realize surplus value."

Much has been made of this new thinking on the problem of the capitalist system. The "Keynesian Revolution" came to describe dominant economic opinion from the 1930s to the present. However, it was no revolution at all. Keynes and his followers have not sought to end capitalism but to save it. The central features of capitalism—private property, production for profit, wage labor, the business system and all the rest—were retained. Indeed, as business leaders came to appreciate the profit (surplus value) possibilities of enlarged government spending during World War II and the trial-and-error Keynesian years after the war, corporate America enthusiastically accepted the new economics. The frequent Liberal posturing against big business should be recognized as pure political rhetoric. In the 1964 Johnson-Goldwater electoral contest, big business showed its colors by rejecting the conservative, laissez-faire Republican in favor of the big-spending Democrat from Texas. Giant corporations poured millions of dollars into LBJ's campaign.

STAGNATION IS IMMINENT

Rather than competing with the private sector, as classical and neoclassical theory had held, government spending (by all levels of government) reduced the pressures of chronic unemployment and excess capacity. It absorbed output and made the private realization of surplus value possible. As Table 9.1 shows, both the absolute magnitude of this spending and government outlays as a share of GNP have continued to grow. Absorbing a mere 7.4 percent of national output in 1903, the government now accounts for 32.9 percent of the GNP.

Despite the growth of government spending, the contours of crisis remain evident for those willing to go beyond conventional economic rhetoric. As we shall see in later discussions, fiscal policy has not smoothed out the bumps of the business cycle, unemployment has been growing steadily, and inflation has become chronic—all this as

Table 9.1 Government in the Economy, 1903–1978 (in billions of dollars)

Year	GNP	All government spending	Government spending as % of GNP
1903	$ 23.0	$ 1.7	7.4
1913	40.0	3.1	7.7
1929	103.4	10.3	9.9
1939	90.8	17.6	19.4
1949	258.0	59.3	22.9
1959	486.5	131.0	26.9
1969	935.5	285.6	30.5
1978	1890.4	621.2	32.9

Source: Economic Report of the President, 1978.

Keynesian stabilization policies enlarged government's role in propping up the economy.

Looking at the American economy this way, it is evident that the post-1929 growth of government did slow the speed of the system's deterioration into crisis, but it has not eliminated the tendency toward stagnation. Meanwhile, government spending must be financed either out of growing deficits or by rising taxes. The former method is inflationary and is severely testing the limits of the financial structure to carry the burden of debt, especially since the private sector is expanding its borrowing even more swiftly than government. The latter method is pushing the taxpayer to the wall. At any rate, both inflation and rising taxes as ways of financing growing government spending are adding to working class misery. Thus, the growth of government has not ended the exploitative effects of chronic capitalist crisis but has only changed the forms of exploitation.

The current energy problem and deepening recession increase demands for state spending to maintain both corporate profitability and the political legitimacy of the system. The capitalist system has reached the limits of fiscal policy expansionism as a device for realizing surplus value.

Is another "Great Depression" possible? *Very definitely!* But this time, it is unclear just how the capitalist system will be able to recover from a deep stagnation. With the capacity of government to absorb surplus production limited and the political fabric torn by the chronic exploitative character of capitalism, depression may well be fatal for the system as we now know it. Such pessimism (or optimism from a Radical perspective) may not yet seem well founded. However, the following discussions of such issues as stabilization policy, unemployment, inflation, state fiscal crisis, and international trade should give a clearer picture of the economic contradictions confronting capitalism and the limited options available for dealing with the system's fundamental crises.

ISSUE 10

Stabilization Policy
How Well Has It Been Working?

We must recognize that only experience can show how far the
common will, embodied in the policy of the state, ought to be
directed to increasing and supplementing the inducement to
invest.

John Maynard Keynes, 1935

Is fiscal policy being oversold? Is monetary policy being oversold? . . . My answer is yes to both of those questions. . . . What
I believe is that fine tuning has been oversold.

Milton Friedman, 1968

The potency of fiscal policy—both good and bad—has been
demonstrated time and again in the past couple of decades.

Walter W. Heller, 1968

There have been a lot of surprises in the 1970s—things that we
had very little experience with before.

Robert M. Solow, 1979

THE PROBLEM

While the larger and more spectacular questions of whether or not the economy is depression-proof always loom in the background, the problems of short-run economic performance attract greater attention from economists and public officials. In other words, more day-to-day concern is placed upon the trim of the economic ship than upon what might be done if it actually capsized. Obviously the two concerns are not unrelated; however, in this section we shall look more closely at the overall performance of public policy rather than its application to the extremes of the business cycle. The questions for examination are: How has stabilization policy developed, and how effective has it been?

In 1946, after extensive debate, Congress passed the Employment Act, which President Harry Truman signed. With memory of the Depression years still vivid, the act committed the federal government to the principle of national economic intervention. In heavy and careful legal jargon, the act proclaimed:

> The Congress hereby declares that it is the continuing policy and responsibility of the Federal Government to use all practicable means consistent with its needs and obligations and other essential considerations of national policy, with assistance and cooperation of industry, agriculture, labor and State and local governments, to coordinate and utilize all its plans, functions, and resources for the purpose of creating and maintaining, in a manner calculated to foster and promote free competitive enterprise and general welfare, conditions under which there will be afforded useful employment opportunities, including self-employment, for those able, willing and seeking to work and to promote maximum employment, production and purchasing power.

Alvin Hansen, a leading American economist and one of the new breed of Keynesians who had actively urged passage of this bill, called it the Magna Carta of government economic planning. The act itself was quite general. Aside from creating a Council of Economic Advisers to assist the president and a Joint Economic Committee for Congress, it had no specific content. Over the years, however, it became accepted as the legal and moral foundation for commitment to a three-pronged macro policy—providing high levels of employment, maintaining stable prices, and encouraging economic growth.

Although presidential comprehension of and adherence to the public policy objectives of the act have varied with intellect and ideology since 1946, these goals have, for most mainstream economists, been the essence of government economic policy for the past three decades. They were the great trinity of modern macro policy thought and analysis.

By the 1960s the dominant economic doctrine held that the New Economics could fine tune the economy to meet desired employment, price, and output objectives. The *Economic Report of the President* in 1965 put it this way: "Fiscal and monetary policies must be continually adjusted to keep the aggregate demand for goods and services in line with the economy's growing capacity to produce them." Experience during the early and mid-1960s seemed to support the view that stabilization policy worked. Employment and growth were up, and prices remained constant.

Beginning in the early 1970s, however, stagflation (high prices, high unemployment, and near-zero growth) caused serious rethinking about the tools and limits of modern public policy. For the first time, Americans suffered under the "depressionary" burden of unemployment and the "expansionary" cost of inflation. At least until the 1970s, we had thought of these two tendencies as being common to different stages of business cycle activity.

The stabilization doctrines of the 1960s were now debatable, and the New Economics was placed upon the defensive. Did stagflation signal the need to rethink economic policy? Or, was the new situation something unique, an exception to all the rules and merely a short-run redirection in the economy's performance?

SYNOPSIS The Conservative argument holds that stabilization policy attempts not only have failed to fine tune the economy but have been instrumental in creating the present stagflation. Liberals interpret the stabilization record quite differently, pointing to the successes of fiscal and monetary policy in the 1960s and arguing that a policy of monetary and fiscal restraint would worsen current economic conditions. While admitting the short-term effectiveness of stabilization policy in counteracting depression tendencies, Radicals see the enlargement of government intervention in the economy as working on behalf of only business and the ruling class and as having created an increasingly irrational system of production and consumption.

The Conservative Argument

Having incorrectly assumed that massive injections of government spending were the cures to any drastic economic downturn, Liberal Keynesians have elaborated equally spurious doctrines about fine tuning the economy in "normal" times. According to their view, expansionary monetary and fiscal policy could effectively offset minor but troublesome downturns in output and employment. Conversely, contractionary actions could lessen inflationary pressures. The public policy spigot need only be adjusted to produce the desired flow. This idea has been one of the most dangerous frauds ever perpetrated upon a free people, and it demands to be exposed.

THE RECORD OF FAILURE

First, there is no proof that a free economy will not correct its own expansion or contraction tendency (see the last issue). Second, the effectiveness of fine tuning and general macroeconomic management of the economy is unproved, and the record of failure and of creating even greater economic problems than the original ones is easily documented. Since the Keynesian ascendancy in the 1960s, stabilization policy has been synonymous with rising federal expenditures and a growing mountain of debt. As Table 10.1 shows, federal spending has increased by 500 percent in this period. Meanwhile, the almost annual deficits have expanded government debt by about 300 percent.

Although this "activist" fiscal expansionism has been defended by most Liberals as essential to maintaining a full employment economy, Figure 10.1 shows that employment difficulties have worsened over the years *and* that the excessive growth of government debt has triggered a long inflationary spiral (more on the last point in Issue 12).

OVERSELLING FISCAL POLICY

Americans have been oversold on the possibilities of a better life through fiscal expansion, just as they have been oversold on the idea that regulated markets work better than free ones. The fine-tuning proponents hold that fiscal policy is the most immediate and direct means to adjust the economic spigot. However, the failure of this tool

Table 10.1   Federal Receipts, Outlays, and Deficits, 1960–1980 (in millions of dollars)

Fiscal year	Receipts	Outlays	Surplus or deficit (−)
1960	$ 92,492	$ 92,223	$ 269
1961	94,389	97,795	−3,406
1962	99,676	106,813	−7,137
1963	106,560	111,311	−4,751
1964	112,662	118,584	−5,922
1965	116,833	118,430	−1,596
1966	130,856	134,652	−3,796
1967	149,552	158,254	−8,702
1968	153,671	178,833	−25,161
1969	187,784	184,548	3,236
1970	193,743	196,588	−2,845
1971	188,392	211,425	−23,033
1972	208,649	232,021	−23,373
1973	232,225	247,074	−14,849
1974	264,932	269,620	−4,688
1975	280,997	326,185	−45,188
1976	300,005	366,439	−66,434
1977	357,762	402,725	−44,963
1978	401,997	450,836	−48,839
1979[1]	455,989	493,368	−37,379
1980[1]	502,553	531,566	−29,013

Source: *Economic Report of the President*, 1979.

[1]Estimates.

is demonstrated explicitly in the Liberals' own most cited proof of their case—the tax cut of 1964. According to their interpretation, this timely tax reduction pulled the economy out of the doldrums of the 1960–1961 recession and began the long expansion of the 1960s. First of all, the timeliness thesis is unconvincing. Initially, the tax cut was said to be absolutely essential in 1962; but it was proposed in 1963, did not pass until 1964, and could not have had much effect before early 1965. Second, and most important, before the tax cut became law, the economy was clearly on the road to recovery.

The problem of lags in fiscal policy should not be underestimated. The functional view of fiscal policy advanced by Keynesians assumes an immediacy to public policy and an infallibility in forecasting

FIGURE 10.1   INFLATION AND EMPLOYMENT RATES, 1960–1979

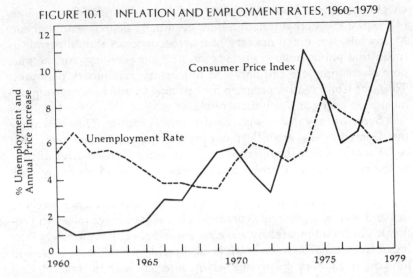

Source: *Economic Report of the President, 1979.*

that are impossible to attain. As a result, any particular government action may actually take effect when the condition calling forth the policy has been reversed. Thus, the expansionary effect of the 1964 tax cut only added impetus to an already existing expansion and contributed to the inflationary crisis with which we still live.

Another adverse effect of the overselling of fiscal policy is the undue emphasis on lessening unemployment. With an incredible disregard for the majority of citizens, Liberals have argued that inflation is a small price to pay for full employment. But they have failed to deliver on their full-employment promise, and more important, the growth of "stagflation" is mostly of their own making.

ATTACK INFLATION FIRST

From a Conservative outlook, inflation is clearly the greater enemy. Not only does it gnaw at purchasing power and lower real demand, but it also interferes with business investment decisions, foreign trade, and financial and securities markets. The result is lowered business expectations and production levels that throw millions of people out of work. No one has ever argued the case that unemployment causes inflation; usually it is assumed to have some depressing effect upon prices. But evidence from all the great inflationary spirals of the past shows that inflation *does* eventually depress employment. Meanwhile, a minimal mastery of macroeconomics should permit us to see that public policy efforts to heat up the economy for the purpose of creating jobs can only add to existing inflationary pressures. Thus, the Conservative program for bringing an end to the unemployment problem begins with fiscal restraint.

Some will say that this is a hard-hearted position. They will argue that Conservatives care little about people who are unemployed. That is not true. Solving the inflation problem is the Conservative answer to the unemployment problem. A privately oriented economy with low interest rates, reasonably assured business expectations, and a slow but steady rate of money expansion to support higher levels of demand will be a growing economy. That means more jobs. An economic system dominated by government, where either monetary policy or fiscal expansion (or both) is used recklessly to create jobs, will limit the freedom of the private sector, interfere with the market, and sooner or later worsen the employment problem. This is because excessive expansion has undesired effects. Expansion is generally associated with a growth of debt. This debt, if supported by an increased money supply, means inflation and, if funded by new government bonds sold at high and attractive interest rates, leads to generally high interest rates and lower investment in the economy. Either way the citizen loses.

If this argument is accepted, we must direct our attention toward decreasing inflation in order to decrease unemployment. Alas, the dominant thought in the economics profession moves in the other direction. The issue of unemployment is seen as the *first* problem to be tackled by public policy through selective monetary and fiscal actions. On the fiscal side this means enlarged government spending and government debt to create more private spending, investment, and jobs. Never mind that all this tends to be inflationary; that is supposed to be acceptable if full employment is reached. The catch is that inflation, whether or not promoted by the government, leads to unemployment. The result is like a kitten chasing its tail. Inflation (among other things, like market imperfections and short-run technological effects) leads to unemployment, and direct economic intervention to halt this unemployment generates further inflationary pressure, which in turn results in more unemployment, and so on. The more the kitten tries to catch its tail, the faster it must run.

THE POLITICIZING OF FISCAL POLICY

Although Keynesians are loath to admit it, politics rather than economics is largely responsible for our fiscal mess. For instance, much of the largely wasteful welfare and other social spending by government would be unnecessary if people were not paid a premium not to work or to work at pointless jobs. To be sure, the chronically poor and unskilled who can find no work must receive some support. But there are also many able-bodied Americans whose incentive to work has been diminished. Over time these people, together with the bureaucrats created to administer poverty and unemployment programs, have developed political clout. They are a voting constituency bought and paid for by government expenditures on welfare or make-work projects, just as votes were bought by political bosses a hundred years ago. Meanwhile, other individuals who owe their jobs to selective government spending—such as the unionized construction workers employed on unneeded public works—similarly become a permanent lobby for higher government spending. For such Americans, as well as for those on welfare, jobs could be found in an economy that was freely expanding rather than burdened by debt and inflation. Nor is the dole limited to these groups. Businesspeople, farmers, and doctors are on the welfare rolls too, since they receive guaranteed subsidies, tax deductions, and fees from government. In their own way they too form a powerful lobby for government expenditure on their behalf.

The politicization of government spending and resulting economic chaos are perfect examples of how well-intentioned efforts to improve upon free market operations destroy both market effectiveness and individual freedom. The Liberal program to lift people out of unemployment and poverty (and in a few cases to make the rich richer) by setting them up as permanent feeders from the public trough is a cruel hoax. It is passed off as a social and economic remedy to economic problems when it is in fact a growing problem in itself.

All this is not to say there should not be a national fiscal policy. Of course there must be, but the best one is the most neutral one. It is one that does the least damage to business and individual freedom. A proper fiscal policy would include the following: (1) a balanced budget; (2) overall fiscal restraint on the size of expenditures and receipts; and (3) in time of recessionary pressures, cutting both taxes and expenditures to increase private demand. Given our present fiscal state of affairs, adopting this policy would mean holding the line on virtually all spending except that which is essential for national defense and at the same time making sizable tax reductions.

The Liberal Argument

In the last issue, we laid out the case for fiscal and monetary policy to counter depressions. In brief, the argument held that, since the Great Depression and the appearance of the Keynesian critique, we do possess adequate policy tools to manage the general level of economic activity. However, possessing the tools and using them correctly are different matters. In the case of fiscal policy, how effective have we really been and what should we presently be doing?

Conservatives, who do not believe in the efficacy of fiscal policy, are in fact long on theory and short on evidence. What evidence they do offer begs correct interpretation. Far from being "proven" ineffective in the past and the "cause" of present stagflation problems, fiscal management of the general level of economic activity has a good record.

THE FISCAL POLICY RECORD EXAMINED

The general framework of antidepressionary policy making was in place by the beginning of the post–World War II period. Steps to end the Depression, wartime spending, and the legal commitment of the Employment Act of 1946 helped to end the traditional government commitment to a balanced budget. Nevertheless, between 1946 and the early 1960s, the political leadership of the nation showed little mastery of the new policy possibilities. Both Harry Truman and Dwight Eisenhower held a strong predilection toward balanced budgets. Largely unnecessarily, the economy went through four recessions (1949, 1954, 1958, and 1960). Fiscal policy, as it was practiced, was unplanned and ill-timed. Deficits or surpluses appeared at the wrong times or quite accidentally at the right time. Manipulative monetary policy was not practiced at all.

With John Kennedy's election in 1960, as we noted in the last issue, countercyclical fiscal policy was to get its chance. First in 1962, with a tax reduction for businesses investing in new plant and equipment, and second in 1963, with a proposed $11 billion tax cut ($9 billion to individuals and $2 billion to corporations), Kennedy sought to expand aggregate demand and stimulate employment. With Kennedy's death, Lyndon Johnson quickly enacted the tax cut. There followed several years of economic growth, falling unemployment rates, and steady prices—precisely what the Employment Act of 1946 called for and Keynesian economists promised they could deliver.

The experiment in stabilization, however, was to be short-lived. The expanded war in Vietnam coupled with Johnson's adamant stance that the economy could produce guns *and* butter began to pump up excess demand. Richard Nixon's continuation of the war after 1969 and his own timidity in dealing with growing excess demand brought the short era of stabilization policy to an end.

The failure of fiscal policy in the late 1960s, however, was not a defeat for theory. If Johnson had shared his war intentions with his economic advisers and also shown more political courage, a tax increase in 1966 or 1967 could have cooled the economy down. Nixon, too, failed to utilize the fiscal brakes, fearing political reaction to a tax increase. Instead he sought to deal with the inflationary push by wage and price controls (see Issue 12) and by having the monetary authorities put a squeeze on demand through tight money.

As a consequence of these political developments, we have only a comparatively short period, roughly from 1962 to 1969, to evaluate countercyclical fiscal policy. However, as Table 10.2 shows, these years stand out boldly in attaining the objectives of the Employment Act of 1946. Per capita income growth was high (a 25 percent increase in eight years compared to 13 percent over the previous eight years). Unemployment fell from nearly 6 percent to 3.5 percent. Prices rose about 19 percent, higher than during the Eisenhower years but were still acceptable, considering the employment and growth gains. Alas, Camelot was all too brief, but it did provide proof of the efficacy of modern fiscal policy management.

THE CASE AGAINST "RESTRAINT"

The current disrepute of fiscal policy, especially expansionary fiscal policy, is paradoxical, for the lagging economy is sadly in need of stimulation. However, hostility to fiscal fine tuning in general and fis-

Table 10.2 Per Capita Income, Unemployment Rate, and Price Index, 1929–1978

Year	Per capita income (in 1972 $)	Unemployment Rate	Consumer price index (CPI) (1967=100)	Changes in CPI
1929	$1,886	3.2	51.3	
1939	1,756	17.9	41.6	10.3
1949	2,253	5.9	71.4	29.8
1954	2,476	5.5	80.5	9.1
1959	2,696	5.5	87.3	6.8
1960	2,697	5.5	88.7	1.4
1961	2,725	6.7	89.6	.9
1962	2,796	5.5	90.6	1.0
1963	2,849	5.7	91.7	1.1
1964	3,009	5.2	92.9	1.2
1965	3,152	4.5	94.5	1.6
1966	3,274	3.8	97.2	2.7
1967	3,371	3.8	100.0	2.8
1968	3,464	3.6	104.2	4.2
1969	3,515	3.5	109.8	5.6
1970	3,619	4.9	116.3	6.5
1971	3,714	5.9	121.3	5.0
1972	3,837	5.6	123.3	2.0
1973	4,062	4.9	133.1	9.8
1974	3,973	5.6	147.7	14.6
1975	4,014	8.5	161.2	13.5
1976	4,137	7.7	170.5	8.7
1977	4,290	7.0	181.5	11.0
1978	4,418	6.0	202.0	10.5

Source: *Economic Report of the President*, 1979.

cal expansionism in particular has grown during the Nixon–Ford and Carter administrations.

Only an expansive fiscal policy can provide full employment. Expansion must come primarily but not exclusively through rising expenditures by the public sector and, at least in the short run, a growth of federal deficits. The federal budget must "lean against the winds of the business cycle." Elementary Keynesian analysis tells us that the level of total demand $(C + I + G)$ determines the level of employment in the economy. Clearly an increase in government (G) is essential to offset secular declines or relatively insufficient consumption (C) or investment (I) which result in unemployment. While this is dogma to all Liberals, it is incorrectly practiced, if not preached, by politicians identified as Conservative in fiscal affairs. Indeed, it is ironic that under President Ford, whose 1976 campaign dwelt ceaselessly on fiscal restraint, the federal budget grew to record highs and the annual national debt increase was the greatest it had ever been in peacetime. Leaving aside this contradiction between ideology and practice, why did the inadvertent fiscal expansion under Nixon and Ford not provide the jobs a Liberal believes should come from such expansion?

The answer is simple. The Conservative debt-expenditure approach rested on budgeting errors involving both expenditures and receipts and was preoccupied with monetary policy efforts to deal with inflation. These errors of judgment cost us dearly. The unemployment crisis that Carter faced was aggravated, if not in fact caused, by the Conservatives' failure to understand and use fiscal policy tools correctly.

First, while government spending rose, it rose in areas that have little effect on the unemployment problem. Rather than public jobs and aid to construction programs, which would have increased employment directly, the government focused on such items as military spending. By 1977 such spending accounted for more than 27 percent of the budget (for a total of $104 billion). In two years defense spending had grown by 20 percent, while funds for commerce, transportation, community development, and job training (for those lacking skills even to get into the labor force) remained virtually unchanged. Because of the structure of the industry, defense spending does not have the same employment effect as government expenditures in most other industries (construction, for example) or in government-funded job programs. Thus, though federal expenditures rise, income distribution and the structure of employment are only minimally altered. While we know that, everything else being equal, an increase in government spending should increase total demand, it is a perversion and misuse of modern Keynesian arguments to say that all increases in demand via government expenditures will have the same employment effects. Dollars spent in different ways have different results on employment.

A second problem posed by the "fiscal restraint" of the Nixon-Ford years was the decision to rely on tax cuts rather than on increased expenditures to attack unemployment. Again this is a perversion of modern employment theory. Under certain circumstances, tax cutting can be a stimulus to the economy: witness the 1964 Kennedy-Johnson tax cut. However, tax cutting at any time has a slower and smaller multiplier effect on labor markets than does direct spending. Moreover, the impact of the cut depends on whose taxes are involved. Cutting taxes in the upper-income brackets (and these are the ones that benefited most from past Conservative economic policies) has less of an effect in creating demand and thus cutting unemployment than reducing middle- and lower-income bracket taxes. For instance, the tax cut of 1975, which totaled $23 billion, is estimated to have had only a $30 billion effect. There is also much truth to one wag's comment that a tax cut on zero income does not help much. In any case, and especially when there is a general economic slowdown and high unemployment, the surer, more direct fiscal route to job creation is the intelligent expansion of expenditures.

The Nixon-Ford budgets and tax cuts showed a notable bias in favor of upper-income Americans and corporations. As far as spending was concerned, a very sizable portion consisted of transfers to wealthy individuals and corporations; transfers to the poor decreased, relatively speaking. On the revenue side, corporations and the wealthy were the major beneficiaries of tax reductions and existing tax loopholes; middle- and low-income families had few income tax reductions or tax loopholes, and faced rising payroll taxes as well. As a result, the proponents of so-called fiscal restraint not only failed to generate jobs, but actually made things worse for many Americans by reneging on the commitments of the early 1960s to narrowing income differences.

A third limitation on the Nixon-Ford approach to the ideal of full employment was their Conservative belief that inflation was the greater evil in any unemployment-inflation dilemma. This meant that the government tended to tighten the screws of monetary policy in an effort to hold down prices. Thus even if the expansion effects of Conservative budgets and tax cuts had been significant, they were overwhelmed by tight money. As interest rates were forced upward, economic activity declined and unemployment was accelerated.

Nor were the Carter years much better. Initially promising a tax cut of $31 billion to stimulate the economy, the president accepted less than $14 billion. By 1978–1979 Carter seemed to have adopted the Conservative "inflation first" analysis and began to reduce government job programs and social spending. Like his predecessors he defended a tight monetary policy and fiscal restraint as the best course.

To summarize, failure to follow a truly expansionary fiscal policy aimed directly at unemployment, coupled with the belief that inflation had to be tackled before unemployment, meant that workers paid for all recent efforts to deal with stagflation. For those who reject this logic, there is the uncomfortable weight of the evidence. During recent years, while unemployment was high and often rising and real income fell, profits for big business grew, and prices—supposedly the real enemy—stayed up. The case for so-called fiscal restraint stands not only unproved but unfounded.

IN DEFENSE OF EXPANSIONISM

A common criticism of expansionary fiscal policy is that it creates or adds to "the crushing burden of federal debt" and that it is necessarily inflationary. The answer to this charge is simple: The $70 billion deficit of the last year of the Ford Administration did not represent the cost of fiscal policy; it was the cost of a less than fully employed society. In recession, we lost $50 billion in uncollected taxes, $15 billion in unemployment insurance, and $5 billion in welfare payments. When growth of the federal debt is seen this way, it is indeed "crushing"—but not because of fiscal expansionism. As to the inflationary impact of debt, it is interesting to note that, while the new debt piled up in 1976, price inflation actually slowed down. Growth of the debt (even the bad Ford debt) is not very inflationary in a less than fully employed economy. Indeed, the inflationary "cost" of government spending has been uncritically accepted (see Issue 12).

For those Conservatives and Radicals who would argue that the Liberal case for fiscal expansion is disproved by the supposed collapse of Keynesian policy making in the stagflation after 1971, we offer the following arguments. First, as former presidential adviser Arthur Okun has argued, measured against the standards that prevailed at the time of the passage of the Employment Act of 1946, fiscal-monetary policy has been a resounding success throughout the postwar period.* Second, the recent so-called failure of fiscal policy had nothing to do with fiscal theory. Stagflation resulted from abandoning theory.

Finally, only fiscal expansion (coupled with massive job training for the "unemployable") offers any reasonable social solution to the

*See Arthur Okun, The Political Economy of Prosperity (New York: Norton, 1970), pp. 37–61.

deep and growing unemployment problem. Any other alternatives will tear the fabric of our society. Faced with the problem of the Great Depression, Herbert Hoover, a president deeply committed to a conservative fiscal outlook, once lectured a visiting delegation of mayors on the evils of deficits and enlarged government spending. "Gentlemen," he asked, "can you think of anything worse than an unbalanced budget?" James Curley of Boston, thinking of the bread lines, ugly social disorders, and misery in his city, raised his hand. "Well, Mr. President," he said, "how about a revolution?"* Radicals advocate revolution. Conservatives, in their ignorant rejection of several decades of proven fiscal policy effectiveness, would unwittingly bring it about by their insensitivity to the problems of the unemployed.

The Radical Argument

In the preceding issue, we examined the significance of enlarged government spending in absorbing a surplus, or to use Keynesian terms, in maintaining demand. We noted that without this expansion of government spending the capitalist economy would have confronted a fatal crisis of overproduction and underconsumption long ago. Yet, this is not the end of the question of managing the capitalist business cycle. Over the past thirty years Keynesians have enlarged the scope of their claims: not only can the depression extremes be eliminated but general economic stability may be secured through an adroit mix of monetary and fiscal policy measures. The successful application of so-called stabilization policy supposedly eliminates all of the violent swings of the market economy. Steady prices, full employment, and continued growth would then be a permanent state of economic affairs.

Given the present economic condition of the United States (and the fact that we shall examine the unemployment and inflation problems separately in succeeding issues), little needs to be said here about these claims except to point out that they are unfounded and untrue. With unemployment exceeding 6 percent, inflation in double digits, and real income declining, only the most obtuse Liberal Keynesian can claim much recent success in fine tuning the economy.

*Cited in *Viewpoint*, Industrial Union Department Quarterly of AFL–CIO, vol. 6, no. 2 (1976), p. 13.

The most important aspect of stabilization policy efforts, however, is not their record of failure but their social impact on the economic system. Thirty years of unrelenting Keynesianism in the classroom and about two decades of stabilization debates in political circles have deceived Americans about the nature and effects of monetary and fiscal policy. Not only has a false sense of security been created about the quantitative effectiveness of stabilization policy, but the qualitative impact of these policies on American life has not been examined. While countercyclical policy may have bought some time for American capitalism, it has been purchased at the cost of greater ruling class and corporate domination and greater irrationality in production and consumption.

STABILIZATION POLICY
AND CLASS DOMINATION

The economic composition and social impact of public policy is rarely examined by Liberal defenders and Conservative critics. For good or ill, public policy is presented as largely impartial in its social and political effects. This misses an important aspect of public policy making—namely, that it is a class instrument, a tool for perpetuating ruling class domination. The social inequalities of stabilization policy are better appreciated by ordinary Americans than most economists admit, but they might usefully be laid out in detail.

First, there is the upper-income bias in taxation policy. A brief survey of important tax-cutting efforts to stimulate expansion—either the cuts of 1964 or those of 1976, for example—indicates that upper-middle and upper-income taxpayers received the largest percentage reduction and the bulk of the total cut. These same groups, of course, benefit the most from the legal loopholes of the tax system, such as the ability to deduct interest payments and business expenses from their tax bill. The poor and the lower-middle class, without the benefits of tax loopholes (or even much opportunity to cheat), have lost economic ground in the tax-cutting efforts of expansionary fiscal policy. In the case of tax increases, the poor are again hit hardest. The recent increase in social security withholding taxes is a good example. Over the past few years both the taxable base and the rate of the taxes have risen at the lower end of the income scale. (By 1980 the rate was 6.13

percent on incomes up to $25,900.) Such taxes are regressive, since they fall heaviest on lower incomes.

Second, low-income Americans have also lost out on the spending side. While Conservatives and Liberals (for different reasons) point to the magnitude of federal transfers to the poor and indigent, this is a massive deception. The federal government's spending in this area amounts to about the same percentage of the GNP today that it did in the pre-Keynesian 1930s.* At the same time, transfers to large farmers, business, and to professional workers have grown. Government spending for goods, meanwhile, directly benefits the ruling class and higher-income workers. A good example of the upper-income and monopoly capital bias of such expenditures is military and space spending. The recipient firms are among the largest in the nation and also the most capital and skill intensive. Spending funneled into these firms strengthens monopoly power and has little or no impact on creating jobs for less skilled and lower-paid workers (see the next issue). Looked at this way, government spending, even for stabilization purposes, is not neutral at all. It actually heightens class divisions in the society. Spending on low-income housing, medical care, and other social goods that would improve the poor's quality of life has always ranked very low among fiscal priorities. This is because the poor, regardless of their numbers, are not yet a powerful constituency and also because spending for certain social goods would actually create competition with the private sector. Subsidized public housing would destroy the lucrative low-income housing market in the private sector, free clinics would bankrupt private hospitals, and so on. Moreover, when the stabilization experts call for a contraction in government spending (to balance the budget or reduce aggregate demand), services and transfers to the poor are the first items sacrificed.

Third, monetary policy is equally selective and unfair in its class effects. For instance, the recent pursuit of high interest rates (a tight money policy) as an anti-inflation tool especially burdens the working class. For consumers high interest rates mean greater portions of their income must be paid for such necessities as home mortgages and for

*This fact may seem startling to Americans, who are constantly bombarded with propaganda about the alleged extravagance of social spending on the poor. In reality, we spend only a little over 2 percent of our GNP on programs directed specifically to low income groups (about $55 billion in 1979). In 1938, for example, the $1.5 billion spent on various poor relief programs by federal, state, and local governments amounted to a little less than 2 percent of the GNP.

the "luxuries" provided by credit buying. Upper-income groups, of course, face the same interest rates, but their burdens are a much smaller proportion of their income and more easily borne without sacrifice of their living standards. Meanwhile, for workers, tight money translates into reduced business output and fewer jobs or lower pay.

Thus, stabilization policy perpetuates and accentuates the normal class inequalities of capitalism. Expansionary policy never benefits the poor as much as the rich. And contraction always demands that the least affluent American citizens must tighten their belts the most. The normal exploitative tendencies of traditional capitalism have merely been reinforced under the arrangements of Keynesian stabilization policy.

THE IRRATIONALITY OF STABILIZATION POLICY

Apart from the inherent injustices of stabilization policy, there is also the problem of irrational production and consumption that it encourages. As American capitalism has steadily enlarged its productive capacity—or, in Paul Baran and Paul Sweezy's analysis, its ability to produce surplus—it has had to develop equivalent devices to absorb the surplus. Leaving government aside for a minute, the private sector has devised a number of important ways to "waste" (absorb) output. Developing socially useless goods (hygienic and cosmetic goods come to mind) and expending considerable resources to distribute, advertise, and sell these goods help create jobs and income, but such activities do not elevate society much. Yet, such needless and irrational production and consumption, with the attendant creation of needless and alienated labor, do absorb the surplus.

Government spending has pushed along the absorption of surplus through irrational means. Presently, we are spending well over $120 billion a year on military goods—a beautiful way to absorb the surplus. We build machines that have no social usefulness, do not compete with private enterprise, and hopefully will be quickly outmoded so that we can build more. However, people are put to work, corporations earn profits, and the GNP is increased by the spending.

With the coming of the energy crisis, we have discovered an equally irrational example of government spending in the case of our highway network. The building of the massive interstate highway system was a direct boon to construction companies and suppliers of resource materials such as cement and steel. Indirectly, it spurred auto buying and gasoline consumption. When gasoline was 29 cents a gallon, it seemed like an extremely good way to stimulate the economy. Very quickly we relocated our residences and our industries to adjust to the highway (another piece of economic stimulation), and we allowed mass transportation to disintegrate. This was the "price of progress," some said. Suddenly, to everyone's surprise, we ran out of gas. The transportation system faces collapse and with it the entire industrial economy.

Rather than reconstructing a stable economy, uncritical and unplanned government spending policy has reinforced the irrational production and consumption patterns of a capitalist system.

THE EMERGING CONTRADICTION

We shall examine the specific failure of public policy to deal with the unemployment problem in the next issue. Nevertheless, our examination of the composition and social outcome of modern stabilization policy is by itself sufficiently damning to dismiss any belief that Keynesian economics offers capitalism a way out of the woods.

Overall, the past twenty or thirty years of public policy have heightened internal capitalist contradictions. The unequal distribution of benefits and losses has produced growing conflicts—big business versus little business, capital versus labor, worker versus worker, worker versus nonworker, and always rich against poor. And, overarching everything is the mounting evidence that government cannot deliver on any of its promises of full employment, growth, and price stability.

The result is a growing public reaction against Liberal government. Proposition 13, the balanced budget amendment, and similar popular reactions reflect particular groups' exasperation with the failures of the Keynesian era. Meanwhile, traditional economists remain captives of their own theories of aggregates, unable to comprehend the many conflicting parts of the crisis. Nevertheless, they know that even if government intervention in the economy has not succeeded, nonintervention will ensure an even greater failure.

For Radicals the immediate effects of the collapse of Keynesianism are uncertain, though chronic stagnation problems point toward economic collapse (see the last issue). The growth of political Conservatism and the resurgence of worn-out laissez-faire economics do not lead toward the socialist reconstruction of the American economy. At least they do not lead there immediately. However, as Marx remarked, when history repeats itself, it first appears as tragedy and then as farce. The reappearance of right-wing politics and economics is real enough, but their solutions to the basic capitalist contradictions are comic. Once that is understood, the Radical critique must be taken seriously.

ISSUE 11

Chronic Unemployment:
Is a National "Full-Employment" Program Needed?

Once I built a railroad, made it run
Made it race against time
Once I built a railroad, now its done
Brother can you spare a dime?
Popular song by Jay Gorney, 1932

Capitalism forms an industrial reserve army that belongs to
capital quite as absolute as if the latter had bred it at its own
cost. Independently of the limits of the actual increase of
population, it . . . creates a mass of human material always
ready for exploitation.
Karl Marx, 1867

There are not enough private sector slots even if employers
were given 100 percent subsidies to hire the disadvantaged.
Arnold Packer, Assistant Secretary of Labor, 1979

THE PROBLEM

In late 1979 unemployment in the United States stood at about 6 percent. In human terms that meant over 6 million people in the labor force were without work. Moreover, these official figures probably underestimated the real unemployment problem. Some economists have speculated that the real unemployment rate was between 50 and 100 percent higher than the one reported.

In any case, a 6 percent unemployment rate is considerably higher than what economists had earlier accepted as "normal unemployment." "Full employment" had never meant that everyone was working. In the 1950s full employment translated into 3 percent unemployment. By the 1960s normal unemployment had been revised upward to about 4 percent. Most economists during these periods would have expected that any public policy efforts to reduce unemployment much below these figures would have produced a trade-off with rising prices. By the 1970s some were saying the same about a 6 percent unemployment rate. In other words, given the skills of workers and the demand for labor, 6 percent unemployment was "full employment," and any effort to pump up demand to decrease unemployment would only stimulate inflation without materially affecting joblessness.

The stubborn rise of unemployment rates has directed considerable attention to identifying the unemployed and determining why they cannot find jobs in the economy. Looking closer at unemployment, we can see it is unevenly distributed. It is greater among blacks than whites, among women than men, among teen-agers than those twenty-five to forty, and among the unskilled than the skilled. It is higher in the older industrial states of the East and the Midwest than it is in the South and Southwest.

Moreover, as Figure 11.1 indicates, the problems of the chronically unemployed have not diminished much when the economy periodically has picked up. Unemployment for minorities, teen-agers, and women has consistently remained high even during the comparatively good years of 1973–1974 and 1976–1978.

If this persistent joblessness is not responsive to economic growth, what are the means to solving the chronic unemployment riddle? American unemployment rates are well above those of most industrialized na-

FIGURE 11.1   THE NATION'S STRUCTURALLY UNEMPLOYED

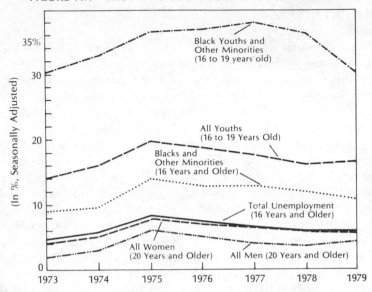

Source: Bureau of Labor Statistics.

tions. They simply would not be tolerated in Scandinavia, Germany, or Japan. Whatever the solution, all of us must realize that a society that cannot or does not find work for its people is in deep trouble. The ideological battle over how to attack the problem of chronic unemployment is more than just an intellectual debate.

SYNOPSIS Conservatives see the present unemployment problem as largely the result of government efforts to manage labor markets. They therefore advocate minimum government as the only long-run solution to joblessness. Liberal arguments hold that much of our current unemployment is beyond the reach of usual stabilization policy tools. Thus, new and enlarged job programs are necessary to remove the "structural" limitations of the economy that have created chronic unemployment. For Radicals, unemployment is characteristic of capitalism, a natural outgrowth of the system's tendency to produce surplus labor.

The Conservative Argument

From the Conservative point of view, unemployment is logically unnecessary. In an economy left to its own devices, involuntary unemployment can result only from short-run market readjustments. The classical economist Jean Baptiste Say (1767–1832) argued long ago that supply creates its own demand. Say presumed that demand would naturally remain high and that work would be available for everyone who was willing and able. Say's world, of course, no longer exists. As has been pointed out before, massive interruptions in the market have become institutionalized. In the world of labor unions, big government, and discretionary fiscal policy, Say's Law has little relevance. The Conservative critique must therefore begin with the macro economy as it is.

THE CAUSES OF UNEMPLOYMENT

Rather than leading to Liberal renunciation of past policies, the failure of fiscal policy to reduce unemployment (see the preceding issue) has produced even more exotic unemployment theories. Liberal opinion now holds that much of our current unemployment is beyond the reach of expansionary fiscal and monetary policy. Thus, chronic unemployment supposedly results from workers having inadequate skills or from discrimination or from workers being in the wrong places. The Liberal response is to enlarge direct government intervention in labor markets.

In fact, less government meddling, not more, offers the best solution. Liberal tinkering with the economy is the *cause* of, not the cure for, unemployment.

Because they presume that free markets do not work, Liberals have attempted to improve upon the market mechanism. But their efforts have stimulated an increase in resource misallocation and unemployment. A few examples rather than a detailed analysis should be sufficient to make this point clear.

Liberal support for labor unions in this century, while benefiting some workers, has cost many their jobs. Unions, by instinct and design, restrict the number of jobs as they force wages upward for their members. The older craft unions specifically used the tactic of exclusion in forcing higher wages. By having long periods of apprenticeship and limiting the number of apprentices, unions in the building trades, for instance, purposely reduced the supply of available labor. This kept carpenters', masons', and hod carriers' wages up, but it also kept large numbers of would-be workers out of the labor force. Meanwhile, large industrial unions also reduce employment. By forcing upon management an industry wage that is higher than would otherwise prevail in a free labor market, the industry's total demand for labor is reduced. Thus both wages and unemployed workers increase.

Legally mandated social legislation (unemployment insurance, workers' compensation, social security contributions, etc.) also depresses employment. Ironically, many of those programs aimed specifically at the poorest and least secure workers have worsened rather than improved their lot. For instance, Liberals invariably cite the passage of minimum-wage laws as one of their greatest triumphs; yet such laws probably have had the largest negative impact on employment of all of their efforts at social engineering. Setting minimum-wage rates above a market-determined wage has two immediate effects. First, more individuals enter the labor market, now willing to work at the higher wage whereas they opted for leisure before. Second, the number of jobs available is reduced, since employers reduce their hiring. While minimum-wage legislation has been defended by Liberals as a boon to the less skilled workers, it has actually had the opposite effect. The least skilled jobs, those with the lowest marginal contribution to a firm's earnings, must be the first eliminated as the result of raising the minimum-wage floor. Thus, part-time employment for teen-agers and unskilled factory work for women and minorities have declined as the minimum wage advanced.

The Liberal charge that discrimination is a major cause of unemployment has brought forth a number of elaborate affirmative action programs, all of which produce expensive paperwork for corporations but have not reduced minority unemployment. (In mid 1980 black unemployment was reported at about 15 percent, more than twice that of whites and higher than it was two decades earlier.) The trouble with the Liberal analysis is that it misinterprets minority unemployment. While Conservatives admit the existence of past discrimination in education and in the general society, they reject the argument that employers consciously discriminate. For that to be the case, employers, who are, after all, profit maximizers, would have to pay additional costs for the act of discrimination. Excluding certain elements of the work force as undesirable (minorities or women, for instance) would reduce the supply of available labor and force up the price of labor in general. This would not benefit employers. However, it would benefit white male workers in general and unions in particular.

LABOR POLICIES HAVE FAILED

Failing to comprehend that most unemployment is the direct or indirect effect of government intervention in the economy, Liberal economists and politicians have identified most current unemployment as resulting from structural changes in the economy. Geographic shifts in industrial sites, technological advances with resulting changes in the skills demanded, changes in the population profile and labor participation rate are all cited as factors producing chronic "structural unemployment." According to Liberal doctrine since the Kennedy-Johnson years, these developments demand the introduction of special labor policies by government—specific efforts aimed at upgrading skills or creating specially funded hiring programs.

The Liberal proposal for special job programs is both unnecessary and counterproductive. Despite a decade and a half of federal expenditures for the education of young people, the retraining of older workers, and elaborate public service programs, as well as affirmative action programs to increase the employment of minorities and women, there is virtually no evidence that significant numbers of would-be workers have been aided. In fact, the tax bill for funding and operating these programs has probably had a negative impact on jobs, because private sector funds had to be shifted to these employment efforts.

The best cure for so-called structural unemployment would be to free up labor markets, to reduce union power, and to eliminate the minimum wage. If there is structural unemployment, it is caused by imposed higher wages, not the fact there is a real shortage of potential jobs for workers.

UNEMPLOYMENT IS OVERSTATED

Unemployment is certainly higher than it should be and than it would be without current government policies. However, the level of joblessness is overstated rather than understated. The advantages of welfare and unemployment compensation have attracted many who would not otherwise enter the labor market. More than that, certain types of job seekers—particularly those who are merely supplementing the family income—should not be counted in the same way as the primary jobholder in a family. Married women seeking work to pay for the family vacation are not qualitatively or quantitatively the same as men seeking work to pay for the groceries. While they should indeed have work if they want it—and could in a society freed from fiscal interference and such labor market constraints as unions, minimum-wage laws, and social "protections"—unemployment as presently reported overstates the importance of their problem. It suggests incorrectly that work for all is impossible under capitalism. Under pure capitalism there would be jobs; under the present mixed economy there is unemployment. The same is very much true of so-called unemployables. Technology should create jobs. All past technological advances have. But an unfree labor market (that is, one dominated by union power and unwarranted government interference) and subsidies for the unemployable limit rather than encourage those who want to find work and develop new skills.

The overreaction to unemployment statistics has also tended to direct attention away from positive employment developments. Even with the high unemployment statistics of recent years, the number of *employed* workers has been steadily growing. Between 1971 and 1979, all supposedly high unemployment years, the total number of employed workers grew by 23 percent, from 79 million to 97 million. This growth is unsurpassed in any similar peacetime period in our history.

Thus, if we understand who is unemployed and why and if we also recognize the real vitality of the economy in employing workers, the so-called unemployment problem vanishes.

The Liberal Argument

Recently, Liberals have been unfairly attacked for the current problems of stagflation. According to Conservative rhetoric, the appearance of both high levels of unemployment *and* rising prices is "proof" that public policy has failed. As we pointed out in the last issue, such a conclusion is simplistic and unproven. Properly applied, public policy has worked well against both unemployment and inflation. The trouble is that much of our current unemployment and our upward price pushes is not to be explained by business cycle tendencies. Rather, it is the result of subtle institutional changes in the American economy. The problems of unemployment demand a new approach. Not only do we need an expansive fiscal policy to cure lack-of-demand joblessness, but we must recognize that some unemployment is structural and not responsive to demand increases.

STRUCTURAL UNEMPLOYMENT

Since World War II the American economy has enjoyed, with a few brief interruptions, phenomenal economic growth. However, the expansion has produced important technological changes and regional economic shifts that have contributed to national unemployment. The demand for older jobs and skills has declined as new goods and production techniques have revolutionized labor. At the same time, the geographic distribution of manufacturing has been altered. The result has been to change the structure of labor markets.

Some examples of these structural shifts are:

1. The continued decline in agricultural employment as farm production was increasingly mechanized

2. The increased use of more and more sophisticated technology in industrial production, thus reducing the relative demand for industrial labor in general and unskilled labor in particular

3. The migration of many businesses and factories from the inner cities to suburban locations

4. The greater concentration of economic activity in large metropolitan areas and the decline of employment in smaller cities

5. The shift in the geographic location of industry to the West and South as new industries grew up in these areas and old plants left the industrial Northeast

6. The sectoral shift in employment patterns as service industries and government increased employment and the old employers—in manufacturing, transportation, mining, and construction—declined. (In 1950 manufacturing, transportation, mining, and construction employed more than half the work force; by 1980 these industries em-

ployed less than a third. Meanwhile, over the same period, service and government employment grew from 25 percent to over 40 percent of all employment.)

An example of how these structural changes could affect an area can be seen in the state of Pennsylvania. At the close of World War II the primary employment industries in Pennsylvania were mining, transportation (particularly the railroads), steel, and agriculture. By the mid-1960s employment in coal mining had sagged as other energy resources replaced coal and as coal mining became increasingly automated. The decline of small farms in the Northeast squeezed hundreds of thousands out of agriculture. Meanwhile, railroads, once the bulwark of the nation's transportation system, began a long period of contraction. The steel industry began to automate its old plants in the Pittsburgh area, and many firms shifted operation to southern states (Alabama and Maryland, for instance), which were closer to new buyers. By 1965 Pennsylvania's unemployment rate was about twice the national average. Even in an improving economy, there were few jobs for former miners, railroad workers, and small farmers.

The Pennsylvania experience was common throughout much of the old industrial Northeast and Midwest. Men and women seeking work either were located in areas where industry had closed or no longer possessed skills that were in much demand. These dislocations were made worse by the postwar migration northward of large numbers of southern blacks. Formerly agricultural workers, blacks encountered two problems—job demands that exceeded their level of skill and plain old-fashioned prejudice.

Across the nation the structural changes in employment produced large pockets of chronic unemployment. Since most of those unemployed lacked sufficient skills, or at least the skills needed, economic expansion of the economy had little effect on their work status. Pumping up aggregate demand would not have much effect on an unemployed railroad worker in Altoona, Pennsylvania, or an out-of-work miner in Kentucky.

THE CHANGE IN LABOR FORCE COMPOSITION

Changes in the composition of the labor force have added to the structural problems. Beginning in the 1960s larger numbers of women began to look for work. Most of these new entrants possessed minimal skills and took, when they could get them, low-paying jobs with little employment security in the service sector. Many of the female job seekers were extremely immobile. Many were wives and mothers who had to seek work near their homes. This added a further restriction to their general lack of skills in obtaining work. Meanwhile, the entrance into the job market of the large number of people born in the post–World War II baby boom increased unemployment. As with women entrants, many of the youthful job seekers did not meet the new employment demands. For urban, primarily black, youths, there were virtually no jobs at all. They had no desired skills and, anyway, they did not live near or have access to the few unskilled jobs available.

The addition of these new entrants precisely at the time of great structural changes in employment markets inflated unemployment rates. The incorrect impression was created and championed by Radicals that the growing unemployment reflected the chronic incapacity of the system to create jobs. However, if we understand the real causes of unemployment, the problem lay with the workers and not the economy in general. Quite simply, too many would-be workers lacked the education, or were in the wrong location, to find work.

The Conservative argument that unions and minimum-wage laws have restricted employment is utterly false. For most of the chronically unemployed, there would be no jobs however low the wage level. Industry no longer hires just bodies but demands a highly educated labor force. There are serious shortages in the labor market for tool and die workers, machinists, accountants, bookkeepers, engineers, computer program operators, and other skilled workers. Lower wages, as Conservatives argue, will not open these jobs to the chronically unemployed. Wages are not the issue; skill levels are. Proof of this may be seen in the fact that the minimum wage, as a percent of average factory earnings, is smaller today than it was during either the long boom of the 1960s or during "Eisenhower normalcy." Evidence does not support the Conservative claim that the minimum-wage law is the cause of our chronic unemployment.

A LIBERAL PROGRAM

As we have noted, structural unemployment and joblessness resulting from changes in the composition of the work force are not responsive to efforts to pump up aggregate demand. Instead, specific job-creating programs are necessary to provide full employment. However, unlike the make-work efforts of the past (such as WPA in the 1930s), these programs should not be mere Band-Aids. Since the lack of skills is the primary cause of chronic unemployment, federal programs should be constructed to improve the hirability of would-be workers. Three specific job programs, discussed below, should be supported.

Youth programs   With unemployment among teen-agers the highest of all groups (13 percent among white teen-age males and 35 percent among black teen-age males), youth unemployment demands special attention. Teen-agers account for about one-fourth of all the unemployed. Most teen-age unemployment, especially among blacks, is found in urban areas. Also, among the teen-age unemployed there is a high educational dropout rate. Thus, employment programs for this group should be urban in focus and organized to encourage completion of public education. In January 1978 the Labor Department began demonstration programs in six cities providing twenty hours of part-time public service work during the school year for urban teen-agers and forty hours of minimum-wage employment per week in the summer. Expansion of these projects (President Carter asked for $2.3 billion in his 1979 budget) as well as continued support for the Job Corps and the Young Adult Conservation Corps should lower youthful unemployment. While learning useful skills, many youths will learn the workplace discipline that is necessary for retaining employment. At any rate, a long-run improvement of youthful unemployment problems is fairly certain as the past decade's declining birthrate makes itself felt in labor markets. With a modest jobs program now, youthful unemployment can be brought under control.

Public service jobs   Beginning in 1973, the Comprehensive Employment and Training Act (CETA) instituted federal funding for local government hiring of public workers for limited employment periods. Rather than creating an overloaded federal bureaucracy, this approach has allowed local communities to set and meet their own public service needs. Workers meanwhile obtain important on-the-job experience before their CETA jobs expire and should find regular private or public sector employment possibilities improved.

Wage subsidy   A third approach to chronic unemployment is to subsidize private sector employment of the unskilled. In 1978 corporations received up to $2.5 billion in tax credits for hiring the unskilled and underskilled ($2,100 per worker and up to $100,000 total credit per firm). The bonus paid to private corporations is intended to offset the expected lower productivity of workers in this program.

The scale of these programs and their effectiveness in solving the problem of chronic unemployment may be seen in Table 11.1. Readers should be cautioned that the emphasis on retraining and upgrading skills in both public sector and private sector programs will not immediately affect structural unemployment; nevertheless, over time the effects on improving workers' job opportunities and their productivity should be evident in reduced chronic unemployment. However, real changes will only be seen if the commitment to these programs is much greater than at present. Largely a victim of budget-tightening pressures, the employment program that started with great promise has been scaled down in the 1980 budget and in budget estimates for 1981. This amounts to reversing our national commitment to full employment. Unless our full-employment goals are reaffirmed, chronic or structural unemployment will grow, and the nation will be denied the contribution that these would-be workers could make.

More important, extensive and chronic unemployment will tear society apart. Despite the costs of such programs, we can ill afford their dismantling.

Table 11.1   Estimated Federal Outlays and Participation in Training and Employment Programs, 1978

Program	Outlays (millions of dollars)	Person-years (thousands)
Total training and employment	$10,317.0	1,865.3
Training	1,890.7	487.8
Institutional	1,345.7	350.2
On-the-job	545.0	137.6
Public service employment (PSE)	8,426.3	1,377.5
Regular PSE	5,809.1	681.4
Work experience (principally youth)	1,794.9	403.5
Summer youth	672.0	255.0
Older Americans	150.3	37.6

Source: Economic Report of the President, 1978.

The Radical Argument

Both Conservatives and Liberals misunderstand the role of unemployment in a capitalist society. To the Conservative advocating a free market economy, there would be virtually no unemployment if the market were to work freely—that is, unimpeded by government action, labor unions, and so on. To the Liberal, unemployment is at least a periodic, and perhaps a chronic, condition of capitalist economies, but it can be controlled by "enlightened" public policy. Neither position sees unemployment as central to capitalist organization, as necessary to the actual functioning of the system. The simple fact is that capitalism, regulated or unregulated, cannot help but create unemployment.

UNEMPLOYMENT: CAPITALISM AS USUAL

As capitalists accumulate and successfully translate past labor into what they see as profit-producing capital and investment, the need for an absolute or growing volume of labor diminishes. This must be true by simple definition. The object of capital development is to increase production without increased (or with decreased) costs. Labor-saving machinery is cost-saving machinery only because labor is paid less per unit of output. Thus increased capitalization and technological growth, all things being equal, must produce growing surplus labor. This is the historical tendency of capitalism.

The growth of unemployment tends to be in recessionary clusters rather than in a steady, unbroken upward movement; however, the overall unemployment trend is upward over a period of time. Since the mid-1950s we have seen the official unemployment figures move, with annual variations, from around 3 to 6 or 7 percent. In other words, the percentage of the labor force in what Marx called "the reserve army of the unemployed" has about doubled (according to official figures) in the past twenty years. No doubt this unemployment would have been even higher had not government pursued expansionary policies. In other words, the situation has been getting progressively worse despite elaborate governmental efforts to hold unemployment down. Neither the free market nor Keynesian tinkering halts this tendency.

The failure of expansionary fiscal policy to deal with the problem of chronic unemployment is particularly evident if we go back to the tax cut of 1964. This was perhaps the first self-consciously Keynesian effort to use fiscal policy to reduce unemployment (then at 5 or 6 percent). The $11 billion Kennedy-Johnson tax reduction did spur business investment and increase national output. Between 1964 and 1966, investment increased by over 22 percent—more than twice that of the previous two years. GNP grew by 13 percent during the same period, compared to a growth rate of less than 10 percent in the earlier period. However, reported unemployment fell by only 900,000 between 1964 and 1966, despite the fact that government alone increased its payroll by 1.7 million. Thus, any real reduction in unemployment came not from tax cutting à la Keynes but from good old government hiring.

An additional case against the supposed effectiveness of "full-employment" fiscal policy is the hyperexpansion of government spending that took place during the Vietnam war. Although government policy during the war may now be represented by Liberals as unintended and undesired (in other words, determined on political rather than economic grounds), it did not result in the employment growth that modern Keynesians associate with expansionary fiscal policy. Between 1966 and 1969, during the height of war appropriations, unemployment fell by less than 100,000. Meanwhile, direct government employment added an additional 1.6 million to public payrolls. It was direct government hiring, and not private sector job growth, that brought unemployment rates down during the middle and late 1960s.

From the data available we can conclude that an expansionary fiscal policy can increase business investment, profits, and the gross national product, as well as raise average wages for those working. As the explosive effect of Vietnam spending showed, it can also stimulate considerable price inflation (which, of course, gnaws into the wage gains of those working). However, fiscal policy has not changed the chronic tendency in American corporate capitalism toward higher levels and rates of unemployment. It is not surprising that Liberals would therefore turn to special employment and job-creating programs as their ultimate solution for unemployment. Their strategy, however, is an evasion of the truth.

Political rhetoric to the contrary, the fact is that capitalism benefits from surplus labor—at least to a certain point. Surplus labor tends to force wages downward. Nonunion workers compete with one another, and employers have a pleasant buyer's market. Even the prospects of important union wage gains are diminished by the competitive threat of the swelling ranks of unemployed. As wages fall or stagnate, profits rise. Statistical evidence clearly substantiates this point. For example, between 1970 and 1974, real wage earnings stayed about the same (they actually declined 7 percent between 1973 and 1974); meanwhile, corporate profits, discounting inflation, grew by about 30 percent.

UNDERSTATING THE PROBLEM

Bad as it appears to be, our unemployment problem is really much worse than we realize because we understate the number of unemployed in at least four ways. First, the average annual rate does not show the number of people affected by some type of annual unemployment. For instance, in 1976 at least 30 million Americans experienced some unemployment during the year. Second, our statistics tend to overestimate the actual number employed. In 1975, the "employed" included 4 million Americans who worked only part time and another 1.6 million who fell into an "unpaid family labor" category. Such calculations expand the total "employed" category but do not show how slight their employment is. Third, official statistics do not indicate the underemployed. At least 6 million full-time workers earn wages below the official poverty income level. Fourth, the "unemployed" category does not include workers who are "not presently looking for a job," although they may be people who want jobs but have long ago given up looking. According to the editors of *Monthly Review*, an independent socialist monthly, due consideration of all these factors might have revealed unemployment to be nearly 14 percent in 1976, rather than the 8 percent then reported. (This is about what reported unemployment was in the Great Depression year of 1937.)

It is important to understand not only the real size but also the composition of unemployment in the United States. Clearly, job possibilities are poorer if one is black, female, or young. This discrimination in employment is not surprising. Basically, it reflects the general contraction of labor markets and the resulting exclusion of newcomers. On the one hand, such discrimination has served the system well since many of the unemployed are not visible but hidden away in ghetto or home. On the other hand, obvious discrimination of this kind creates considerable political development among the affected groups, who quite consciously and correctly see themselves as an exploited class. The Liberals, aware of this tendency, developed makework and on-the-job-training programs aimed at quashing the discontent of the hard-core unemployed. But such programs have no long-run effect on improving employment.

There is obviously a limit to how large the surplus labor army can grow—not just an economic limit but a political one. Unemployment breeds contempt for the existing order and sows the seeds of revolution. Therefore, capitalism faces the constant problem of devising expensive "legitimation" schemes. Ironically, given our soak-the-poor tax structure and the present fiscal crisis, employed workers are increasingly burdened by taxes to support unemployed workers. As we shall see in Issue 14, this situation has so far only set workers against nonworkers, rather than uniting all against the system that oppresses them.

In any case, modern public policy can do nothing about the threat of long-term unemployment. Short-run manipulation and trade-offs with inflation (see Issue 12) are possible, but the structural foundations of capitalist unemployment remain. Nor do special job-creating programs for the chronically unemployed offer a long-run solution. At best, they only buy a little time through deceptive but unfulfilled promises of future jobs. Small wonder that officials have no wish to tabulate all the unemployed. But their statistical manipulation does not change the historical tendency of capitalism. How great is the real unemployment problem confronting American capitalism? The editors of *Monthly Review,* using Department of Labor data, have estimated that 36 million jobs will be needed in the next decade simply to reduce unemployment to an acceptable and supposedly tolerable 5 percent. This job total results from the following demands:

To reduce current unemployment to 5 percent	8.2 million
To accommodate net increase of those entering the labor force	15.0 million
To compensate for productivity gains	12.8 million

To see how critical the problem is, we need to know only that the American economy succeeded in creating about 18 million jobs over the past ten years, or slightly more than half of those needed in the next decade. To Conservative and Liberal defenders of the "system," the outlook is grimmer than they will admit.

RADICAL STRATEGY: EXPOSE THE SYSTEM

The Radical strategy in the face of such an obvious future must be to halt the self-conscious division of the labor force into workers and nonworkers. As long as the unemployment problem is minimized, either politically or economically, to disguise capitalism's failure, workers will bite each other and not the master as they fight for the system's scraps. A broad educational and political program is necessary to reveal the inability of capitalism to create jobs, and to remove the stigma of uselessness from those who cannot find work. Only then can the mass of citizens see the need to end capitalism as a system. Specifically, this means a coalition of employed and unemployed, one that will reject the idea that there is anything left in the Liberal toolbox to fix things up. Some people will say that this is no solution but mere Radical rhetoric. In the absence of a viable Radical political movement, the accusation is more true than false. But only through such educational struggles can a Radical alternative begin to emerge.

ISSUE 12

Inflation

Can We Have Long-Run Price Stability?

There can be no question that much of what we have considered to be growth in the past many years has, in fact, been artificial in the sense that it has reflected dollar values rather than real values. We have lived through—are living through—a period of credit inflation that is not contributing to the real well-being of the economy.

Tilford Gaines, Vice President,
Manufacturers Hanover Trust, 1975

I believe that the present inflation is rooted deep in the nature of the mixed economy.

Paul Samuelson, 1974

There must be control—permanent control—in the organized sector of the American economy where union settlements act on prices and prices pull up wages.

John Kenneth Galbraith, 1974

If you're going to have the market system work, it has to have some basic stable framework. It has to have something it can count on. The virtue of . . . a constant rate of increase in the quantity of money is that it would provide such a stable monetary framework.

Milton Friedman, 1969

THANKS FOR *NOTHING* KEYNESIANS
Bumper Sticker, 1975

THE PROBLEM

Until comparatively recently, persistent and nagging inflation has rarely been a serious problem in the American economy. This is not to say that the United States did not experience rising price levels from time to time, but these were usually associated with extraordinary wartime conditions. For instance, between the end of the Civil War and the beginning of World War I, prices scarcely changed. Although the "Great War" caused price levels to double, prices fell back to 1916 levels during the 1930s. World War II, the postwar boom, and the Korean War again produced a doubling of prices, but this movement slowed to a gentle but consistent rise through the last half of the 1950s and the early 1960s. Average annual price increases were usually less than 3 percent. This was well below the rate of GNP growth, and most economists, in this period of seemingly endless prosperity, accepted it as tolerable.

Beginning in the late 1960s, however, prices began to take off. Between 1969 and 1979, the price level more than doubled as the consumer price index (based on 1967 = 100) rose from 109.8 to over 220. In very simple and comprehensible terms, that meant wage earners would have had to double their earnings in just ten years merely to stay even with prices. There never has been such a protracted inflationary episode in American history. In the decade after 1969 price increases never fell below 7 percent a year and three times hit double digits—11 percent in 1974, 12 percent in 1978 and over 12 percent in 1979.

History suggests that serious and nagging hyperinflation is always an urgent problem—an economic disease that gnaws deep into a society. Shrinking the wages and savings of workers on the one hand, it also disrupts investment, output, and foreign trade. No less acute an observer of capitalism than V. I. Lenin commented that the quickest way to national political destruction was debasement of a nation's currency. The "flight of the mark" in Germany after World War I, which saw prices increase billions of times over in a few years, precipitated the economic ruin from which Hitlerian fascism arose.

As we noted in the preceding section, American public policy has generally shown greater concern about unemployment than about inflation. The chronic price increases of the past decade, however, have been sobering, and emphasis has begun to shift. In the recent stagflation crisis of rising prices *and* rising unemployment (heretofore viewed as antitheti-cal tendencies), practically all economists recognized that policies aimed at eliminating unemployment had to be scrutinized for their pos-sible inflationary effects. In fact, President Carter, whose platform prom-ise of "putting Americans back to work" was probably the crucial factor in his 1976 victory, initially unveiled a very modest, inflation-conscious fiscal policy and jobs program package to fulfill his promise. Recently, OPEC price actions and the general rise of energy costs have drawn the most attention as causes of consumer price increases. There are, how-ever, many other elements to economists' explanations of the inflation crisis.

Inflation is no longer merely a matter of theoretical dispute among economists but has become one of the most important issues of con-temporary public policy debate. The immediacy of the inflation prob-lem is graphically illustrated in Figure 12.1, where the price line seems

FIGURE 12.1   U.S. CONSUMER PRICE INDEX SINCE THE CIVIL WAR

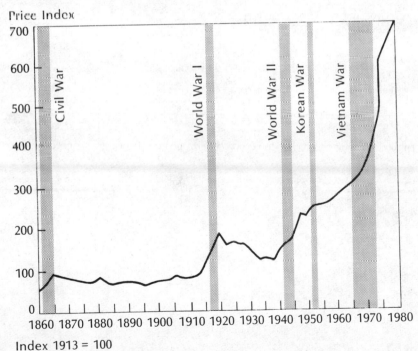

Index 1913 = 100

about to shoot through the ceiling. Increased concern, however, has not produced much agreement on causes and remedies.

SYNOPSIS The Conservative argument sees inflation as resulting primarily from excess demand and advocates rigid control over money creation rather than efforts to tamper with prices. According to the Liberal argument, excess demand, cost-push, and shortages are all factors in the inflationary process, but, in a less than fully employed economy, cost-push and shortages are the major culprits and must be dealt with by some type of government price regulation. The Radical argument traces inflationary pressures to the growth of concentration and monopoly pricing, exacerbated by government expansionary policies.

The Conservative Argument

The long-term growth of output and employment in any economy depends on the society's utilization of resources. Prices are nothing more than the measure by which money is exchanged for commodities. Accordingly, the general tendency of prices in any society will be determined by changes in the stock of money available for transactions. The stock of money, of course, must increase or decrease as the general level of economic output expands or contracts. A relative decrease in money stock compared to output must produce general price reductions. A money expansion rate above the rate of increase in output will lead to price expansion. Quite simply, more money does not and cannot by itself create more goods. Instead, it will be spent on the available goods at higher prices.

THE CAUSE: EXCESS DEMAND

This analysis of the fundamental cause of inflation is amply supported by evidence. Every significant inflationary episode in United States history has followed excessive growth in the supply of money. However, neither logic nor the evidence has succeeded in deflecting modern state policy from pursuing an inflationary course. As we indicated in the preceding sections on stabilization policy and unemployment, public policy has too long been committed to the Keynesian belief that high levels of output can be created and maintained by manipulating aggregate demand. In practice, such an approach has meant fiscal stimulation through government deficits or through liberal expansion of the money supply. The result has been persistent, and sometimes spectacular, excess-demand inflation.

The effects of this inflation are intolerable. Individuals' wages and savings are dissipated. With expectations confused, business reactions are adverse to growth as business leaders try to hedge against the effects of inflation on future profits. Consumers begin to hoard. Foreign trade is disrupted as domestic goods are priced out of foreign markets. Interest rates rise, even with a growing money supply, and investment is discouraged. Meanwhile, inflation pressures are heightened by the catch-up tactics of organized labor's demands for higher wages. Unemployment, the cause of expansionary fiscal and monetary action in the first place, grows. Economic growth ceases.

THE NEED: MONETARY AND FISCAL RESTRAINT

From a Conservative point of view, an economy—at least one that is free to operate according to the economic laws of the market—is inherently stable. Left to itself, it will grow according to its productive potential. Wars, shortages, and changes in business expectations and consumer choices may deflect the economy from its general path of development, but adjustments of prices, resource use, and output will return it to its natural course. Even the current petroleum shortage and its price impact will be absorbed as the economy adjusts to new consumption patterns, new fuels, and new production techniques. Only the failure of government to recognize this fact and its continued interference in energy production and pricing will inhibit the orderly readjustment of the economy. The Conservative anti-inflationary program, then, is to facilitate return of the nation to its normal path of economic development through minimal government interference in economic affairs.

The first item on the Conservative agenda is to end the present public policy efforts to manage aggregate demand. Expansionary fiscal and monetary policy can at best raise employment and output for a very brief period, and this increase is accomplished only by borrowing upon or mortgaging the future. When fiscal authorities allow large budget deficits to pile up, two undesirable effects result. One is that new government financial issues to float the deficit compete with private financial borrowing and reduce productive capital formation. The other is that deficits stimulate the excessive growth of the money supply. When monetary authorities also try to stimulate borrowing and the creation of new money by means of artificially low interest rates, the explosive excess-demand effects of modern macro policy are further accentuated.

The immediate impact of expansionary monetary and fiscal policy will probably be to induce new business investment and additional consumer spending. Thus, an increase in output and employment may occur. However, the expansion is only temporary at best. Tricked by a sudden increase in earnings, businesses and consumers have overspent and overborrowed. While money income has risen, their "real" situation has not improved; indeed, it has probably worsened if they have overspent. Over time, however, people learn. Anticipated discretionary actions by monetary and fiscal authorities merely induce businesses and consumers, who are not stupid after all, to take any action they see fit to protect themselves. Their "rational expectations" negate the impact of the authorities' policies. Over time, expansion of the money supply no longer stimulates economic expansion (even temporarily); it simply fuels demand-inflation without any employment benefits.

The second item on the Conservative agenda is to oppose policies that supposedly deal with so-called cost-push inflation. In fact, cost-push inflation would not exist without government approval of monopoly power in the market—by recognition of union power or the sanctioning of undesirable business concentration. At any rate, most alleged cost-push inflation is just short-run realignment of prices so as to reflect changes in product cost or one-time adjustments in supply (the oil shortage, for instance). The Liberal plan to create wage-price control boards to regulate changes in price is simply overkill.

If prices are left alone and monopoly protection ceases, the natural balancing mechanism of the economy can come into play. For instance, alternative energy sources may be developed to replace costly oil and gas simply because such innovation is profitable. Increases in energy supplies would, of course, cool the upward price push. Ending monopoly practices in labor and some businesses would also allow the market pricing mechanism to work freely. Inordinate pressure on prices from the cost side would simply disappear.

The third and most important element of the Conservative program is the establishment of rigid control over the money supply. Once established, this control should not be subject to political whim. Politicians seeking a quick employment remedy to take back to their restive constituents should not be allowed to tamper with the rules of monetary policy. As we have shown earlier, money expansion should take place at about the same rate as the general expansion of the economy. Thus money growth rates should be legally set at between 3 and 5 percent per year. Historical studies show that this is within the range of our potential annual growth rate. To prohibit meddling with these rules, the powers of the Federal Reserve System must be curtailed sharply. Indeed, abolishing the Fed might be a good move.

Regrettably, these efforts will not end inflation quickly, even if followed religiously. The effects of four decades of super-expansion will not disappear swiftly.

WAGE-PRICE CONTROLS ARE NO SOLUTION

Impatience with inflation and unwillingness to face up to its real causes have led some Liberals into the erroneous belief that wage and price controls are the only long-run answer to the problem of price stability. Old and worthless ideas have a habit of returning dressed up as new, and most defenders of wage-price controls try to sell their wares as a brilliant innovation in public policy. Nothing could be further from the truth. The faltering Roman Empire introduced price and wage controls to deal with chronic inflation in 301 A.D. They did not work. The "just price" administered by Church authorities characterized medieval market activities. It did not work either. In the United States, the Puritans, the Continental Congress, and World War II regulatory boards all experimented with versions of direct control over prices and wages. The record of failure is consistent.

As might be expected, controls distort an economy. They create black markets and gray markets for commodities whose administered prices are too low. Goods that are needed but unprofitable under controls are not produced, and the public suffers. The lesson of price fixing in the natural gas industry should be vivid to all Americans who shivered through the winter of 1977. In labor markets, fixed wages similarly cause resource misallocation and encourage inefficiency and low productivity among disgruntled workers.

Some reformers, seeking solutions to what they see as cost inflation, have proposed profit controls. In point of fact, all wage-price controls amount to profit constraints, but this proposal is especially obnoxious. Plainly, those who suggest it fail to understand that profits are the key to industrial and economic growth. Reductions in profits must mean increases in unemployment.

Wage and price controls are an enormous delusion. Because they appear so easy and innocuous at the beginning, they lead people to believe that they afford a quick and painless solution to chronic price pressures. The plain fact is that curing inflation requires "biting the bullet"—facing up to the excesses of past fiscal and monetary indiscretions that must sooner or later be paid for.

Aside from not solving the inflation problem—or at best only converting it into a general problem of economic stagnation—wage and price controls demand an excessive buildup of government bureaucratic agencies and the legitimation of monopoly power. An enlarged state apparatus now deals with officially recognized business and labor brokers. The entire structure of an individualist economic and political system is undermined.

WHAT ABOUT INDEXING?

One proposed governmental intervention that deserves serious consideration is indexing. Basically this amounts to tying all or some deferred payments to a specific price index—balancing wages and the values of financial obligations and assets with the real rate of price inflation. Milton Friedman has proposed that all payments between the public and the federal government be indexed and that such arrangements be voluntary for the rest of the economy. Other Conservatives would go further.

The benefits are obvious. Uncertainty over the value of future income (retirement savings, for instance) would be removed. The redistributive effects of inflation upon income, especially fixed income, would be reduced. Wage agreements could take on *real* rather than *money* meaning, and contracts anticipating inflation would not be necessary. The result would be greater stability for both business and the employee. In stemming the inflationary wage pressures through automatic, indexed increases in pay, we might eliminate the psychology of "catch up with and get ahead of the next price rise." The excessive wage settlements that contribute mightily to unemployment might eventually be halted. To what lengths the principle of indexing should be extended is a matter of Conservative debate, but most would agree that the idea is worth thoughtful deliberation in the present inflation crisis.

The Liberal Argument

There is no single cause of inflation. Rising prices may result from (1) excess demand for goods—that is, too many dollars pursuing too few commodities; (2) cost-push, better known as the wage-price spiral; or (3) shortages, which, through the levering of supply and demand, push up prices. Knowing this is small consolation to the consumer facing frustration at the grocery checkout counter, but it is important if we are to determine the correct anti-inflationary policy at any given time.

DISSECTING THE THREE TYPES OF INFLATION

Throughout our history, and probably throughout world history, excess-demand inflation has been the most common of the three types. Excess demand is invariably the result of the creation or appearance of "new" money or credit at a time when goods do not increase proportionately. In the sixteenth century, for instance, the Spanish brought back to Europe galleon after galleon loaded with precious metals stolen in the New World. The effect was a sudden increase in Europe's money supply. Spanish gold chased after English woolens and French wines, bidding up prices everywhere it went. While this great price inflation ultimately contributed to the destruction of feudal society and the building of modern capitalism, most excess-demand inflation has had less salutary effects.

Most inflationary periods in the United States have been the result of war-generated excess demand. In other words, government deficits created by war have tended to expand money and credit precisely as wartime shortages reduced available goods. As Figure 12.1 shows, the Civil War, World Wars I and II, and the Korean and Vietnam conflicts accounted for practically all price increases up to 1970. The post–World War II price spurt (1946–1948) was not really an exception but a carryover from the massive spending of the war years. Post–Vietnam inflation, however, is another matter. Debt and spending for that conflict were not enough to account for the recent steep and steady price rise. This does not fit the model of excess-demand inflation, especially since it has been accompanied by high levels of unemployment.

The point here is an important one, since Conservatives tend to offer a simple generalization explaining all inflationary movements, seeing them almost exclusively as the result of government deficits and/or expansionary money policies. Such an analysis makes government and monetary authorities the culprits and proposes tight-money policies and balanced budgets as the cures for all inflation. The economics of this view is wrong in both theory and fact, and the policy implications actually weaken efforts to solve price problems (not to mention causing greater unemployment misery). Rather than less government intervention, we need more in order to deal with inflation. Government can create jobs *and* hold the price line if we understand that our present inflation comes from cost-push pressures and shortages.

The cost-push element of inflation has become very significant over the past decade because of important structural changes in the American economy. First of all, wage pressures have to some extent been heightened by growing union power, especially in certain critical industries. Contracts with built-in cost-of-living escalators, plus the ever-present desire to catch up with yesterday's inflation, have added to tomorrow's higher prices. As a rule, whenever wage gains or, more accurately, increased wage costs exceed productivity increases, prices must go up.

Unions, however, should not be singled out in analyzing cost-push inflation. The increased concentration and monopoly pricing tactics of American industry bear an equal, if not greater, share of the guilt in pushing prices upward. Administered prices dominate market structures. That is, firms establish prices jointly and without any thought of future reductions as they attempt to meet profit targets. While profits are essential to industry, they are very often obtained through price increases rather than attempts to improve productivity or efficiency. Thus, cost increases—and labor is only one among many costs—are passed on as prices are adjusted to assure profit goals.

Logic should tell us that these higher prices might be expected to lower demand, and they do; however, market control by industry can still keep aggregate profits up. In some industries (such as oil) profits have actually been rising as production fell and prices advanced. Such production declines mean greater unemployment. Given the existing structure of American industry, cost-push inflation actually causes economic stagnation. Thus, we see that the situation is quite different from that posited in the Conservative argument, which emphasizes excess demand as the ultimate destroyer of jobs.

Shortages are the other crucial force in creating the recent inflationary spiral. Too little oil and gas because of the Arab embargo, OPEC production limitations, worldwide depletion, and our own gluttony have driven all production costs upward. Presently, the Department of Energy calculates that about one-third of our inflation rate is solely the result of rising petroleum prices. While part of this price rise may reflect the market monopoly power of oil companies, most of it reflects shortages of fuel. Food prices, another leader in the recent inflation, have gone up as world shortages developed. Even the coffee "holdup" of 1976–1977 was largely the result of weather conditions. The list of commodities in short supply goes on and on.

Before leaving this discussion of inflationary causes, it should be noted that the current episode of price increases has a certain uniqueness. By past standards, the inflationary period has been quite long and the length has produced a stubborn psychology of "inflationary expectations." Thus, wage demands by labor and pricing policies by corporations increasingly reflect efforts to hedge against future inflationary losses, but in fact these efforts to offset inflation's effects only spur greater price increases. Meanwhile, consumer decisions to spend more and save less, since inflation destroys the value of accumulated savings, also push prices upward. Once established the vicious cycle created by inflationary expectations is not easily or quickly halted. The Conservative program of simply standing back and waiting until readjustment takes place is an absurd policy; rather, direct and firm government intervention is needed now.

WHY MORE GOVERNMENT ACTION IS NEEDED

If cost-push and shortages are the primary causes of our present inflation, what does this suggest in terms of an anti-inflationary policy? Labor must agree to tie its wage demands to productivity increases, and business must be induced or compelled to rely on productivity increases rather than simple-minded price hikes in its search for profits. Failing this, profits themselves may have to be regulated. All of these public policy efforts demand enlargement of state authority—at a minimum the creation of wage-price guidelines.

Shortage inflation, even more than cost-push inflation, demands direct government action through both price setting and direct rationing. Energy prices cannot be set in the market by the laws of supply and demand. Conservatives may argue that these are "one time" price adjustments resulting from changes in technology and supply. But it is obvious that prices will rise many more times in the future. There must be comprehensive energy policies, not simply to solve the problems that shortages create in specific markets but also to control the effects of shortages on the whole economy.

While our experience with enforced wage-price controls in the 1971–1973 era of "Nixonomics" did little to enhance the concept of direct government price regulation, there are really no other reasonable options in solving the inflation problem. The voluntary wage-price guidelines initiated by the Carter Administration in 1977 were notably ineffective in slowing the inflation rate. As we shall argue in Issue 16 on economic planning, federal control and direction of the economy's general performance in the area of prices and employment must expand. We need rational planning. The nation's public policy can no longer be a haphazard reaction to this or that emerging economic crisis.

A note of caution might be added here. Despite our strong arguments on behalf of a dual cost and shortage explanation of modern inflation, Liberals do not discount the fact that excess demand *can* be a problem. Obviously a fiscal and monetary policy that thoughtlessly turns up the heat of aggregate demand in an effort to reduce unemployment runs the risk of creating excess-demand price pressures. Liberals do not believe that unbalanced federal budgets should be a fact of life. But budget balance and fiscal restraint are not God-given commandments either. President Carter's promised plan to balance the budget by the 1980s was perfectly consistent with Liberal philosophy as long as that balancing does not sacrifice the commitment to full employment.

A WORD ON INDEXING

Some economists have proposed indexing as a solution to the inflation dilemma. This technique would tie the dollar value of deferred payments to the price index. It is now a fairly common device in nations undergoing super-inflation. Proponents (who include both Conservatives and Liberals) argue that it would remove uncertainties about income and wealth. Values would supposedly be maintained even if inflation continued. Since indexing requires comparatively little government intervention, it appeals to those who oppose broadening government powers. Whatever its painkilling effects, however, indexing is a sedative and not an antibiotic. It will not cure inflation since it does not deal with its causes.

Even if indexing were adopted, we would still have to deal with the structural problems of cost-push and shortage inflation. These are not likely to go away by themselves, and we still cannot evade the issue of direct government controls to maintain price stability. Advocates of indexing—a proposal that does have merit—should not believe that they have found an easy way out of a difficult problem.

The Radical Argument

Capitalism did not invent inflation, nor does it have an unchallenged claim on it today. Precapitalist societies knew the anguish of rising prices and debased money, and even socialist economies have faced inflationary pressures. But the present American inflation problem is unique to our economic system. To put the issue directly, our problems of rising prices are the unwanted but unavoidable result of monopoly domination in our society. Although apologists for the system can point to inadequate public policy, labor unions, or Arab sheiks as causes, a far more important factor is the growth of economic concentration.

The inflation record supports this position. Except in times of wars and their immediate aftermath, inflation is a purely modern problem in the United States. Inflationary growth since the mid-1960s exactly parallels the greatest merger and concentration period in American history. Liberals understand the general relationship between business integration and price increases, but, as we have seen, they believe that government regulation can offset monopoly price activity. They are naive about political relations in modern monopoly capitalism. Their belief that monopoly pricing can be corrected in economic terms indicates an ignorance of how essential such pricing is to the existing economic order.

HOW MONOPOLY POWER CAUSES INFLATION

How, precisely, does monopoly create inflation? First of all, monopolists (or "collusive oligopolists," as some purists would have it) have the ability to raise prices irrespective of supply and demand conditions. Conventional theory tells us that monopoly prices will always be higher than those in a competitive situation. As price makers, monopolists will always set their prices to assure maximum profits. Competitive firms, subject to market conditions beyond their control, cannot do this. That monopoly prices are higher than those in a competitive system is a textbook truth and a standard condemnation of monopoly power. In the real world, though, upward price pressures are more spectacular than theory suggests.

Let's take the case of the highly concentrated auto industry. In 1973 and 1976, good years by recent industry standards, prices went up about 3.5 and 5.5 percent respectively. In terms of traditional theory, this rise would be expectable as demand increases created an upward price push. However, in 1974, when demand fell by more than 20 percent (from 9.7 to 7.4 million American autos sold), prices actually increased 9 percent. When 1975 demand fell another 6 percent, prices went up 8.6 percent over the previous year. The pattern is not unique to the auto industry. In the past few years, pricing has followed similar paths in aluminum, glass, rubber, and steel. In fact, with perfectly straight faces, steel executives explained their November 1976 price increases as the result of falling demand and increased foreign competition. Supposedly, higher prices would mean improved profits, greater capital accumulation, and, ultimately, higher productivity.

If all this sounds a bit odd, it's because it flies in the face of all we have learned about the behavior of markets. Theory tells us that lower demand should reduce prices. In fact, prices rise no matter what the demand. Prices are flexible—but only upward.

Monopolistic industries today are not the monopolists of legend. Unlike the Robber Barons, they do not seek at any given time *all* the profits they might obtain. They operate under the constraints of public opinion, foreign competition, pressure from other businesses, and fear that the antitrust laws might actually be dusted off. Thus, while monopoly price inflation is insidious, it is rarely outrageous, at least at any particular time. Bit by bit, though, it bleeds consumers and cheats workers of their wages.

Manufacturers' explanations that prices must go up because of higher wage costs, or energy prices—or even as the result of environmental and consumer protection actions—are basically deceptions. Monopolists set their profit goals independent of these costs and generally reach them. While real wages actually fell as prices consistently rose between 1969 and 1976, total profits and profit rates steadily advanced in most industries. While the public was directed to take off after labor unions, Arabs, Russians, and lovers of wildlife, corporate profits grew without much fanfare. Whatever else inflation has done, it has not hurt profits; this fact reveals a good deal about the relationship between monopoly capital and price increases.

As we noted before, most Liberal economists and politicians are aware of the relation between business concentration and profits. But, with their usual attitude of "a plague on both your houses," they point an accusing finger at both capital and labor in their efforts to explain cost-push inflation. This line of argument evades the evidence. Having failed to understand the central role of monopoly profit seeking in causing inflation, Liberals compound their error in macroeconomic policy making.

HOW GOVERNMENT MAKES THINGS WORSE

Aside from its roots in monopoly pricing, inflation is also generated by government actions to offset and legitimize monopoly capitalist production. As we noted in Issue 11, advances in production and business concentration have meant the release of more and more workers from goods production, and, therefore, chronic unemployment. For instance, between 1947 and 1980 manufacturing employment grew by only about a third. During the same time GNP about doubled. To take up the unemployment and stagnation slack in the economy, government spending in real dollars grew by over 500 percent. In short, vastly increased state spending was necessary to offset monopoly capitalism's production crises by absorbing and sustaining unemployment and by cranking up aggregate demand for goods.

Without these steps, recession would have degenerated into serious depression. However, government spending and other expansionary moves produced their own inflationary effects. Debt expansion has meant money supply growth and inflation of the demand-pull type. Yet government has no option but to continue spending (usually in socially destructive areas such as defense). The alternative would be massive unemployment or falling business profits or both.

To summarize the Radical view: Initially our inflation problem began with business concentration and monopoly pricing. Concentration of business also created problems of unemployment and sagging demand. To counteract these tendencies, state spending had to be pumped up. That, of course, has added further fuel to inflation. In all of this, monopoly is the key.

Unable and unwilling to face the real significance of this fact, Liberals turn to their last resort—government. Their only remedy is wage and price controls. Control mechanisms are, of course, bound to fail since they continue to support the profit motives of business. Nixon's Phase I–Phase IV efforts from 1971 to 1973 are a grim reminder that state wage-price controls mean that workers' wages are now "officially" sacrificed to provide corporate profits. Under Ford's WIN (Whip Inflation Now) program, the element of patriotism and the appeal to a stiff upper lip were thrown in to gain workers' collaboration with their own exploitation.

Nor were Carter's 1977 "voluntary" wage-price guidelines any less exploitative. By setting a 7 percent per year "voluntary" guideline for wage increases, the Carter Administration gave management a club to hold over labor's head. Corporations could now tell workers, whose real income was falling, that they were powerless to help them. In fact, if they granted increases deemed "inflationary" by the government, corporations were told by Washington that federal purchasers would shun their goods. While workers were caught in a wage restraint of no more than a 7 percent increase a year, corporate profits (which were unaffected by the Carter decrees) grew by more than 25 percent a year through 1978 and 1979. Thus, corporations could both appear as patriots and improve their profit position by complying with the Carter guidelines. But all the bleeding of labor through wage freezes did not stop the bleeding of consumers through price increases. Despite the supposed controls and all the official jawboning, monopoly-inspired price increases scarcely slowed down. Controls have meant only that most Americans get a double dose of exploitation to keep the monopoly capitalist system afloat. One ripoff comes in the paycheck, the other at the cash register.

The Military-Industrial Complex

How Much for Defense?

In the councils of government, we guard against the acquisition of unwarranted influence, whether sought or unsought, by the military-industrial complex. The potential for the disastrous rise of misplaced power exists and will exist.

Dwight D. Eisenhower, 1961

Today it is more likely that the military requirement is the result of joint participation of military and industrial personnel, and it is not unusual for industry's solution to be a key factor. Indeed, there are highly placed military men who sincerely feel that industry is currently setting the pace in the research and development of new weapons systems.

Peter Schenck, Raytheon Corporation, 1969

National solid waste treatment program	=	$43.5 billion	=	B-1 bomber program
Total environmental cleanup	=	$105.2 billion	=	New weapons systems in development or procurement
To eliminate hunger in America	=	$5 billion	=	C-5A aircraft program

Seymour Melman, National Co-Chairman of SANE, 1974

THE PROBLEM

There was a time—long forgotten by most of us—when military spending took a very small proportion of a very tiny federal budget. That was, of course, before World War II and the three decades of cold war anxiety that have left an indelible mark upon recent American history. To see the economic impact of national security spending, we need only know that the United States has spent nearly $2 trillion on war, threats of war, and anticipated wars over the past forty years. But how much is too much, and how much is enough spending for national defense? The answer is not an easy one. As Table 13.1 indicates, total defense spending has been growing steadily since the Vietnam War period even though the United States has been at peace, made efforts to relieve Sino-American tensions, and until recently been negotiating arms limitations (SALT) with the Russians. Such data, however, can be misleading. While military spending has been going up, Figure 13.1 shows that its increase has generally lagged behind national economic growth. Thus, we have been spending a smaller share of our output on defense. Is this wise policy or does it invite war? Critics of our defense spending are divided.

From a macroeconomic point of view, defense spending plays a very large role in the maintenance of total demand in the economy (in Keynesian terms: $C + I + G$). The jobs of millions of Americans and the well-being of entire regions are presently dependent on the fortunes of

Table 13.1   National Defense Spending, Selected Years, 1939–1978

Year	Amount (in billions of $)	Year	Amount (in billions of $)
1939	$ 1.9	1970	$ 73.5
1944	84.4	1971	70.2
1949	13.2	1972	73.5
1955	38.4	1973	73.5
1960	44.5	1974	77.0
1965	49.4	1975	83.9
1966	60.3	1976	86.8
1967	71.5	1977	94.3
1968	76.9	1978	110.0
1969	76.3	1979	123.9 (est.)

Source: Economic Report of the President, 1979.

FIGURE 13.1   DEFENSE SPENDING AND THE ECONOMY, 1968–1978

the military budget. Through the multiplier effect, other jobs and other locales benefit indirectly from such spending. The microeconomic impact of defense is probably more easily observed. In simplest terms, it means profit or loss for some of America's largest corporations. Given the impact, in scale and duration, of war and defense spending on the economy, it is clear that debate over the size of the defense budget involves much more than the moral and political questions it frequently raises: defense is an economic problem too.

The debate between defenders and critics of the military budget is at least twenty years old now. Although the urgency of the question slackened somewhat after the Vietnam debacle and during the period of detente, the Iranian Crisis and the Soviet invasion of Afghanistan have produced presidential and congressional calls for immediate increases in military spending of from 5 to 10 percent a year (over and above increases for inflation). Even though public opinion has generally supported this appeal for additional arms, economists are by no means of one mind on the matter of military spending.

SYNOPSIS The Conservative argument maintains that defense spending, although probably characterized by some waste, is necessary for national security. The Liberals have tended to be divided on military spending with some opposing the growth of a powerful military-industrial complex and urging that war spending be shifted to social goods, while others, like the Conservatives, have argued for the necessity of a large arms budget. The Radical argument holds that our economy depends on war for profit and maintaining high levels of demand, and that shifting this spending to other areas is politically and economically impossible under the present system.

The Conservative Argument

By any rational calculus, war is wasteful and uneconomical. Human labor, lives, and resources are used not for production but for destruction. Markets are distorted, shortages develop, and the price mechanism fails to direct resource allocation properly. The production of war goods, meanwhile, subtracts from the society's accumulation of capital and its social and private wealth. All of this should be obvious. Yet predominant in most discussions of military spending, or the so-called military-industrial complex, is the charge that war is necessary or that war is good for the economy. Needless to say, this argument is usually advanced by critics of capitalism. It is demonstrably false, but proving logically that war is not essential to a capitalist economy is not the end of the matter. War and threats of war are a reality today. War spending, therefore, is not a function of limited capitalist economic options. It is a necessary political and societal response to an external threat: in this case we are talking about the protection of American capitalism and democracy from the threat of international communism.

Although military spending is basically the political problem of a society protecting itself, such spending clearly has economic effects and so should not be beyond the pale of economic analysis. In this area a great deal of confusion exists.

A NECESSARY EXPENDITURE

A common charge is that defense spending is too high. In absolute magnitude, the defense budget is large. The high technological and capital costs of the nuclear age, however, reflect requirements that have changed a good deal since soldiers threw rocks and spears at one another. It must be remembered too that the limits on military spending are not being determined by how much we want to spend but by how much our adversaries force us to spend for adequate defense. More important, though, is the fact that defense spending is relatively small and growing smaller as a part of our total output.

In 1979 spending on national defense amounted to about $124 billion, 24 percent of total federal spending and only about half what the federal government spent on health, education, and income security.

Defense spending was down from a 29 percent share of the budget in 1974 and a 40 percent share in the Vietnam year of 1970. In the years between 1970 and 1979, human resource spending increased from 37 to 52 percent of the budget. As a share of our total economic output (GNP), 1979 defense spending amounted to less than 6 percent. Compare this with, say, 1922. The United States was then at peace, pursuing a foreign policy of isolation, blissfully allowing its army and navy to grow obsolete, and beginning a long period of economic prosperity. Nevertheless, the $1.2 billion spent on defense that year still amounted to 2 percent of our GNP and 35 percent of federal expenditures. The facts simply don't support the alarmist claims of those who oppose defense spending. (One might ask, parenthetically, why these opponents attack military spending—which is small and growing relatively smaller—while showing little concern about government spending in other areas.)

Since defense is primarily a function of how one's adversary reacts, it is important to ask what the Soviet Union is doing. According to estimates of the Department of Defense and private researchers, the Russians are devoting about 10 to 12 percent of their GNP to military outlays. Such an effort is about twice as great as ours in terms of the share of GNP. As Table 13.2 illustrates, the Russians have been increasing their military preparations and offensive capacities precisely as our defense has contracted. The Soviet readiness exceeds ours in such important categories as men under arms, ICBMs, missile subs, tanks, and combat ships. However, the bottom line points up our real prob-

Table 13.2   Changes in U.S.S.R.-U.S. Military Balance, 1960–1961 and 1978–1979

	U.S.S.R.		U.S.A.	
	1960–1961	1978–1979	1960–1961	1978–1979
Men under arms (in millions)	3.6	4.4	2.5	2.1
ICBMs	50	1,477	13	1,054
Missile subs	0	90	3	41
Tanks	35,000	45,000	12,500	12,500
Surface combat ships	160	243	416	172
Budget (in billions of 1979 $)	$91	$162	$125	$123.7

Source: U.S. government and the International Institute for Strategic Studies.

lem. The Soviets spend about 30 percent more than the United States for war and war preparations. Moreover, the offensive purposes of this spending should be evident to all doubters after the Soviet intervention in Afghanistan.

IN DEFENSE OF DEFENSE

A second charge leveled at military spending is that it is inefficient. This is somewhat harder to refute, since there is evidence of cost overruns and technological failures. The problem is calculating efficiency in making military hardware. The production and sale of sophisticated war goods cannot take place in a competitive market; things have changed since Lincoln's secretary of war took bids on horse blankets and salt pork. No rational executive will risk capital by speculating in the tank or missile business.

Secrecy, complex technology, and capital demands set constraints on the supply side of the military market, while the demand side is limited to a single domestic buyer and a few overseas purchasers. Given the reality of monopoly in the supply and purchase of military goods, the record of waste does not seem extraordinary. (One might ask again why critics single out the inefficiency of military spending but neglect to apply the same standards to government purchases from other industries. Is there no waste in highway construction or in federally funded and managed urban renewal and housing projects? Of course war is a waste, but the charge of economic inefficiency is another matter.)

This same obsession with the military and the so-called military-industrial complex appears in charges of conflict of interest and political manipulation. Opponents of military spending talk darkly about the "Senator from Boeing," disproportionately high outlays in the districts of certain congresspersons, and the ease with which retiring Pentagon colonels slide behind corporate desks. Yet they rarely identify other congressional figures as the "Senator from Corn" or the "Congressman for the AFL-CIO." No one expects Interstate Commerce Commissioners to be former Boy Scout executives. It should surprise no one that military officers drift toward defense industry jobs.

This is not to defend inefficiency or conflict of interest. Neither should be allowed. But the military is no more guilty than other sectors that deal with government. Such problems are not unique to the "military-industrial complex."

A final word might be said on behalf of indirect benefits from the military budget. Despite the ultimate waste of war and some probable inefficiency in procurement and production, defense spending has produced useful inventions and innovations. Military research and development has made possible, among many other things, Boeing 707s and 747s, our satellite communications network, and the transistor.

Lest readers mistakenly conclude that the Conservatives' position on military spending is inconsistent with their attitude toward government, it should be pointed out that war and defense are decisions that transcend the marketplace. A permanent war economy certainly extends government into areas of social activity better left to the people. This issue calls for vigilance, but defense of the society is essential. This stubborn fact is totally ignored by the opponents of defense spending.

The Liberal Argument

Conservatives correctly argue that adequate military defense is not a matter of purely economic choice or of frivolous luxury. Quite simply, it is necessary in the cold war (and sometimes hot war) environment in which we have lived for more than three decades. However, the abstract need for defense and the present dimensions of the military-industrial complex are two different questions. As retiring President Eisenhower prophesied in 1961, big military budgets have created a dangerous symbiotic relationship between the Pentagon and broad areas of the American economy. Because of the political influence of the MIC, serious examinations of its extent and inner workings have been difficult. Despite these difficulties, we *must* ask such questions as: How much defense is needed? How well is defense spending managed? How much should defense claim as a share of our national output?

A MATTER OF OVERKILL

Although Liberals are not in agreement on how much defense is necessary in dollar terms, some have made a convincing argument that our preparedness for total war has already reached the overkill stage—that absolute numbers of missiles, bombers, and other weapons are no longer a significant measure of our well-being. There is no such thing as a comparative advantage in weapons after a certain point in defense development. When the overkill stage is reached, additional amounts bring no additional security.

No part of the federal budget is vulnerable to as much intensive congressional and industrial lobbying. The public is fed a steady diet of information and misinformation about new and wonderful weapons systems, missile gaps, and the intentions of our adversaries. Behind the patriotic appeals is the simple matter of dollars and cents. A great many giant American corporations are dependent for their existence on military orders. Lockheed, General Dynamics, McDonnell-Douglas, Rockwell International, Raytheon, and Ling-Temco-Vought—all among the nation's top hundred manufacturers—have depended on national defense spending for more than half their total sales for the past fifteen years. To a lesser degree, dozens of other firms feed at the Pentagon trough.

Naturally, the military economy affects many citizens. Some 7 percent of all employed Americans work in defense industries; over 20 percent of all manufacturing personnel are involved directly in military hardware. In states such as Connecticut, California, and Washington, about 40 percent of the manufacturing workers are in defense-related industries.

With this kind of political and economic muscle, the Pentagon budget has long been sacrosanct. The public purse is ever open to ill-planned and unneeded weapons. Between 1953 and 1968, more than $10 billion was spent on weapons that proved useless. Meanwhile, provided with public capital, prime contractors continually piled up cost overruns that sometimes doubled and tripled the original estimates. Even when faced with bankruptcy due to their own mismanagement, prime military suppliers have received government loans and grants to bail them out.

Condemnation of military waste, however, is not pacifism. While attacking the political clout of the MIC, Liberals are not naive about the real need for an adequate defense. Weakness may well invite war and provoke Soviet adventurism, as we presently see in the Middle East and in Southwest Asia. Nevertheless, defensive strength must not be confused with domination by the MIC.

There is no question that the power of the military-industrial complex makes it dangerous. The foremost concern is that war has become "easier." Overheated patriotism and the self-fulfilling prophecies of cold war supporters (in the Pentagon, Congress, and the defense business) make it that much easier to look for military solutions.

DEFENSE SPENDING AND THE ECONOMY

Radicals have long charged that war is the only way a capitalist economy can cure its periodic problems of recession and depression. According to this view, government spending for war helps maintain high levels of aggregate demand $(C + I + G)$. Moreover, as military spending and war goods investment continue over time, there is a steady shift in production possibilities toward a permanent war goods foundation. The economy is supposedly geared to a certain war production that must be maintained for industry's sake.

Such a view is highly mechanical. It fails to realize that government spending (G) could also be allocated for social goods. Moreover, war goods always diminish a society. In a fully employed society, war goods can be produced only by giving up civilian goods. In our present stagflation economy, persistently large military budgets lead to a serious trade-off with other social spending. When overall federal spending is held down by fears of inflation and limited revenues, big military budgets mean less for education, health, welfare, and other social spending.

With such costs forced upon the society by military spending, it would seem that a shift of G from war to social goods is not only possible but essential if MIC power is to be controlled. While such a move may cause some grief and readjustment at General Dynamics, it is not the end of the capitalist economy.

Spending on bombs, tanks, and missiles could just as well be spending on hospitals, parks, or the environment. And, unlike war spending, which does not create beneficial or consumable goods, spending in social areas not only benefits the public but also stimulates consumption (C) spending for private goods. This in turn encourages private investment (I), which is not stimulated (except in defense industries) in a war economy.

Spending on social goods could more than make up for any general economic contraction that might result from reducing the military component of G. Economic growth does not depend on war, cold or hot; it would, in fact, be enhanced by a shift toward "peace" goods.

In the debate over whether national priorities should favor defense spending or social spending, Liberals feel that social goods must be given preference—short of reducing American defense to ineffectiveness. Specifically, this means taking a hard line against the overzealous MIC lobby. The government must be rigorous in setting standards for procurement policies and enforcing contract terms. Such measures should deter bribery and collusion and stimulate cost efficiency in the firms that do defense business. Steps should be taken to curb the special influence of congressmen representing regions that depend on defense spending. The deleterious effects on business of reducing or holding the line on military spending could be offset if the government directed other government spending into affected locales and instituted job-retraining programs.

Basically, this program is political, not economic. It is primarily a matter of convincing people to spend money for social goods rather than for war. Its success ultimately depends on the popular will.

The Radical Argument

America's high levels of military spending are not simply the consequence of maintaining an "adequate" defensive position, as Conservatives argue. Nor, as Liberals would have it, are they the largely accidental result of efforts by a self-aggrandizing and small political clique known as the military-industrial complex. On the contrary, military spending and/or war is essential to American capitalist development.

AN OFFENSIVE DEFENSE

In the first place, military spending is not purely defensive—at least not in the sense of building a retaliatory force to negate the "Russian threat." Although the possibility of a Russian attack has been emphasized for three decades to justify military budgets, defense preparations have always entailed much more than a threatened confrontation between the United States and the Soviet Union. When American policy makers have spoken of defense, it has usually been in terms of "defense of the free world." The "free world," of course, is that part of the globe where American capital has interests to protect. Freedom—other than the freedom of American business to manufacture and sell profitably and to obtain resources cheaply—has very little to do with this defensive strategy. Friendly repressive regimes in Chile, Brazil, the Philippines, and elsewhere must be defended from national revolutions that would seize or nationalize United States corporate assets.

When necessary, as in Korea and Vietnam, the United States has shown a willingness to invest its young men and its military might to protect its international economic interests. This aspect of military policy is neatly avoided by Conservatives and Liberals. Forgetful they may be, but it is not difficult to recall that both world wars in this century—and most smaller wars in the last two centuries—were either between expansive and competing capitalist powers or between capitalist powers and developing economies that were challenging their hegemony. The basis for war has been capitalist imperialism.

Armies and navies are crucial for capitalist countries in defending their overseas interests. The costs of maintaining these forces and of fighting actual wars are extraordinary. In fact, in any rational sense, the total expenses are usually far in excess of any benefits gained through overseas profits. In the case of Vietnam, a recent study has indicated that the war may have cost as much as $1 trillion.* While the actual budget for direct war spending was only about $171 billion, to this amount should be added $305 billion for future budget drains for equipment replacement, $71 billion for calculable human losses to Americans, and about $380 billion for the costs of war-generated inflation, recession, and foreign trade problems. Such spending in a war we didn't even win indicates that capitalist "defensive" policies are not rational. Nonetheless, in terms of the system's views of its overseas needs, military waste is essential, even when the waste is a crushing blow to the nation's economy and people.

WAR, A CRUTCH FOR THE DOMESTIC ECONOMY

Leaving aside the supposed overseas benefits from "defense," it is also important in stabilizing the domestic economy. In a microeconomic sense, many firms and some entire industries are wholly depen-

*Robert Warren Stevens, *Vain Hopes, Grim Realities* (New York: New Viewpoints, 1976), pp. 163–196.

dent on the Pentagon budget for their profit margins. This is not simply a matter of firms that do 50 percent or more of their business with government. Large companies such as General Motors, General Electric, Ford, and Chrysler—which gain less than 20 percent of their sales from military contracts—depend on these contracts for the lion's share of the profits they earn in the United States.

In a macroeconomic sense, high levels of defense spending are a crutch for the whole economy—a fact acknowledged by the Liberals. They argue that the G in the $C + I + G$ equation for maintaining high levels of demand could be used for social rather than war goods. Theoretically this argument is true, but it fails to consider the political nature of the military budget and the powerful role of corporations in determining governmental fiscal priorities.

The Liberal argument, in underestimating the importance of war spending, neglects history. As even Liberals will admit, it was not the elegant theories of Lord Keynes that led our economy out of the Depression. It was massive wartime spending, not the purchase of social goods, that pumped up aggregate demand and created full employment. While social spending might have had the same effect—at least in theory—the point to remember is that war spending was the route the nation followed. Nor has it altered that course.

Military spending, from the corporate point of view, is especially attractive because it is wasteful. In other words, it produces income and profits while doing nothing to improve or change the society's stock of consumable goods. There is no need to worry about gluts of commodities that will sooner or later be blown up or abandoned. Social spending, on the other hand, is particularly disruptive. In producing certain goods (public power or public housing, for instance), it competes directly with the private sector. Too extensive social outlays also interfere with labor markets, driving labor costs upward.

The profitability of wasteful government spending on military hardware is, from business's point of view, an undeniable factor in its constant lobbying for more "defense" and its cold war "educational" efforts. The public treasury is opened in the names of patriotism and national security for corporate plunder and profit. Business will not easily give all this up.

Up to this point the arms makers have enjoyed much support from labor and certain defense-oriented regions of the nation as they work to maintain military spending and trade it off against social outlays. While the AFL-CIO leadership still remains strongly defense oriented, there are signs that American labor in general is reexamining the blind commitments to defense spending.

World political developments such as detente, the Strategic Arms Limitation Treaties (SALT), Chinese-American rapprochement, and the bitter aftertaste of the Vietnam struggle have weakened the "better dead than Red" mentality that gripped the United States for so long. While the Russian incursion into Afghanistan showed that Cold War hysteria has not ceased entirely, it is important to remember that Afghanistan did not escalate into a Korea or a Vietnam. Popular support for a direct confrontation with the Soviets was less than universal, despite the ample efforts of 1980 presidential candidates to stir up American jingoism.

At home, the growing power of the MIC aggravates the problems of ordinary citizens in an already troubled economy. Military spending, going primarily as it does to large firms, strengthens monopoly power. Since most war suppliers also produce civilian goods, monopoly pricing power is enhanced in the market for civilian goods as well. Meanwhile, since war production is capital intensive and complex in its technology, each defense dollar spent produces very few employment gains. Among the hard-core unemployed, military outlays produce no job gains at all. Even for skilled workers, military purchasing and the arms industry are having a declining impact. Thus the long enjoyed "jobs effect" of the MIC is on the wane.

If Americans can gain a more reasoned understanding of the phony ideological arguments upon which the MIC has been built and perpetuates itself, they can appreciate its real economic effects. Contrary to Liberal rhetoric, however, there are few possibilities of simply shifting public outlays to other areas. At least there are few possibilities without restructuring the entire economy and society. War is waste, but capitalism depends on waste. The capitalist system is inherently unable to opt for rational and humane production. The ability to wage war protects capitalism's interests overseas, and the system cannot exist without these interests. Realization of these facts, along with an understanding of capitalism's chronic tendency toward unemployment and inflation, reveals the profound irrationality of the American social and economic order.

The Fiscal Crisis
of the State

On New York City's Collapse, Proposition 13, and Deciding to Bite the Bullet

Annual income twenty pounds, annual expenditure nineteen, nineteen and six; result happiness. Annual income twenty pounds, annual expenditure twenty pounds ought and six; result misery.

Charles Dickens's Mister Micawber, 1849

New York City people got used to certain luxuries like free tuition at the City University of New York and big and easy welfare which they will just have to learn to live without.

A New York banker, 1975

The whole banking industry is most intimately interwoven with public credit. Part of their business capital must be invested in interest-bearing government securities that are promptly convertible into money. . . . The whole money market . . . is part and parcel of this "aristocracy of finance," and in every epoch the stability of government is synonymous to them with Moses and the Prophets.

Karl Marx, 1869

FORD TO NYC: DROP DEAD!

New York Daily News *headline, 1975*

THE PROBLEM

As the national economy drifted downward after the 1974–1975 recession and as stagflation became a "normal" fact of economic life, governmental finance began to face serious problems. After almost two and a half decades of practically uninterrupted expansion of spending and deficits at all levels of government, severe expenditure and debt constraints emerged. At the federal level (as we have already seen in Issues 10 and 12) inflationary fears have slightly dampened the earlier tendencies. At the state and local levels, however, the burdens of past debt and the increasing bite of higher taxes to cover enlarged services have sparked far greater controversy and concern.

As Figures 14.1 and 14.2 illustrate, federal spending and debt still dwarf state and local annual expenditures and debt. However, in terms of percentages and compared to past experience, the growth of state and local spending and debt was astounding. Between 1950 and 1975, state and local debt grew by nearly 1,000 percent, compared to a little over 100 percent for the federal debt. Meanwhile, annual spending for

FIGURE 14.1   GROWTH OF GOVERNMENT DEBT SINCE 1940

Source: *Economic Report of the President,* 1978.

FIGURE 14.2   GROWTH OF GOVERNMENT SPENDING SINCE 1902

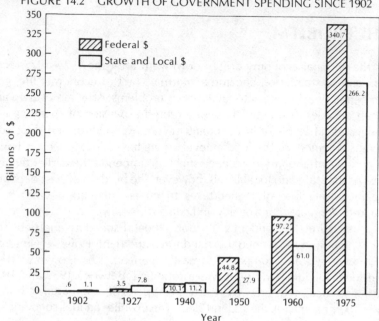

Source: *Economic Report of the President,* 1978.

states and localities grew by 950 percent, compared to 750 percent at the federal level.

The rising debt structure, especially in the recessionary economy after 1974, created grave concern in financial circles about the ability of many governments to honor their municipal and state bonds. At the same time, ordinary citizens, who generally feel closer to and more affected by their state and local tax burdens than the rather distant and unassailable federal tax structures, reacted against rising state and local taxes (the other side of rising debt and spending) by joining in a number of taxpayer revolts.* The seriousness of the problem was pointed out in two separate but yet related events—New York City's virtual bankruptcy and California's Proposition 13.

On May 24, 1975, Elmore C. Patterson, representing the New York City financial consortium that serviced the city's debt, reported to

*Reaction to federal debts and spending, however, is still significant. As we noted in Issue 10, considerable pressure is growing for a "balanced budget" amendment to the Constitution.

Mayor Abraham Beame that the city would receive no further loans until it adopted a balanced budget satisfactory to the banks. Patterson argued that the city's $12.2 billion in outstanding debt was endangered by the growing gap between city revenues and expenditures. From the point of view of the banks, credit could be offered to the city only if there were deep slashes in city services and sweeping reductions in city payrolls. New York's financial rating among banking establishments plunged from "AAA" to "ZZZ." Borrowing was now impossible, and the city moved close to bankruptcy. Only a series of spectacular last-minute "rescues" by the state government and, finally, federal promises of aid kept the "Big Apple" from going under.

The financial crisis of New York City highlighted a problem largely ignored until then—the growing fiscal crisis of urban and state governments in the United States. Through the recession of 1974–1975, most of them had seen their revenues fall or their tax bases contract. Meanwhile expenditures were increasing, especially for social services for the growing number of unemployed. The widening budget imbalance had to be closed by borrowing or by reducing expenses. As the New York City crisis was to show, borrowing was no longer an alternative. Money markets were simply closed to governments with "dangerous" expenditure-revenue gaps.

Yet bankers were not alone in their efforts to impose restraint on what many considered to be runaway state and local spending. In June 1978 California citizens sent a message throughout the nation when Proposition 13 was passed by popular referendum. Proposition 13 set property taxes at a maximum of 1 percent of assessed value and set a 2 percent ceiling on annual increases of assessed values. Support for the proposal was broad based among practically all income and social groups in the population. The message was clear: Stop the growth of government spending and taxing. The economic implications were equally clear—greater fiscal crisis for state and local governments.

After years of expansion in the areas of education, highway construction, and social welfare programs, the bubble had burst. Virtually every American mayor and governor began to tell constituents that the days of wine and roses had passed. Governments were compelled not just to hold the line but to reduce or cut out programs that had long been regarded as essential. Public employee wages and benefits generally were frozen (which meant an actual decline because of inflation). Thousands of public workers were discharged or retired, and those lost through normal attrition were not replaced. By the end of 1976, New

York City, for example, had laid off over 60,000 workers, reduced its City University faculty by 20 percent, and was preparing to cut even deeper into social expenditures.

In California the immediate impact of Proposition 13 on government jobs and spending was less pronounced than originally feared. Largely because of an enormous surplus in the state treasury, the drying up of local property tax income was offset. However, many thought this was only a temporary breather. When the state monies ran out, the revenue-expenditure squeeze would cut deeply into services and employment. In anticipation, most local governments introduced user fees to cover the operation of libraries, art centers, and in some cases, sanitation.

The fiscal crisis is here to stay. But there is wide disagreement about how it has come about and how it should be resolved.

SYNOPSIS The Conservative argument lays the blame for the current fiscal crisis on the unwise reliance on deficits to expand governmental capital and social programs. The Liberal argument sees the fiscal crisis as emerging from basic structural shifts in the economy that have placed heavy burdens on many older cities and states. The Radical argument asserts that present fiscal problems reflect the entire society's dependence upon debt to maintain economic growth and that the crisis of New York City was engineered by banks to protect their precarious financial position.

The Conservative Argument

The present crisis in the public finance of states and municipalities is the result of phenomenal debt growth over the past three decades. As late as 1950, state and local debt totaled only $24 billion in the entire nation. This was a scant 8 percent of the GNP and only about a tenth the size of the war-bloated federal debt. By 1975 state and local debt had grown nearly tenfold. It stood at 16 percent of the GNP and was a third as large as the federal debt—now swollen by welfare as well as warfare. Such statistics show how close most government units in the United States have come to bankrupting themselves.

HOW DID THE CRISIS ARISE?

How did all this happen? How was it possible in a little more than a generation for state and local governments to move from solvency to a fiscal profligacy that was nearly fatal (at least in the case of New York)?

Basically, it was the result of learning too well the erroneous economics of modern Keynesianism. Keynes belittled the significance of government debt. To him it was a small cost for ending unemployment and thus stimulating economic growth. Of course, Keynes was speaking of national debt, which he believed could always be made good by the broad taxing powers of the national government and by its ability to create money. The federal government could literally print currency to "pay" its debt service. We have already examined the inflationary effects of such federal actions, which were bad enough. Another unhappy result was the spread of Keynesian debt psychology to other units of government.

If federal debt expansion could create jobs and provide goods and services not otherwise possible under current tax revenues, why couldn't cities and states develop massive capital programs and defer *their* payments for goods and services? Economic stimulation in the public sector was apparently possible without paying a very high price. After all, in an expanding economy, tax revenues should be quite enough to cover debt service charges. Eureka, the economist had become alchemist and could turn everything to gold!

Bad as unlimited federal debt creation has been, the state and local explosion could lead only to catastrophe. Debt not only amounted to a mortgaging of the future, but also had its impact on current government spending. Whether created for capital purposes or to cover tax-revenue shortfalls, it loosened public purse strings. State and local debt grew by nearly 1,000 percent between 1950 and 1975, and state and local spending grew at exactly the same rate. Long-time constraints on public spending dissolved as state and local governments engaged in massive education, highway, public works, and welfare projects. Between 1950 and 1979 state payrolls grew from 4 million to 13 million. Some 15 percent of the total nonagricultural labor force was employed by state and local governments.

As in all "something for nothing" schemes, the bill had to fall due sooner or later. Although persistent inflation did help a bit by constantly devaluing past borrowings, rising debt burdens claimed an ever-larger share of revenues. Meanwhile, expenditures of all kinds had pushed people and governments to their taxing limits.

It should be understood that many government units were actually lowering their taxing limits by their own spending. In the case of New York City, rising taxes to cover rising expenditures had the predictable effect of driving business and middle-income taxpayers from the city. When they left, the tax base went with them. As jobs began to disappear, social spending requirements grew. Ironically, many cities and states found themselves having to tax more, even though each increase meant a reduction in the tax base. As in *Alice in Wonderland*, they had to run faster and faster just to stay in place.

When stagflation gripped the economy after 1970, state and local governments faced serious revenue losses. Borrowing was now essential to close the revenue-expenditure gap. But it became increasingly difficult as tight financial markets recognized the precarious solvency of these local governments. The good old tax-free municipal bonds developed a very bad odor. When the mortgage finally fell due, city and state governments were faced with four options: (1) stand hat in hand and wait for a federal bail-out through easy loans or free transfers, (2) drastically reduce spending, (3) go into bankruptcy, or (4) try some combination of the three (New York City's experience).

Federal guarantees of state and local finances offer very limited alternatives because of the national government's own deficit position—currently about $700 billion in total debt and going up; across-the-board guarantees of state and local debt might also trigger a new expansion of unwise spending at a time when reduction is necessary. The alternative of reduced spending is politically painful since so many Americans have become clients of state and local governments in their roles as students, employees, welfare recipients, and so on. But it is the only possible alternative, because bankruptcy would forever impair state and local credit and, more important, would cause financial panic and collapse.

THE ONLY SOLUTION

As philosopher George Santayana wisely observed, those who do not remember the past are condemned to repeat it. History is replete with examples of governments that have spent beyond their means. The result has always been political and economic chaos.

Unless governments balance their budgets, they face serious consequences. At the national level, as we have pointed out, deficits debase the value of money. Moreover, public credit instruments compete with private financial borrowing and therefore interfere with credit markets and the allocation of capital funds. Balanced budgets have a salubrious effect on governments. If a budget must be balanced, the pain of taxation tends to restrain budget growth. Taxes hurt more than deficits, and they restrain government expansion.

Balancing the budget for New York City—or any other city or state—will mean a vast reduction in the services to which people have become accustomed over the past twenty-five years. Generous welfare expenditures and luxuries such as free or underpriced higher education must be terminated. Overpaid public employment must be trimmed. There must be serious efforts to increase productivity in the public sector. The ultimate object of all these actions is to retire government debt and lower taxes.

Balancing the budget, however, is not the end of the matter. Absolute reductions in state and local government spending are essential. Before California's Proposition 13 proved the contrary, it was an article of economic faith that tax revenues simply could not be reduced at the state and local level. Now under the pressure of voter sentiment, conventional economists have been compelled to ponder the unthinkable—the gradual shrinkage of the public sector. Indeed, as the scope of government inefficiency and bureaucratic management contracts, economic conditions should improve. A year after Proposition 13, California was reporting not the chaos Liberals and Radicals projected but considerably better economic conditions.

In such an improved economic environment, the blight of over-taxed and economically declining cities and states can be replaced by growth. Increasing investment and job opportunities in the private sector will take up the slack from the presently overdeveloped public sector. There is no alternative if local governments are to return to a sound economic footing. Continuing the same policies we have followed for the past twenty-five years is no longer fiscally possible.

The Liberal Argument

The so-called fiscal crisis of the state has been overemphasized and inadequately understood. The "lessons" of the New York City crisis that politicians and the public have learned were the wrong lessons. Present efforts to solve urban and state, and even federal, public finance problems through massive pullbacks in spending will not work. In fact, fiscal stringency may actually worsen the economic problems many of these governments face. This is not to say that many government units do not have serious revenue-expenditure difficulties. They do. But the cause of these problems has been misunderstood. So has the cure.

ANOTHER VIEW OF STATE AND LOCAL DEBT

In the Conservative view, the fiscal crisis of cities and states in particular is the penalty for failing to walk the balanced-budget path; this is another version of the usual Conservative attack on the growth of federal deficits. With uncommon shortsightedness, Conservatives see deficits as the *cause* rather than the *result* of deteriorating economic conditions. In fact state and local budgets and debt (as in the federal case) have grown largely because of governmental efforts to ameliorate economic conditions created by the private economy or to provide needed goods and services that the private economy fails to deliver.

Debt is not the problem that Conservatives maintain it is. First of all, in the aggregate it is not that big. While the state and local debt burden has been growing, it has not outstripped our national ability to carry it. Federal debt, as compared to the GNP, has been declining— except during the recent Conservative administrations of Ford and

Nixon, when it grew because there was no fiscal policy to fight recession. In "affluent" 1965 the ratio of government debt (of all kinds) to GNP was .62. By "recessionary" 1975, the ratio was .51. In short, our national ability to handle debt has improved, not declined.

Second, the popular Conservative view of debt is quite inconsistent. Conservatives see government deficits, like personal debts, as somehow wrong, perhaps evil. Government debts for colleges, roads, and broadened public services are viewed as signs of economic weakness. Corporate debt, on the other hand, is a measure of strength. When General Motors announces a new debt issue, it is taken as an indication of expansion and business vitality. Why is debt that brings us more cars *good* while debt to build roads for the cars to run on is *bad*? On the basis of this logical inconsistency alone, much of the power of Conservative analysis is lost.

ANOTHER VIEW OF THE FISCAL CRUNCH

We must look beyond the question of debt to understand problems facing New York City and other cities and states. Let us look at their fiscal crisis from a more realistic perspective.

Between 1945 and 1976, when state and local debts were growing, American metropolitan areas were undergoing profound changes, not all for the better. In a mass migration, businesses and people moved to suburban locations beyond urban political limits. Businesses relocated because, with the introduction of new production technologies, many old inner-city factories became inefficient, and cheap land outside the city was usually taxed at a lower rate. Urban workers were encouraged to move because of rising incomes, which enabled them to buy houses and automobiles. An improving highway network stimulated the development of suburban shopping centers, with a concomitant decline in downtown shopping.

Meanwhile another mass migration brought southern rural blacks, and a few whites, to the central cities of the North and West. All the ingredients of what might be called "core-city disease" were now assembled. The urban tax base fell just as heavier demands were placed on the public sector. The new city immigrants, unable to find inner-city jobs after the flight of industry, became increasingly dependent on social services. Urban centers also needed monies for public housing, urban renewal, and expanded police and fire protection. The shrinking tax base was hit even harder by new levies. Higher taxes stimulated the flight from the city, which in turn increased the income-expenditure gap. In such a situation, the growth of debt was the only alternative.

There were also increasing demands for expenditures at the state level. New road systems had to be built to accommodate proliferating autos and trucks. Additional social services had to be provided for the poor, both in the inner cities and in rural areas. The social burdens of the North were aggravated by the classic solution of southern states to their welfare problems: let George do it. (In the late 1950s in Mississippi, one option open to welfare recipients was a hundred dollars and a one-way ticket to Chicago.) The point to be stressed here is that the old northern industrial states were accumulating gigantic social and economic development costs. By the 1970s they were in serious trouble. Many were losing their most educated and skilled workers and their industries to the faster-growing Far West and Sunbelt regions. Just as cities were losing people and industry to the suburbs, so some states were losing to other states. Then came the familiar sequence of declining ability to tax and rising demands for expenditures.

What we see as the important long-term trend after 1950, then, is not careless finance but deep structural and geographic changes affecting the economy. From a fiscal point of view, the claims on local and state governments were everywhere rising; most cities (especially the old industrial cities) and many states (again the older industrial states) simply could not meet them. New York City could not tap the wealth of Westchester County, nor could New York State share in the affluence of Texas. Increasing debt and growing budget gaps were the only alternative. The recession of 1974–1975 finally forced this growing crisis to the surface, with spending demands shooting upward just as revenues turned sharply down.

It is very probable that many cities and states added to their fiscal problems by imprudent budgeting. New York City budgets for a long time were subject to demands by the strong municipal unions and construction interests. It is very likely that municipal wages and capital projects were tainted by politics. Nevertheless, the real problem did not arise from these obvious errors in fiscal judgment, nor was it unique to New York City. The Big Apple's collapse simply brought into sharp focus a serious national economic problem.

A LIBERAL PROPOSAL

Given this analysis, what is the solution to the so-called fiscal crisis? One obvious alternative is the Conservative proposal to balance the budgets of all governments and end debt expansion. While this sounds easy and attractive, the result would be disastrous. Budgets may indeed be balanced, but at the cost of diminishing the quality of life, with debilitating poverty and deprivation for millions.

Despite glowing reports by Conservatives that Proposition 13 has not hurt California, their evaluation is premature. Touted as a boon to hard-pressed home owners, about two-thirds of the $7 billion in tax relief actually went to landlords and industry. Only action by the state in spending its huge surplus prevented massive job reductions and curtailment of programs. However, the future will reveal the inequities of Proposition 13 thinking. As state sources of income dry up, communities will have to (1) reduce certain essential services or (2) enact highly regressive user fees or sales taxes to finance necessary operations. Both techniques will fall disproportionately upon the lower-income groups who will either lose certain public services or have to pay a larger share of their income for them.

It is indeed possible to shrink the size of local and state government operation or to bias state and local taxing and spending to aid the middle- and upper-income groups, but this will sharpen the sense of income and economic inequality in the United States. The result will not be the idyllic return to a no-government era that Conservatives talk about but the creation of an increasingly unstable social dynamite within society.

The only realistic solution to the fiscal pressures on urban and local governments is to recognize them as national and not just local problems. New York City's poor and unemployed are not simply New York's dilemma, nor is New York's dwindling tax base. These are national responsibilities, and they require national shouldering of them. Several options are available in developing a "new federalism" to equalize the regional unevenness in revenues and outlays. Certain local programs might be funded entirely by the federal government. The most prominent of these are the welfare system and the educational system, which together absorb 45 percent of all state and local expenditures. Federalization of these programs need not mean complete federal control. It could take the form of loosely administered federal revenue-sharing arrangements, though these must go beyond the largely unsuccessful revenue-sharing schemes of the past ten years.

Another area in which regional balance could be restored is that of existing federal taxation and spending. At present, the federal government actually makes regional imbalance worse. A recent state-by-state study of federal spending and taxation reveals that the hard-pressed Northeast and Midwest lose about $40 billion each year to other areas of the country through federal transfers.* Neither region can afford such a drain on its resources.

The Liberal program does shift greater tax burdens to the federal level, but this is essential if we are to eliminate the economic inequalities that have caused the present difficulty. At any rate, added federal taxes should reduce local taxes where the burden is heavy. In undertaxed areas, added costs should not create any great inconvenience, although they will put an end to the present favored fiscal status of such regions.

While we are developing these long-range programs, the federal government should be prepared for short-run emergencies. The machinery for bailing out overburdened urban governments like that of New York City should be established through long-term grants or loans or through federal guarantees of municipal debt.

In the long run, of course, the end of the fiscal problem is possible only if there is general economic expansion. The budget crisis of local governments is really the economic crisis of the whole society in a different form. From a Liberal point of view, the best way to solve it is to stimulate economic expansion and create new jobs throughout the economy. Even if tax burdens and spending were not perfectly equalized, many of the fiscal problems faced by states and cities would at least recede to a point where they could be dealt with locally.

The Radical Argument

As we have argued in earlier discussions of unemployment, inflation, and military spending, fiscal policy in the United States is a captive of the private sector. Contrary to the Conservative argument the

*The National Journal, June 1976.

public sector does not exist independently, with its own bureaucratic objectives. If this is understood, a quite different explanation of the present fiscal crisis emerges. It enables us to see quite clearly how the collapse of New York City and the perpetration of the Proposition 13 hoax can be traced directly to the needs of the business and financial sectors of the economy.

FULFILLING THE NEEDS OF CORPORATE CAPITAL

The growth of government budgets (at all levels) has paralleled the growth of monopoly capital in the United States. Precisely as business has become more centralized, state expenditures and debt at all levels of government have grown. The connection is not accidental. The monopoly elements of the economy have utilized government to perform two important tasks: (1) facilitate capital accumulation, and (2) legitimize the whole system by providing enough social welfare to prevent political disorder.

To carry on these essential tasks, the state has become more and more involved in the entire economy. Whether we look at huge military spending by the federal government or at the highway and education expenses of individual states and localities, all amount to the support of the business sector. The people who build weapons, roads, and schools depend on the state as their source of profits. This, of course, is quite a different scenario for business-government relations than that advanced by the Conservatives or even the Liberals.

In the particular case of state and local governments, it is quite clear that the debt expansion between 1950 and 1975 was almost exclusively for capital spending, provided cheerfully by American business. No one ever heard of a contractor who accepted a job from the state—say the building of a university campus—and then lamented the growth of bonded debt. This was not an evil but a bonanza.

While spending and debt expanded as a direct subsidy to industry, other government spending grew to protect the business system itself. As we have already noted, economic growth in the 1960s was achieved with a dwindling number of workers. This surplus labor became the direct responsibility of the government, of the state in general. To legitimize growing unemployment and income inequality, elaborate and expensive transfer systems had to be developed. By the early

1970s public welfare was the fastest-growing expenditure item in state and local (as well as federal) budgets.

CONTRACTION—ON CAPITAL'S TERMS

As the entire economy began to contract in the early 1970s, the result was an extraordinary demand on government funds, both from corporate capital, which depended on state expenditures, and from a growing surplus labor force, which needed support for its very survival. At the same time, of course, revenues were decreasing. Taxpayer revolts had become common in the late 1960s as governments bit deeper into middle-class incomes. In the growing recession conditions after 1970, revenue pressures and taxpayers' ability to pay were moving in opposite directions. Most state and local governments began to face revenue-expenditure shortfalls that could not be closed by the deficit finance measures resorted to by the federal government. Unable to print money and lacking broad taxation powers, state and local governments could not enlarge their debts without aggravating the situation.

As a direct result, the debt of state and local governments was threatened. Greater budget pressure would have required suspension of debt service unless, of course, more debt was created to refinance present deficits. From the perspective of bankers, this was obviously unwise. In fact, in an economy already carrying $2.5 trillion in public and private financial obligations, debt had itself become a serious problem in the private as well as the public sector. The expansion capacity of debt, which had fueled the economic growth of the post–World War II years, was stretched nearly to its limit. The debt economy was threatened by serious solvency and liquidity problems, not just in state and local governments but in the corporate sector as well.

By 1974 it was obvious to bankers and other capitalists that the government sector, at least at the state and local level, had to be scaled down. Irrespective of its earlier role in providing for capital accumulation and social legitimation of the system, retrenchment was now necessary to protect financial markets. The actions of bankers in closing off credit to these governments effectively drove them to the brink of bankruptcy. But better New York City than General Motors and better a little painful belt tightening than national and international financial collapse—or at least so banker logic ran. Just as the expansion of the government sector had served the needs of corporate capital, so would its enforced contraction.

CORPORATE BENEFITS FROM NEW YORK'S CRISIS AND PROPOSITION 13

In early 1975 the twelve major New York banks alone held $4 billion in bad debts—$2 billion in New York City obligations, $1 billion in loans to hard-pressed airlines, $500 million in bankrupt W. T. Grant and Company loans, and $500 million in loans to other municipalities threatened with bankruptcy. On top of this, the banks held over $11 billion in unguaranteed real estate loans and investment trusts. Meanwhile their protection amounted to only $1.8 billion in reserves and $9.5 billion in other resources. Since bank collapse was a real possibility, the bankers' decision to shut off credit to New York City was predictable.

By holding off credit, the bankers forced the city to go through a series of crises to avoid bankruptcy. As city notes were about to come due, the banks would take up the paper only at the last minute, and then only after gaining concessions from the city and the state. Without going into detail, these scare tactics allowed the banks to obtain the following: (1) access to New York State revenues in case of the city's failure to pay its debt, (2) creation of a new financial agency that would exchange the "worthless" city notes for state-guaranteed bonds paying between 8 and 14 percent tax-free interest, (3) creation of the banker-dominated Emergency Financial Control Board to oversee the city's budget for two years, and (4) a federal loan to buttress the city's ability to pay its debt obligations.

The banks had saved themselves from bankruptcy and, the bankers argued, they had "saved" the city. New Yorkers might wonder about the price. They had seen state and federal funds go directly to support the banks' holdings of New York bonds. Meanwhile wages for city workers were frozen and at least 60,000 lost their jobs. Union pension funds were put up as collateral to support city notes. And, to all intents and purposes, the city surrendered control of its own taxing and spending power to a banker-dominated control board. Meanwhile, New York State was dragged into the whirlpool, as it had to pledge its own tax revenues to support the city's debt service. After it was over, New York City's debt was greater than before, and the cost of its debt service was about four times higher.

All in all, it would be difficult to find a more blatant example of how capital dominates the public sector and how its domination will be used to protect its own interests, not those of the people. New York, of course, was an object lesson, the protagonist in a drama that would have to be played out in varying degrees by other governments. Reduced social services and reduced public payrolls and wages, as well as efforts to increase public sector productivity, would be the more obvious effects of capital's demands. While these moves may be justified as belt tightening, they are an obvious sacrifice of people's needs to the requirements of capital. It is capitalist exploitation in a new guise.

The passage of California's Proposition 13 in a 1978 popular referendum illustrates the extent to which the fiscal crisis can be manipulated for corporate advantage even when voters believe they are acting in their own interest. Tax reductions are, after all, a reasonable and logical demand, especially among middle-income voters whose standards of living are being eroded by both inflation and rising tax bills. But reduced tax revenues must mean the eventual reduction of state services, particularly vital services to the poor and low-income groups. Proposition 13, therefore, set the interests of one part of the working class against another part. This division effectively masked the real winners in the so-called tax reform—business and industry.

The first year of property tax reductions produced a windfall of $3 billion for corporations operating in California. During debates on Proposition 13 many business leaders had promised price reductions for consumers resulting from their tax savings. However, a year after passage, the *Wall Street Journal*, hardly a Radical forum, reported that there was no evidence that any significant proportion of the tax savings had been passed on. By the careful use of people's concerns over the fiscal crisis, business had obtained increased profits. Meanwhile, all segments of the population faced the reality of reduced state services (though, of course, the poor confronted greater problems as state spending contracted).

In summary, the fiscal crisis of the state is not accidental. It is not the result of fast and loose public finance. It is most assuredly not the fault of the people. It is the inevitable outcome of using the public sector to subsidize and maintain private capital. The crisis appears now because the possibility of further mortgaging the society through public debt is simply closed off. Debts sooner or later must be paid off or refinanced. Only economic expansion can facilitate debt retirement, but our expansion is built on debt creation. The fiscal crisis is thus a reflection of general economic contraction. The crisis, however, will be managed by the financial and business community to minimize its effects on them.

The Radical strategy must be to expose the capital-government connection and to oppose the use of state finances to subsidize banks and corporations. Bankruptcy for state and local governments—which really means bankruptcy for the banks—is not without its political benefits from a Radical perspective. After all, "solvency" for New York and tax reductions for California have meant greater economic exploitation of the people, for the benefit of the banks and corporations.

ISSUE 15

Crisis in International Trade
Rising Deficits and Shrinking Dollars

Under a system of a perfectly free commerce, each country
naturally devotes its capital and labor to such employments as
are most beneficial to each. This pursuit of individual advantage
is admirably connected with the universal good of the whole.

David Ricardo, 1817

If nations can learn to provide themselves with full employment
by their domestic policy . . . (i)nternational trade would cease to
be what it is, namely a desperate expedient to maintain employment at home by forcing sales on foreign markets and restricting
purchases which if successful will merely shift the problem of
unemployment to the neighbor.

John Maynard Keynes, 1936

On the whole, capitalism is growing far more rapidly than
before; but this growth is not only becoming more and more
uneven in general, its unevenness also manifests itself, in particular, in the decay of countries richest in capital.

V. I. Lenin, 1916

In the 1950s and 1960s, the world was easier.

Paul A. Volcker, Chairman of the Federal Reserve Board, 1979

THE PROBLEM

Until recently, Americans have not paid much attention to international economic affairs. Displaying a strong sense of insularity, Americans perceived their economy as above or beyond the trade and currency crises that surfaced elsewhere. Since the 1960s all this has changed. Today, Americans, in their roles either as consumers or workers, are well aware of the growth of foreign imports to the United States, the precarious trade balance of the nation, and the international decline of the American dollar's purchasing power.

Indeed, the nation seems to have tumbled a long way from its international economic pinnacle after World War II. At the close of hostilities the United States was the only economy that had escaped the shambles of war and had in fact grown stronger during the war years. Through the late 1940s the United States was exporting two to three times as many goods as it was importing. Even while offering outright grants to rebuild Western Europe, our international balance of payments (the dollar sum of all goods and cash inflows and outflows) remained in surplus. Meanwhile, under the Bretton Woods system,* the American dollar effectively replaced gold as the means of measuring and making international payments. To oversee these international transactions, the International Monetary Fund (IMF) was created. The pound, the franc, the mark, the yen, and all other currencies were valued by the IMF against the dollar. Thus, when a nation experienced domestic inflation that raised the price of its goods relative to those of other nations, it was obliged, for international money exchange purposes, to devalue its currency in relation to the dollar. If, for instance, the British experienced an inflation that doubled the price (in pounds) of British goods, then the only way to bring the inflated British currency into proper balance with unchanged dollars (and other currencies) would be to devalue the pound by one-half. Each dollar would now buy twice as many pounds and twice as much British goods as was possible before the revaluing. If the British did not devalue their currency, trading nations would shun either their products or their currency, and the domestic crisis would be

*Meeting at Bretton Woods, New Hampshire, toward the end of World War II, the Allied powers agreed to an "adjustable-peg" system. While exchange rates for individual currencies were pegged to the dollar, their value in dollar terms could be changed to reflect overvaluation or undervaluation.

worsened. To forestall short-term shortages of funds for international payments and to avoid the anarchy of devaluation wars as each nation sought to gain a brief currency advantage over others, the trading nations maintained reserve balances with the International Monetary Fund or could borrow from the fund. Meanwhile, the fund pegged currencies to the dollar, adjusting values from time to time as economic conditions within nations changed. So long as the dollar was sound, the problems of inflation or unemployment could be limited to the affected country.

The system's weakness, however, was what everyone had thought to be its strength—the dollar. During the 1950s the United States began to experience chronic deficits in its balance of payments: we owed more each year than others owed us. By the late 1960s and early 1970s the deficits had become staggering (almost $30 billion in 1971). Table 15.1 illustrates how the payment accounting is set up and what it looked like in 1977 (the worst balance of payments year in our history).

The primary factors in the worsening payment situation were: (1) overseas military and economic spending by the U.S. government, (2) continued movement of U.S. private capital to overseas investment, (3) the greatly increased productivity of foreign labor and capital, (4) the rising prices of U.S. goods relative to foreign goods, and (5) the incredible increase in the cost of oil imports after OPEC's 1973 price hike. With foreigners now holding more dollars than they wanted—dollars that were believed overvalued by the old Bretton Woods pegging system—the United States was forced to take action. On August 15, 1971, President Nixon suspended the dollar's convertibility to gold. At the time foreign dollar holdings were four times greater than the value of the U.S. gold stock, the price of which was then officially stated as $35 per ounce. Gold henceforth became a speculative commodity having no official

Table 15.1   U.S. Balance of Payments, 1977 (in billions of dollars)

Basic transactions	Amount
Exports of goods and services	+177
Imports of goods and services	−192
Balance of trade (exports + imports)	− 15
Net unilateral transfers from U.S.	− 5
Net capital movement from U.S.	− 12
Surplus or deficit in balance of payments	− 32

Source: Department of Commerce, *Survey of Current Business.*

role in international payments. By early 1980 its commodity price had climbed to over $800 an ounce.

After the United States ceased gold conversion, there were periodic efforts to revalue the dollar under the old pegging system. However, even after several devaluations of the dollar, it became obvious that the era of fixed exchange rates was over. Each nation now let its currency "float" to whatever value the market established, and neither gold nor U.S. dollars served as the international currency. Instead, the IMF kept national payment accounts in order through a kind of "paper gold" (SDRs, or Special Drawing Rights), which were made available to members on a quota system. The value of the paper gold is based upon an average of sixteen different nations' currencies.

While the advantages and disadvantages of such a floating system of exchange rates are a matter of some disagreement among economists, there is agreement that the present "managed floating system" has not ended special trade and dollar problems of the United States. The nation is still plagued by trade deficits ($34 billion in 1978) and depreciating dollars. (Between 1970 and 1978 the dollar's value had fallen against the mark, the yen, and the Swiss franc by 40, 35, and 55 percent respectively.) As Table 15.2 shows, the dollar has continued its decline.

Strategies to end the balance of payments and dollar crisis, as well as explanations for the crisis itself, vary among economists. Moreover,

Table 15.2 Percentage Change in the Value of the U.S. Dollar in Relation to Selected Foreign Currencies, Year Ended August 31, 1978

Currency	Percentage change
Swiss franc	−31.50%
Japanese yen	−29.65
German mark	−14.15
Belgian franc	−12.16
French franc	−11.31
British pound	−10.39
Mexican peso	− 0.71
Canadian dollar	+ 3.55
Brazilian cruzeiro	+21.30
Average of fifteen currencies*	− 9.15

Source: American Enterprise Institute Newsletter, April, 1979.

*Currencies of fifteen major industrial countries, weighted by U.S. trade with each, as computed by Morgan Guaranty Trust Co.

as we shall see next, any effort to solve these international economic problems has serious domestic repercussions. No longer are we withdrawn from international economic issues.

SYNOPSIS Conservatives argue that U.S. trade and currency problems are traceable to protectionism, pegged exchange rates, and ill-conceived domestic economic policy. Liberals oppose the Conservative remedy of free trade and floating exchange rates, maintaining that the cost in terms of jobs and industrial decline in the United States would surpass any benefits. They hold that only stimulation of the domestic economy will assure international vitality. To Radicals, the present international trade and finance problems of the United States are a gauge of the nation's decline from power and a further measure of the chronic capitalist crisis of production and distribution.

The Conservative Argument

Perhaps the severest test of commitment to a free and open capitalist economy arises with respect to international trade and finance. Economists, politicians, and especially business leaders who perceive the advantages of competition and the market and who ardently oppose any type of controls or intervention in domestic activities are ever tempted to abandon their philosophy at the national borders. Perhaps it is a narrow nationalism or a basic parochialism in economic thought, but the logic of free markets is too easily abandoned when international issues are raised. For the consistent Conservative, however, there should be no exception in such a case. Free economic arrangements are as crucial internationally as they are domestically.

THE NECESSITY OF FREE TRADE

The first requirement for a free trade arrangement is the elimination of all tariffs, quotas, and bilateral or multilateral trade agreements that inhibit the free operation of international markets. Each nation must be free to sell its goods to any other, and each nation must be open to any other's goods. Regrettably, however, the desire for protectionism runs very deep among nations. This remnant of outmoded mercantilist philosophy persistently reappears when one nation gains a production or price advantage over another in a particular product or line of products. In the United States it appears when firms or industries act as special interest groups lobbying Congress to raise duties on hated imports or to set quotas on these imports. Supposedly, by limiting the ability of foreign firms to compete through price or other means, the American industry's position is enhanced.

Ironically (in terms of the long-run effects), labor unions in affected industries very often ally themselves with the corporation in their lobbying effort. For example, in 1976 the United Steel Workers joined with industry to urge import restraints on certain "specialty steel" items. From the union's point of view, the object is always to protect jobs. The real outcome is quite different, however, for several reasons.

First, protectionism is costly. It raises the prices of imported goods for all consumers or artificially holds up the price of competing domestic goods. This may mean jobs and income for steelworkers and steel companies in Gary, Indiana, but it means reduced buying power and lost jobs elsewhere. Tariffs and quotas have not protected American earnings but have merely redistributed income and jobs and raised prices for everybody.

Second, protectionism encourages inefficiency. Without the incentive provided by competition, neither business nor labor are induced to increase productivity or to modernize production techniques. In turn, consumers must pay for an industry's protected inefficiency, which can be quite costly over time, since it tends to grow cumulatively. The limits on foreign competition are very often increased as the production gaps between a vibrant overseas producer and a lethargic domestic industry grow.

Third, protectionism invites retaliation. Other nations will be induced to follow the same protectionist path if their goods are effectively priced out of our domestic markets. Thus, we may find the threat of foreign steel eliminated at the cost of being unable to sell U.S. tractors in foreign markets. The ultimate result is the end of trade altogether.

Aside from the usual tariff and trade-quota solutions to the balance of payments crisis, some Liberal economists have encouraged direct government controls over American capital outflow. Practically disregarding the favorable effect on the balance of payments of inflows of foreign earnings by U.S. businesses, many Liberals have incorrectly singled out the export of U.S. capital as a primary cause for balance of payment deficits. Their shortsighted cure is to restrict U.S. overseas investment. Beginning in 1964, through special taxes on American purchases of foreign securities, overseas investment has been discouraged. As with all protectionist actions, the effect has been counterproductive for the economy. American businesses are placed at a competitive disadvantage in world markets at precisely the time when they should be strengthened.

Free trade and free overseas movement of U.S. capital may indeed mean the end of some American industries and may throw some workers out of jobs. However, other production possibilities are opened. Let the Koreans concentrate on toy or textile production and the United States exploit its computer technology. Indeed, let each nation develop its comparative advantages so that trade between the two is possible.

Milton Friedman has emphasized the significance of a commitment to free trade this way:

> There are few measures we could take that would do more to promote the cause of freedom at home and abroad. Instead of making grants to foreign governments in the name of economic aid—and thereby promoting socialism—while at the same time imposing restrictions on the products they succeed in producing—and thereby hindering free enterprise—we could assume a consistent and principled stance. We could say to the rest of the world: We believe in freedom and intend to practice it. No one can force you to be free. That is your business. But we can offer you full co-operation on equal terms to all. Our market is open to you. Sell here what you can and wish to. Use the proceeds to buy what you wish. In this way co-operation among individuals can be world wide yet free.*

THE NECESSITY OF FLOATING
EXCHANGE RATES

The other side of the free trade coin is the establishment of freely floating exchange rates. Indeed, the two *must* proceed together.

In the past, pegged currency exchanges, which were established to create international financial order, have had precisely the opposite effect. For the United States the pegged exchange rate meant maintaining an overvalued dollar. The result was a growing balance of payments deficit during the 1960s and 1970s. Under a pegged system the only options to eliminate the balance of payments deficits were: (1) to pay out gold to creditors (so long as we were on an international gold standard), (2) to engineer a domestic recession to lower import demand and reduce the prices of exported goods (thus increasing export volume), (3) to establish import controls, or (4) to resort to an official devaluation of the nation's currency. For a variety of reasons each of these options has such serious political or economic effects that the balance of payments deficit could not be eliminated. As a result, the worsening U.S. payments situation through the early 1970s was directly traceable to the Bretton Woods–IMF system of fixed exchange rates.

*Milton Friedman, *Capitalism and Freedom* (Chicago: University of Chicago Press, 1962), p. 74.

Furthermore, the flow of dollars into European markets and the effects of U.S. government efforts to impose exchange controls created extensive internal currency problems for all nations. The initial flood of U.S. dollars and the attempt to maintain the value of these dollars forced an unwanted inflation on many European nations as their central banks purchased all dollars presented to them.

Flexible exchange rates, however, will eliminate balance of payments deficits and associated problems. The market forces of supply and demand for a nation's currency will create an equilibrium. Assume that two nations are trading. An excess of imports over exports in nation A will bid up the price of the exporting nation B's currency (or lower the value of the importer's currency relative to that of the exporter). The importing nation A's currency is now devalued. However, this means its goods are now lower-priced than before, and its exports to B will rise while its imports from B will fall until equilibrium between the two trading nations is reached.

From a Conservative point of view, the abandonment of pegged exchange rates and the international gold standard has freed international trade from some of the tyrannies of the past. Gold prices may fluctuate as a matter of speculative supply and demand. Floating exchange rates can reflect increasingly the real value of a nation's currency against that of other nations. However, this latter situation has not yet been attained. The present managed float system still allows member nations great latitude in determining their own exchange rates and in taking individual actions to bolster their currency. Until exchange rates are freely flexible and until free trade principles are generally accepted, international trade and currency crises will continue.

THE INTERNATIONAL CRISIS AS FAILURE
OF DOMESTIC POLICIES

Before turning from the question of the international trade and money crisis of the United States, it is necessary to point out that the problems are primarily an extension of domestic macroeconomic policies. The economy's bias toward expansionary fiscal and monetary policy triggered the inflation that priced American exports out of foreign markets. Any solution to our trade problem demands initially that we begin to pay the piper. Domestic inflation, accompanied by growing deficits in international payments balances, requires a contractionary domestic policy. The cost is a reduced rate of economic growth, thus lessening income growth and employment, but the long-run effect will be to restore economic order.

The Liberal Argument

Conservative proposals for free trade and freely flexible exchange rates as solutions to American trade and international currency problems sound seductively simple and logical. They fail, however, to grasp the economic world as it is—incredibly complex and unresponsive to quick and simplistic solutions. As we shall see, the elimination, or even the relaxation, of either domestic or international administrative controls over trade and exchange arrangements will produce immediate short-term problems and no assurance that a favorable equilibrium in trade conditions will result.

THE CASE FOR MODIFIED PROTECTIONISM

Conservatives would have us believe that the United States has recklessly followed high-tariff protectionism. In point of fact, U.S. tariffs have steadily fallen since World War II and stand at historic lows. Duties collected amount to less than 10 percent of the value of imports. Forty years ago duties stood at about 60 percent. Moreover, the U.S. government has conducted, since the Kennedy years, serious trade negotiations to reduce restrictive tariffs and import quotas throughout the trading world.

But reduction of trade restraints must be a two-way street. Reductions of restrictions on U.S. goods should be expected from nations desiring or obtaining benefits from the United States. Otherwise, the United States throws its doors open to foreign goods while our own are effectively excluded from foreign ports. Nor are tariffs and quotas the only devices nations use for creating trade advantages. The Japanese, for instance, have provided extensive governmental subsidies for their manufacturers, thus creating artificially low prices. Their notorious "dumping" of such underpriced commodities as TVs, cameras, specialty steel items, and the like must cease or the United States will be obliged to take restrictive trade actions.

When these real-world obstacles to trade are considered, it is apparent that the road to free trade is much bumpier than Conservatives admit. And, apart from the difficulty of inducing all trading nations to accept the principles of free trade (which would be a minimum requirement even under Conservative logic), the serious domestic problems that might follow the hurried or reckless adoption of free trade must be considered.

First, the ending of all protective tariffs might deal a death blow to many American industries. Among these would be firms that are critical to our capacity to defend ourselves militarily or to our continued economic well-being if world trade was interrupted in the future. In brief, the military and political significance of self-sufficiency in certain goods and raw materials would out-weigh the free trade argument of greater efficiency resulting from free trade.

Second, concentrating production efforts only in those industrial areas where a nation may have a comparative trade advantage would tend to create an incomplete and possibly unstable economy. As our own production mix became more specialized and concentrated, we would become more vulnerable (not stronger as Conservatives argue) when there was any interruption in world markets. The serious impact that overseas shortages of critical goods might have domestically is amply demonstrated currently by the crisis caused by the OPEC energy cartel. Similarly, we might experience interruptions in the purchase of our specialized production when buyers disappeared. The result would be massive layoffs and recession at home.

Third, and closely associated with the first two points, free trade might have the effect of closing off the development of new ("infant") industries. Already established firms would enjoy marketing and capital advantages that could not be overcome. Limited tariff protection would allow new industries to emerge and mature.

Fourth, and probably the most well-known argument against absolute trade freedom, American firms might be priced out of the market by cheaper foreign labor or by foreign dumping, causing domestic economic upheaval and unemployment. In the short run, free trade would probably produce massive unemployment in such basic industries as steel and autos. Even if, in the long run, new industries emerged to fill the employment gap, billions would be spent on unemployment insurance, welfare, and job retraining. Whole areas of the nation would be disrupted as our nation's production mix changed. Such costs would more than offset the efficiency advantages proposed by Conservatives.

A frequent and persuasive argument of free traders on behalf of eliminating tariff and quota protections is that restricted trade is inflationary. Presumably, consumers pay more for higher-priced and protected U.S. goods or heavily taxed or scarce foreign goods. The argument fails to take a broad macro view of the problem. If we correctly calculated the costs of recklessly abandoning all trade protection, we would see that free trade would be inflationary. The economic burdens taxpayers would have to shoulder to sustain displaced labor and encourage areas of economic production in which we possessed advantages would be far greater than the tariffs presently paid.

SOLVING THE PROBLEMS OF PAYMENTS IMBALANCES AND EXCHANGE RATES

The international payments and exchange problems of the United States call for maintaining market controls, not developing anarchic "free floating" exchange rates. The chronic payments imbalance of the United States is not simply a matter of money and its value, as the Conservatives maintain. Rather, it reflects the need to create a productive and fully employed economy at home. Public policies aimed at stimulating economic growth (see Issues 10 and 11) are the only long-run solutions.

Aside from the appropriate fiscal and monetary policies for growth and stabilization discussed earlier, government should encourage greater American productivity. New research and development and the broader use of new kinds of technology are critical. Public policy should encourage American firms in these areas. At the same time the huge multinationals should be discouraged both from making massive capital transfers to overseas plants and from exporting technology since these erode our trade position by creating our own foreign competition.

Some other short-term actions that would improve our balance of payments include: (1) asking other developed nations to take up the cost of their own defense rather than depending on the United States to pay the cost of NATO and other defense systems; (2) having these nations increase their aid to developing nations, thus allowing the United States to reduce its overseas transfers; and (3) requiring nations that have trade surpluses with the United States to increase their direct trade with us and to remove all tariffs and quotas on U.S. goods. The last point seems quite obvious, but many nations now having a trade surplus purposely exclude U.S. goods. While protection is defensible, prohibitive tariff restrictions by nations with a trade surplus have the overall effect of "theft."

Of course, the fundamental cause of our current trade and payments imbalances is OPEC. Failure to see this fact has led many observers to encourage more radical trade and currency policies than is justified. Oil alone accounts for 40 percent of our imports. An energy policy that shifted us away from dependence on foreign oil would eliminate our trade imbalance almost overnight.

By looking at trade problems in light of the above, it becomes apparent that the current balance of payments crisis does not stem from a basic failure of our mixed economy. The present situation certainly does not prove the need for free trade and flexible exchange rates, as the Conservatives contend. Indeed, to provide order in international transactions and to avoid the violent price swings that freely flexible exchange rates would create, stronger (not weaker) international money management is needed. Creation of a standardized international currency (which Keynes would have called "Bancor"), establishment of an agency within the IMF to make short-term loans to nations in balance of payments distress, and improvement in the process of setting and adjusting currency exchange rates would bring stability to international money markets. The current practice of hedging and speculating in national currencies, which always worsens the balance of payments problem, would then become less frequent. With greater order provided by these changes, we might then attack our balance of payments problems effectively.

CHOOSING BETWEEN DOMESTIC AND INTERNATIONAL PRIORITIES

Probably the most significant problem posed by free trade and floating exchange rates is that the domestic economy is subordinated to international economic affairs. Policies aimed at correcting balance of payments and exchange problems may actually worsen domestic problems. For instance, unemployment in the United States would have to grow and an extended domestic recession would be required as the price of ending our international payments deficit.

Free traders may resolve this conflict between needed expansionary policies at home and the required contractionary actions to put our international payments in balance by glibly saying, "We must bite the bullet." Matters are not that simple. Indeed, the contraction might be so unbearable as to trigger extensive political reaction in the United States that would destroy not only our political institutions but even the market economy so beloved by Conservatives.

Perhaps, the easiest way to resolve the problems that exist is to be pragmatic. How big is the domestic economic problem of stagnation? How big is the international problem of payments imbalance? Since foreign trade amounts to only 10 to 12 percent of our GNP, it seems self-evident that domestic economic problems demand attention first, whatever their international effect. To do otherwise, as one economist has put it, "would be to let the tail wag the dog."*

The Radical Argument

While the Conservative and Liberal scenarios of international trade and exchange problems seem to be quite different, a closer examination indicates they are similar. Both arguments accept, as a matter of fact, the continued domination of the United States in world trade. The remedies that they suggest for current problems, whether it be the free trade approach of the Conservative or the administrative emphasis of the Liberals, are primarily intended to restore and strengthen the American position. Moreover, their underestimation of the significance of international trade and finance and of the degree of crisis now existing in these areas is a dangerous error of judgment.

Capitalist nations do not trade and expand their international influence merely "to improve efficiency" or "to benefit mutually from each nation's exploitation of its comparative advantage." Profit making, pure and simple, is the engine that drives overseas trade and investment. Indeed, the overseas search for markets, cheap resources, and profitable investment is absolutely essential for any capitalist system's continued expansion. Rather than trade and international economic affairs being mere aspects of capitalism, as Conservatives and Liberals suggest, they are the central *features* of modern production-

*Campbell R. McConnell, *Economics: Principles, Problems, and Policies*, 7th ed. (New York: McGraw-Hill, 1977), p. 918.

for-profit economies. The international trade and exchange crisis is thus the result of the insatiable drive of individual capitalist nations to exploit the rest of the world for their own gains.

THE RISE OF THE AMERICAN EMPIRE

While Americans tend to think of themselves as reluctant internationalists drawn into world affairs only to save the rest of the world from itself, the facts support quite a different explanation. By the turn of the twentieth century, American capitalism had really exhausted its domestic markets. The long decade of depression in the 1890s suggested to many the need for overseas expansion either to obtain markets for our surplus goods or to gain access to cheap raw materials and foreign labor. The United States steadily enlarged its world trade between the 1890s and the 1960s, exporting ever-larger amounts of expensive manufactured goods and importing greater quantities of cheap raw materials. At the same time, to secure markets and assume control over raw materials, Americans exported vast amounts of capital (see Table 15.3).

The old trading powers of Europe exhausted themselves in two world wars, which had been fundamentally economic wars for trade

Table 15.3   Value of Overseas U.S. Investment, Selected Years, 1880–1978 (in billions of dollars)

Year	Amount
1880	$ 1.6
1890	2.9
1900	2.5
1914	3.5
1920	7.0
1930	17.2
1940	12.2
1950	19.0
1960	40.2
1970	75.5
1978	175.2

Source: U.S. Bureau of Census, *Historical Statistics of the United States,* and *Economic Report of the President,* 1979.

supremacy, while the United States continued to expand its overseas sales, purchases, and investment. By the 1960s the United States, in terms of comparative development, had reached the peak of its international economic power.

In 1950 U.S. gross domestic output was about equal to that of the rest of the world combined. Great Britain's output was only 13 percent of this country's, while that of France, West Germany, and Japan was 10, 8, and 4 percent respectively. During World War II, the United States, as principal supplier of arms, had accumulated almost the entire world's gold stock as well as many other overseas assets. Our exports accounted for about one-third of all the world's exports and more than a quarter of all manufactured exports.

Meanwhile, as a result of Marshall Plan aid and other dollar grants to "free" European economies, other capitalist nations fell into a simple client relationship with the United States. Dependent economically on aid and trade programs and militarily (in the cold war years) on America's armed forces and mutual defense treaties (such as NATO) that were dominated by the United States, the older capitalist nations became part of the American economic sphere. At the same time, the United States expanded its penetration into the Third World, establishing a new, informal colonial system. Within this imperial system the resource-rich remnants of the former European colonial empire in Africa and Asia joined Latin America as part of our sphere of influence. Through development aid and especially through the habit of supporting friendly repressive regimes with military assistance, the United States established a neocolonial system that included emerging nations without resorting to the old tactic of territorial seizure.

By the late 1960s a *Pax Americana* had been established. West European and Japanese economies and much of the Third World were under American economic hegemony. Supposedly international agencies such as the International Monetary Fund and the World Bank, as well as the United Nations, became arms of American foreign economic and political policy. Under such conditions it is small wonder that the American dollar became the international medium of exchange and that the international financial situation of the United States appeared so secure. We could virtually dictate exchange rates, and we could hide any balance of payments problem by compelling foreign governments to accept and hold dollars rather than demand gold. The ultimate fall from this pinnacle of international power was to be a terrifying experience for Americans.

THE COLLAPSE OF THE EMPIRE

The fall from power was speeded by events overseas and at home. First, the Soviet challenge failed to disappear. The Soviet economy rose swiftly from the ruins of World War II. Despite the Korean War and dozens of other cold war confrontations, the power of cold war ideology in holding the American–West European alliance together waned as Europeans reevaluated their position within the American empire. This, as much as anything, directed Europe to a more middle-ground approach.

Second, the European economies made their own rapid recoveries in the 1960s. By 1972 Western Europe's and Japan's combined gross domestic output exceeded that of the United States. Accordingly, the U.S. share of world markets declined drastically. Between 1950 and 1972 our share of passenger vehicle production fell from 82 to 29 percent; similarly, steel production fell from 55 to 20 percent, and energy production from 50 to 33 percent. At the same time, the other industrial nations began to claim larger shares of the American market. Finished manufactured imports increased almost 300 percent between 1965 and 1970, while U.S. exports of manufactured goods grew by only 80 percent in the same period.

Third, U.S. domination of the Third World declined. Wars of national liberation and the emergence of new regimes committed to an independent political course destroyed the *Pax Americana*. The failure of our effort in Vietnam to stem the tide of Third World nationalism only accelerated the decline of the empire. By 1973 the United States was helpless in dealing with the OPEC embargo. In 1979 it could only stand aside quietly as Iran, perhaps one of the most important parts of our earlier neocolonial system, threw out its pro-American government.

Fourth, the emergence of American multinational corporations further weakened the United States. The flight of U.S. capital overseas to the expanding economies in Europe and the Third World accelerated the decline of the U.S. balance of payments. The multinationals' flight left investment and employment gaps at home, with which the nation was ill prepared to deal. By 1971 the United States registered the first trade imbalance in the century as imports exceeded exports.

A GRIM SCENARIO

For a nation long accustomed to world domination, the future is not bright. The revitalization of other capitalist nations raises the old specter of capitalist trade wars, which, after all, have already led to two world wars in this century. International trade competition increases, and it threatens to set capitalist nation against capitalist nation. In the United States, as foreign imports erode the nation's balance of payments and cause domestic unemployment, protection is again championed, and protection has always been the first step in the breakdown of international trade and the appearance of worldwide depression.

Meanwhile, the industrial nations' dependence upon the raw materials of the Third World has grown precisely as Third World independence has increased. Because of U.S. dependence on the rest of the world for most of its iron ore and petroleum and practically all of its lead and bauxite (items in which we were self-sufficient four decades ago), this country is vulnerable to political and economic crises beyond its control.

As the political and economic strength of the United States declines, the balance of payments problem worsens, and favorable American exchange rates cannot be sustained. The cost of importing grows, but the need for imports also grows. As a result, prices for American goods continue to rise, stimulating domestic inflation and further worsening our international trade position. To cover these costs, an increasingly devalued dollar floods international financial centers, endangering liquidity throughout the capitalist world. This country's trading partners are obliged to accept our growing international debt or risk a world financial crisis. If American dollars failed to attract holders, the entire capitalist international financial structure would topple. Thus "business as usual" is carried on by international bankers simply to protect themselves. It is necessary to pretend that everything is fine so that it will be. But, the increase of U.S. debt, which causes inflation throughout the capitalist world, cannot go on forever. As one British observer has argued, "America is the centre of what is potentially the most dangerous monetary and trading crisis since 1931."*

From a Radical perspective the problem was predictable. The internationalization of capital is only a further step in capitalism's irrational development. The strength of the American overseas economic operations of the 1950s and 1960s was the result of its power to exploit the so-called free world. This country's gains were others' losses. What we saw as a normal situation was an exceptional one. As our capacity to exploit has been challenged by other capitalist economies, by the development of socialist countries, and by Third World independence, our premiere position in world trade and finance has declined. As overseas growth ends, domestic contraction sets in. The specter of another worldwide capitalist depression looms larger. The crisis is, of course, a production crisis—too many goods and too few buyers. It cannot be resolved by dealing purely with money, balance of payments, and exchange rates. Rather than being the causes of our international economic crisis, our balance of payments and exchange problems merely reflect the basic production-distribution problem of the capitalist system. Neither free trade nor protection, and neither floating exchange rates nor pegged rates, offers a long-term solution. Conservative and Liberal solutions are equally irrelevant.

*Manchester Guardian Weekly, August 25, 1973.

ISSUE 16

National Economic Planning
Is Central Control Inevitable?

In area after area of our national life, we have adopted
policies that unnecessarily threaten the integrity of the individual. . . . There runs through them the common element:
the substitution of bureaucratic organization and control
for market arrangements, the rejection of Adam Smith's great
insight.

Milton Friedman, 1970

The premise that under presently existing circumstances,
the country has to husband its resources more carefully, allocate
them more prudently, and match its financial capabilities with
its social priorities would appear to be worth considering.
What many will call state planning would, to the average
family, be no more than prudent budgeting.

A New York Banker, 1974

Whenever the legislature attempts to regulate the differences
between the masters and their workmen, its counsellors are
always the masters.

Adam Smith, 1776

THE PROBLEM

After studying the economic problems we have discussed in the foregoing chapters, the reader knows that, irrespective of the particular ideological positions expressed, in the real world the "burning issues" of our society and economy have created a more active and vastly enlarged federal role. From the energy crisis to unemployment, from inflation to welfare, government administrative intervention and controls have been constantly enlarging. While the desirability of the direction can be debated by partisans, there is little denying that the local and individual choices of the alleged "good old days" have been replaced by federal administrative constraints.

According to studies by opinion samplers, this development is highly unpopular with most Americans. Nevertheless, independent of the opinions of the people and the rhetoric of their politicians, there is a growing discussion of national economic planning as the only rational way to deal with our complex economic problems. Obviously, effective (not necessarily to be equated with "good") national economic planning would require the extension, not reduction, of government economic and political power. Such planning as is currently being discussed in business, labor, and professional economics circles is not merely another ad hoc effort to resolve a particular problem. It concerns not just an ICC to look after the railroad problem or an energy commission to deal with energy use. National economic planning in its broadest sense presupposes the creation of machinery that will *direct* the whole economy—its macroeconomic performance and to some degree its microeconomic parts—in a rationally calculated way.

Given popular attitudes and political realities, it is highly unlikely that sweeping national planning will be enacted quickly in the United States. If and when it comes, it will come by small increments. In 1976 two bills were introduced in Congress that, in their original form, might have laid the foundation for central planning of the economy—the Humphrey-Javits and the Humphrey-Hawkins resolutions. While neither of these bills would have created the "command" type of economy associated with the Soviet Union and capitalist Japan, they would have moved the United States well beyond the piecemeal regulations and controls that now characterize federal intervention in economic affairs.

Under these proposals a number of immediate steps were called for. First, economic data collection was to be vastly enlarged so that a massive input-output matrix could be constructed to indicate all interindustry, perhaps interfirm, flows of resources, capital, labor, and finished products. Thus, the impact of one discrete event—for example, an oil embargo or a strike—could be calculated on all economic activity. Second, under the Humphrey-Javits bill, an Economic Planning Board was to be created in the Executive Office of the President. Its function was to set economic targets or goals, both microeconomic and macroeconomic. This planning, of course, would be based on economic data and on objectives recommended by Congress and the president. For instance, priorities for mass transit, housing, and the like would be calculated against their effects on industry, labor, and capital, and plans would be drawn accordingly.

A third step in the proposed legislation, specified in the original Humphrey-Hawkins bill, was to update the Employment Act of 1946. As we have noted earlier, this law committed the government only to attaining "maximum feasible" employment. Under the original Humphrey-Hawkins proposal, full employment was defined as 3 percent unemployment, government being directed to attain this goal by fiscal and monetary devices and, failing this, by acting as the employer of last resort.

After extensive debate, the Humphrey-Hawkins Full Employment and Balanced Growth Act passed the Senate by a 70 to 19 margin in October 1978. As the overwhelming vote for the initially controversial piece of legislation showed, political compromise had had its way with this effort to lay the foundation for national economic planning. The idea of input-output data collection was dropped. The separate planning board was abandoned, and the president and Congress were merely to "coordinate" actions with the Federal Reserve Board. While the act did specify the reduction of adult unemployment to 3 percent and all unemployment to 4 percent by 1983, the president could change the timetable, and no specific programs were established to attain the goals.

None of this sounds as if we are about to be transformed into a completely regulated state and society. However, both defenders and opponents of national economic planning point out that this is only a beginning. Each side, of course, has its own views as to what conditions will develop in the future as planning processes grow. Will planning mean direct interference with or extinction of, private capitalist activity? Will legislated full employment solve the jobs and income problem? Is planning on the national level the final and necessary step to bring the piecemeal regulation of our mixed public-private economy together into a national whole? Or is planning merely the last fitful spasm of an economic system that can no longer pretend that capitalism works?

The debate is only beginning, but under the pressures of a growing agenda of national economic issues it is one that will certainly grow in intensity as time passes.

SYNOPSIS For Conservatives the adoption of national economic planning would mean the ending of capitalism as a social system and the imposition of an inefficient dictatorship in its place. Liberals, however, see planning as compatible with our mixed capitalist economy, since the essential elements of the system (private property and economic and political freedom) would actually be enhanced by the increased stability planning would provide. To be sure, Liberals advocate only a limited system of planning. Radicals, meanwhile, see present planning proposals only as efforts to maintain the present inequalities and exploitativeness of the capitalist system. To them planning is essential, but the planning must be done at the level of human needs, not those of the corporation.

The Conservative Argument

At this stage in our discussion of contemporary economic problems, the Conservative response to the idea of national economic planning should be obvious—or, perhaps it would be better to say, familiar. National economic planning, in the sense that it means non-market, administrative decisions on output, pricing, employment, capital, and so on, is to be opposed as vigorously as possible. Planning is the final collectivist victory over freedom and individualism. When economic-political authorities, whether they be fascists or communists or even well-meaning Liberals, have the authority to determine all important matters in the economy, there is little else left in life that is beyond their ability to control. *Brave New World* and *1984* are no longer merely science fiction.

The economic criticism of central planning is fairly quickly summarized. First of all, it is profoundly inefficient in terms of theoretical economic principles. Second, empirical evidence on efforts at national economic planning (and it is abundant) proves that such planning is ineffective.

NATIONAL PLANNING: THEORETICALLY INEFFICIENT

As we know, under a market system, prices are the signals for economic activity. The decision to produce a particular good can be calculated both in terms of the actual production costs in labor, capital, or resources, and in terms of what that particular good costs compared to other goods. As long as the market designates the prices of the factors of production (labor, capital, and resources) and the prices of final goods, we have a rational calculus. As consumers or producers, we can make choices based upon a steady and reliable set of indicators. This is not to say that prices will not fluctuate. Of course they will. They are supposed to fluctuate to show changes in demand and supply and thus changes in the cost structure or in consumer satisfaction.

Far from being anarchistic, the market is a planning mechanism. The market works like a system and, as Adam Smith observed in an essay on astronomy written long before his *Wealth of Nations*, "A system is like a little machine." Like a machine, a market "planned" economy has regulators that keep it in balance.

Administrative planning, on the other hand, has no natural internal or external checks on its effectiveness. In an administered economy, levels of output, employment, and the mix of goods are purely matters of political determination. It is not really important whether these goals are set by commissars, Harvard economists, or the duly elected representatives of the people; they are the result of human judgments. They reflect particular individual or collective biases. Not even a computer can tell what output and employment goals are "correct" unless it is programed (by humans) to respond to certain criteria (selected by humans).

Defenders of planning may point out that high levels of growth and employment have been attained in certain planned economies. There is some truth to this, but the argument misses the point. Administrative planning in the Soviet Union during World War II and afterward, and in developing nations more recently, was bound to have some success because of their very primitive level of economic development. When you have nothing and plan something, you can hardly lose, especially if you have authoritarian control over the labor force. It is quite another matter, however, to maintain efficient administrative planning in an advanced and complex economy. (Lately the Soviets have found this out.)

Like market economies, most administered ones use prices to direct economic activity toward predetermined goals. But it should be remembered that these prices, like the goals themselves, are administratively determined. Prices therefore do not reflect costs as we speak of them but are merely a rationing technique used to direct labor, capital, output, and, ultimately, social behavior to certain objectives.

Space prohibits a more detailed theoretical attack on the output and pricing behavior of planned economies, but a brief survey of some of the problems encountered by them may demonstrate the essence of the Conservative critique.

NATIONAL PLANNING: INEFFECTIVE IN PRACTICE

The Soviet Union is a striking example of what can happen when economic mechanisms are subordinated to clearly political objectives.

Not unlike the implied long-run objectives of Humphrey-Hawkins, Soviet goals also include full employment, enforced price stability, and specific production targets for certain goods.

In the Soviet case, full employment means a job for everyone. In an authoritarian collectivist society this is not a great problem, but there is a big difference between putting people in jobs and having them perform productively. For instance, Soviet plant managers, given output goals by state planners (which must be met or else), may fear a shortage of labor in the future and so "hoard" workers. On other occasions they may have to hire labor as directed by state authorities, whether or not they need it. In either case, the workers in question will be underemployed. In terms of economic analysis, the result is obvious. Workers are hired without any view to their productivity. Wages are set by state planners, who have little or no knowledge of costs of production at a plant. Thus, managers may reach their output targets, with workers "fully employed," but the actual cost of goods (as reckoned by alternative uses of labor and capital) may be much higher than the planners can cover in setting a price. In real terms this means that the whole society must pay the actual costs by forgoing other goods. An inefficiently made tractor may "cost" many thousands of nonproduced consumer items.

The tendency to think only in output (quantitative) terms has qualitative effects, too. Production rushed to meet a planner's goal may encourage defective and shoddy manufacture. Quick and flexible adaptation of production to meet changes in goals is very difficult. Planners lack the signals of prices based on supply and demand to tell them when and how to change the production mix. Plans become rigid, at both the plant and planning levels.

Many of the worst features of central planning have been improved in the past ten years by the introduction of linear programming, input-output analysis, and computers. The incredible lapses of mind that led to production of motor vehicles but not the needed ball bearings for their wheels are now rather rare. In many respects Soviet industry and technology are very advanced. Nevertheless, microeconomic decision making is still hampered by the political administration of prices, wages, and output goals. After years of sacrifice to build the industrial base of the society, ordinary Soviet citizens remain as they always have been, the balancing item in the central plan ledger. The errors of planners, even those with computers, are paid for in relinquished consumer goods and a scarcely improving standard of living. Overarching all of this, of course, is the virtual absence of individual freedom, economic or political.

A LAST WORD

All of this argument may be considered an overreaction to the comparatively innocuous Humphrey-Hawkins Act. To Conservatives, though, the threat of planning is quite real. Talk of national economic planning goes back a long way in American history, and, as is evident in day-to-day government reaction to the issues discussed in this book, the tendency toward collectivist solutions to all economic problems is growing, not diminishing. History shows that, once commenced, the march toward collectivism is hard to reverse. Today we may be talking merely of obtaining additional data for national planning or making "full employment" a law. Tomorrow, the managed-economy objectives may be more personal to all of us—where we live, where we work, what we buy, and so on.

Conservatives are not anarchists. Indeed, they believe in planning, and today we have a high order of acceptable planning in the economy. This planning, however, is a function of individual choices collectively expressed in the market. As Milton Friedman has observed:

> Fundamentally, there are only two ways of coordinating the economic activities of millions. One is central direction involving the use of coercion—the technique of the army and of the modern totalitarian state. The other is voluntary cooperation of individuals—the technique of the market place. . . . Exchange can bring about coordination without coercion.*

The present in-between, never-never land of mixed American capitalism cannot long continue. *We must go either one way or the other in the future.*

The Liberal Argument

The public furor created by discussions of planning arises out of ignorance. Planning as envisioned in the 1976 Senate and House reso-

*Milton Friedman, *Capitalism and Freedom* (Chicago: Univ. of Chicago Press, 1962), p. 13.

lutions was not a sharp divergence from the past. It was basically an elaboration of the principles laid out, but not specifically implemented, in the Employment Act of 1946. Nor is planning in general at all new to the American economy. After all, the government budget is not constructed without calculating the impact of its spending and taxing, nor does General Motors make annual profits of more than $2 billion accidentally. Regrettably, planning calls up the image of a Soviet-type society when in fact it is essential for the improvement of our own democratic capitalism. The type of planning being given serious consideration at present is not an Orwellian nightmare where "Big Brother Is Watching You." Aside from creating jobs and improving efficiency, it is not intended to alter American life very much at all. In fact, planning is intended to protect, as much as possible, the conditions to which we have become accustomed.

IN DEFENSE OF PLANNING

At this point in our discussions, the Liberal defense of planning need not be lengthy. The necessity for some type of general control mechanism has been evident in all of our comments on contemporary policy issues. A shift toward self-conscious national planning would, however, be a major effort to integrate the separate planning and control efforts we now depend upon.

The need for an integrated governmental planning operation will sooner or later be accepted. The crises of energy, employment, inflation, and urban finance cannot be dealt with continually in ad hoc policy making. The multiplication and lack of integration of these separate efforts are wasteful and counterproductive. For instance, an energy conservation policy constructed without specific commitment to employment and price objectives may save us fuel but cost us jobs and investment. The great virtue of national planning efforts is that they recognize the interconnection of all economic problems and hence seek solutions in a broad rather than narrow way.

Collection of adequate production data will make it possible to target general objectives in the economy—say, a certain acceptable level of economic growth in particular industries. Balance can be created among industries, such as that needed between developing public transportation on the one hand and sustaining the private automobile industry on the other.

As a rule, coercion will not be necessary to assure that targets are attained. Careful use of tax-subsidy incentives and participation by capital and labor in the planning process can generate a high order of consensus among the constituent parts of the economy. Meanwhile, with government acting positively as a guarantor of jobs in the last resort, the persistent unemployment problem can be laid to rest.

Of course, we must expect crises from time to time, and mere targets or gentle nudging will not always be enough. War, oil embargoes, and international economic difficulties beyond our control may necessitate some coercive use of planning. Such situations may demand rationing of goods, rigorous wage and price controls, and perhaps more. However, in the face of serious crisis, the nation would have no other alternative—any more than it had an alternative to rationing and controls during World War II.

Critics will say that economic planning in the form of controls, attempted during Nixon's New Economic Policy (NEP), was less than successful. The observation is correct as far as it goes, but it should not be used to condemn planning in general. Nixon's Phase I through Phase IV controls to deal with inflation between 1971 and 1973 never added up to a real planning effort. Wage and price controls were applied unevenly (to business's benefit and labor's loss). Moreover, these controls were not part of a general planning effort to deal with the serious problem of unemployment. The NEP was doomed to failure because of its bias toward business and its lack of comprehensiveness. It is hoped that the bad taste left by that experience can be overcome.

As two Liberal defenders of planning, Lester Thurow and Robert Heilbroner, have observed:

> Planning may well be to our era what the discovery of the Keynesian explanation of depression was to the era of the 1930s. Keynesian policies did not solve the economic difficulties of that era by any matter of means, but they did get us through a period that threatened to plunge us into very serious social and political trouble. Perhaps the proper estimate of planning is much the same. We should not realistically hope that it will solve many of the problems that beset our times—problems of technology, of bureaucracy, of a terrible division of the world between rich and poor—but planning may nevertheless get us through this period of drift and disappointment. That would be quite enough.*

*Robert Heilbroner and Lester Thurow, *The Economic Problem Newsletter* (Englewood Cliffs, N.J.: Prentice-Hall, Spring 1976), p. 3.

The Liberal who is challenged to defend planning in principle and practice has only one answer: "Given where we are, is there any other way?"

PLANNING AND CAPITALISM

We cannot leave this topic without taking up the Conservative charge that "planning" means the end of capitalism. If by capitalism the Conservatives mean the quaint little world of Adam Smith where all men higgled and sold freely and equally, that world passed out of existence a very long time ago—if in fact it ever existed. The tragicomic Conservative defenders of individualism and freedom have failed to adapt these values to a highly complex technological world. The mutual economic interdependence of people, nations, and institutions simply does not allow us to talk of freedom in such a simplistic sense. The freedom to be poor, the freedom to starve, or the freedom to collapse into social anarchy is really the long-run outcome of efforts to return to a marketplace mentality.

Contrary to the Conservative outlook, planning is not necessarily communism, nor is it authoritarianism of any special breed. Planning is essential to maintaining the American democratic capitalist tradition. To the Liberal, of course, "democratic" is much more important than "capitalist" in a generic sense. The economic experience of the United States and all other basically "capitalist" countries indicates quite clearly that only planning can save the private property, production-for-profit system from self-destruction. The perquisites of capitalist production, however, must be limited and subordinated to general social objectives. The only apparatus to protect the general society is the state, and the only means open to the state is planning.

While he has not always been in the mainstream of Liberal opinion, John Kenneth Galbraith's observations of a decade ago fairly represent the Liberal position today. After weighing the growing problems of American industrial society, Galbraith concluded:

> It is through the state that the society must assert the superior claim of aesthetic over economic goals and particularly of environment over cost. It is to the state we must look for freedom of individual choice as to toil. . . . If the state is to serve these ends, the scientific and educational estate and larger intellectual community must be aware of their

power and their opportunity and they must use them. There is no one else.*

The Radical Argument

Planning is the logical conclusion of capitalism's development. The search for profits has exhausted "free market" possibilities, and now the profit system must be protected by law and weighty legal and bureaucratic machinery. Although there is considerable debate as to how close we really are to a formally planned and controlled economy, Radicals would generally agree that it is the next great leap in capitalist development. From laissez faire to monopoly capitalism to state-corporate regulation to formal planning—capitalism has run its course in its effort to secure profit and protect itself. The obvious irony, of course, is that planned capitalism is a contradiction in terms. As the basic economics textbooks tell us, capitalism emerged as a totally free economic philosophy. It ends as a totally authoritarian one.

CAPITALISM NEEDS PLANNING

Ideologies, even after they have proved worthless, die hard, often convulsively. It remains to be seen how the outmoded rhetoric of laissez faire or even the more sophisticated mixed-economy philosophies will pass into history. They are deeply rooted in the individual practice and thought of American citizens, and their public defenders are still loud and shrill. Nevertheless, as our past discussions of contemporary issues should indicate, the use of centralized state planning and controls is everywhere apparent.

This process is not really very new. It originated in the late nineteenth-century response to the growing crises of American capitalism. Troubled by periodic panics or recessions (in 1873, 1885, 1893, and 1907), chronic excess capacity and overproduction, and anarchic market conditions, and threatened by increasingly radicalized labor strife, American capitalism depended more and more on state intervention. We have elaborated on these interventions in our discussions of stabilization policy, inflation, unemployment, and inter-

*John K. Galbraith, The New Industrial State (Boston: Houghton Mifflin, 1967), p. 335.

national trade. As the state became a partner in supporting business, American corporations enlarged their monopoly powers through concentration and control.

This growth of state-corporate integration has been euphemistically termed the "mixed economy" in economics texts. Uninformed Conservatives attacked this integration as the domination of business by the state without even stopping to ask just whose interests the state represented. They fail to see that, quite as Marx had specified, "the State is the form in which the individuals of the ruling class assert their common interests."

Capitalist production has proven to be extraordinarily rational in a microeconomic sense. The organization of production, labor, and capital for any particular firm is governed by economic rules of behavior (we would call it the price system) which, for an individual entrepreneur, give key signals as to how best to attain profit objectives. Yet in totality, the capitalist system is irrational. Though the actions of any given firm are rationally "planned" or calculated with profit in mind, the actions of all firms taken together produce macroeconomic and social disorder. There is a lack of coordination and integration, even among monopolistic capitalists, in dealing with different industries and different sectors of the economy. Rational control of the whole labor force, of total output, and of investment alternatives is lacking.

The boom-bust rhythm of the business cycle, although recently muted when compared to the past, is still evident—but with a difference. Today's highly integrated and automated production is extremely vulnerable to even the slightest variations in sales, profits, and output. In the past, when industry was predominantly labor-intensive, a business downturn amounted mainly to sending the workers home with empty pay envelopes and waiting until things got better. Today, with greater capital usage and production on an international scale, nonproduction presents a firm with greater losses. These, in turn, affect financial markets and the international structure of business.

Moreover, modern capitalism has so penetrated the world that it is limited in its ability to acquire new markets, so essential to its survival. At the same time, as we have noted repeatedly before, capitalist production can be carried on at higher output levels using less labor power. As a result, the crowning irrationality of the system is that it can produce more and more, but labor becomes increasingly redundant and markets harder to find.

The chronic tendency toward unemployment and excess capacity, the steady push of prices, and the worsening balance of trade situation (along with the energy problem) leave few options for American capitalism. As the Liberal John Kenneth Galbraith has argued for years, the next step in capitalist development is to transcend the market and modern Keynesian efforts to correct it, and to move straight toward direct economic planning and controls. Only through such efforts can capitalist irrationality be controlled. Planning presents possibilities for reorganizing the capitalist processes of production and accumulation and at the same time can "legitimize" or bring order to labor markets. The importance of this function of legitimizing was not overlooked in the Humphrey-Hawkins Act, which requires government to maintain full employment (that is, no more than 3 percent unemployed among adults) by 1983.

PLANNING FOR PROFITS, NOT PEOPLE

Although planning is the antithesis of pure capitalist ideology, any imminent American version will certainly retain key elements of capitalist practice. The defenders of the 1976 planning proposals were all quick to point out that their proposals had no similarity to planning as practiced in the Soviet Union, China, or Cuba. Not only is the social confiscation of private property disavowed; there is no intention to set even loose administrative goals over what goods will be produced and how. The principle of private production for profit is to be retained.

Capital planning as presently envisioned by its proponents has two functions. First, the government output "recommendations" are to act as a general guide to business in undertaking specific investment and output decisions. This "indicative" planning can show beforehand where shortages and bottlenecks might appear; it presupposes that rational capitalists will take actions to eliminate such problems. The second aspect of this planning would be selective tax cutting to induce business to move toward certain production goals. This "tax-cutting planning" is really only a dressed-up version of modern Keynesianism. Its main objective remains maintenance of high levels of employment.

At this point readers may ask, "So what's new about all this?" As far as it goes, not very much. To be effective, planning must go much further than indicative and tax-cutting actions, and it very likely will. As we have seen in earlier discussions, there seems to be no end in sight to chronic stagflation. Certainly more specific and direct planning will be needed to lower unemployment and cool inflation. In particular, that means wage-price controls and extensive government hiring as the employer of last resort.

In the latter case, higher taxes will be needed to support the new jobs. The taxes will, of course, be paid by workers and not capital, since payment by capital would offset the technique of tax-cut planning. Moreover, cheap government labor made available to the private sector will subsidize business profits by providing unpaid workers and by acting as a lever against excessive labor union requests.

Wage-price controls, long popular with many Liberals, also amount to a transfer payment from people to business. The bias toward business was readily demonstrated in Nixon's 1971 New Economic Policy. Although a case can be made that the NEP was not a serious effort, it did show that through Phases I to IV, business was able to advance prices slightly and to increase productivity and profits substantially while real labor wages were frozen and employment fell. Without "profit controls," wage-price planning will be simply another device to transfer wealth from workers and consumers to business. And no one in the planning lobby is talking about profit controls.

Planning, then, is only a pretext for doing, under administered arrangements, what capitalism has always done—extract and accumulate surplus value. If the planning is extensive enough, it may in fact put millions back to work and it can slow inflation, but only by lowering the real living standards of American workers. The classical economic doctrine of the "iron law of wages" (that incomes should equal subsistence) would be reintroduced through tax transfers and wage controls. Capitalist planning still assumes that corporate profits are essential to make the system work. We may well have full employment, but only if it is profitable to business and costly to workers in their real wages.

As we have seen repeatedly in our discussions, profit seeking is our basic problem. Humane decisions about the environment, income distribution, and the production of goods will always be shelved if planning is for the profit and well-being of the few rather than for the whole society. Obviously, extensive planning, with the giants of monopoly capitalism increasing their share of power, would end all pretense at expensive and wasteful competition.

1984 ISN'T HERE YET

George Orwell's vision in *1984* of a totally regulated and oppressed society is always a threat. The authoritarian and fascist character of capitalist planning à la *1984* is apparent in the direct controls that such planning would have to take over individuals' working and social lives. The vision has not, however, yet come to pass. Planning is not widely supported in the United States despite its value to monopoly capital.

First of all, American capitalism is uneven in its development. Although we have emphasized the role of large monopoly capitalists, there are millions of small capitalists who are at the same time the victims and the cause of irrational and chaotic market conditions. Few of them would see many gains from central planning, since it would probably mean their end. All capitalist interests are not identical with General Motors. To put it plainly, many American capitalists are not yet willing to accept massive state-capital planning, regardless of the objective demands for planning within the system.

Second, as the 1976 presidential election indicated, most ordinary Americans are suspicious of and perhaps downright antagonistic to big government. Fiscal problems and the Watergate scandal left a deep antipathy to American politics. With the energy crisis and steady inflation-unemployment problems, Americans are not very sympathetic to big business either. Planning entails bigness. It demands a larger bureaucracy and more interference in people's lives. That such planning is needed to "save" capitalism is of much less concern to most Americans than business leaders would like to admit. In fact, a 1975 study by the People's Bicentennial Commission (a private group) found that fewer than half of all Americans could be counted as serious ideological defenders of capitalism as a system.

From a Radical perspective, all this is heartening. While it gives no clear direction as to how to proceed against this final stage of monopoly capitalism, it at least suggests that such an opposition, if properly developed, can be successful.

The Radical, however, does not oppose planning per se. It would be hypocritical and profoundly misleading if the present opponents of state-corporate planning believed that Radicals could or would lead them back to some simple-minded era of complete market freedom. The fact is that *rational* planning is essential. But such planning has the objective of creating a humane society, not maximizing profits. This planning must be by and for the people rather than by bureaucrats for capitalists. Moreover, the planning must be decentralized and democratic. From a Radical perspective, the people must be the architects of their own society. The basic economic decisions of what is produced, how, and for whom must not be entrusted to an elite, whether they be capitalists or political commissars.

The Radical economic and social historian William Appleman Williams put it this way:

> Hence the issue is not whether to decentralize the economy and politics of the country, but rather how to do so. . . . This literal reconstructing and rebuilding of American society offers the only physical and intellectual challenge capable of absorbing and giving focus to the physical and intellectual resources of the country during the next generation. . . .
>
> Throughout such a process, moreover, the participants will be educating themselves . . . for their membership in the truly human community they will be creating. In the end they will have built a physical America which will be beautiful instead of ugly, and which will facilitate human relationships instead of dividing men into separate functional elements. They will have evolved a political system which is democratic in form and social in content. And they will be prepared . . . to function as men and women who can define their own identity, and their relationships with each other, outside the confining limits of property and the bruising and destructive dynamics of the competitive marketplace. They will be ready to explore the frontier of their own humanity.*

*William A. Williams, *The Great Evasion* (Chicago: Quadrangle Books, 1964), pp. 175–176.

PART 4

CONCLUSION

Final Thoughts and Suggested Readings

Having reached the end of this volume of debates on contemporary economic issues, it is probable that the reader expects (perhaps even hopes for) the author to make his own pitch—to say straight out which of the representative paradigms is correct and which is not, perhaps to unveil his own grand program. Indeed, the opportunity is tempting. For an economist, it is practically a reflex to try to get in the last word, especially his own last word. However, after much thought, I decided that such a conclusion would spoil the entire effort. The book was undertaken to present the differing ideological alternatives as objectively as space and writing talents allowed so that the reader would be free to make his or her own hard choices on matters of economic policy.

I can hear some readers complaining: "Cop-out! You're avoiding presenting your own preferences and your own conclusions. You've taken the easy way out of the swamp." Not so. Delivering my own final polemic would in truth be ever so easy. But the book has been about questions and choices. The reader, then, shall be left in the uncomfortable position of making his or her own choice among the paradigms and policy questions surveyed here. And, that is the way it should be.

This perspective, however, must not be misunderstood. The author has not intended to produce a "relativistic" conclusion in which any choice will do and one choice is as good as any other. The point is for the reader to make a *good* choice, and some policy choices *are* better than others. However, only a reasoned analysis of the facts and a critical study of the "truths" of this world will permit any of us to make wise choices.

The British economist Joan Robinson has said it best:

> Social life will always present mankind with a choice of evils. No metaphysical solution that can ever be formulated will seem satisfactory for long. The solutions offered by economists were no less delusory than those of the theologians that they displaced.
>
> All the same we must not abandon the hope that economics can make an advance towards science, or the faith that enlightenment is not useless. It is necessary to clear the decaying remnants of obsolete metaphysics out of the way before we can go forward.
>
> The first essential for economists, arguing amongst themselves, is to "try very seriously," as Professor Popper says that natural scientists do, "to avoid talking at cross purposes."*

Before we can "avoid talking at cross purposes" on economic matters, we must understand our fundamental differences in opinion and interpretation. Hopefully, this book has identified some of these important differences for the reader.

In undertaking this task, any author would find himself or herself sorely tested. While trying to submerge personal biases, he or she must also master the biases of others. Perhaps I have not entirely succeeded on either count. Only the reader can judge. Nevertheless, such an undertaking is extremely educational. It compels a person to work through unfamiliar logic and ideas and weigh them against one's own beliefs. For readers who desire to dig deeper into economic ideologies and their application to contemporary issues, the following bibliography offers some landmark readings in the respective Conservative, Liberal, and Radical schools of economic thought.

---

*Joan Robinson, *Economic Philosophy* (Garden City, N. Y.: Anchor Books, 1964), pp. 147–148.

Conservative

Banfield, Edward C. *The Unheavenly City*. Boston: Little, Brown, and Co., 1970.

Buckley, William. *Up from Liberalism*. New York: Honor Books, 1959.

Friedman, Milton. *Capitalism and Freedom*. Chicago: University of Chicago Press, 1962.

———, and Walter Heller. *Monetary vs. Fiscal Policy*. New York: W. W. Norton & Co., 1969.

Hazlitt, Henry. *The Failure of the "New Economics": An Analysis of the Keynesian Fallacies*. Princeton, N. J.: Van Nostrand Co., 1959.

Kirk, Russell. *The Conservative Mind*. Chicago: H. Regnery & Co., 1954.

Knight, Frank. *Freedom and Reform*. New York: Harper & Row, 1947.

Rand, Ayn. *Capitalism: The Unknown Ideal*. New York: New American Library, Signet Books, 1967.

Simons, Henry C. *A Positive Program for Laissez-Faire*. Chicago: University of Chicago Press, 1934.

Smith, Adam. *An Inquiry into the Nature and Causes of the Wealth of Nations*, 1776.

Von Hayek, Friedrich. *The Road to Serfdom*. Chicago: University of Chicago Press, 1944.

Von Mises, Ludwig. *Socialism: An Economic and Sociological Analysis*. New Haven, Conn.: Yale University Press, 1959.

Liberal

Berle, Adolf A. *The Twentieth Century Capitalist Revolution*. New York: Harcourt Brace Jovanovich, 1954.

Clark, John M. *Alternative to Serfdom*. New York: Vintage Books. 1960.

———. *Social Control of Business*. New York: McGraw-Hill, 1939.

Galbraith, John Kenneth. *The Affluent Society*. Boston: Houghton Mifflin Co., 1971.

———. *Economics and the Public Purpose*. Boston: Houghton Mifflin Co., 1973.

———. *The New Industrial State*. Boston: Houghton Mifflin Co., 1967.

Hansen, Alvin. *The American Economy*. New York: McGraw-Hill, 1957.

Heilbroner, Robert. "The Future of Capitalism," in *The Limits of American Capitalism*. New York: Harper & Row, 1966.

Heller, Walter W. *The Economy: Old Myths and New Realities*. New York: W. W. Norton & Co., 1976.

Keynes, John M. *The General Theory of Employment, Interest, and Money.* New York: Harcourt Brace, 1936.

Lekachman, Robert. *The Age of Keynes.* New York: Random House, 1966.

Okun, Arthur M. *The Political Economy of Prosperity.* New York: W. W. Norton & Co., 1970.

Reagan, Michael D. *The Managed Economy.* New York: Oxford University Press, 1963.

Shonfield, Andres. *Modern Capitalism: The Changing Balance of Public and Private Power.* New York: Oxford University Press, 1965.

Radical

Baran, Paul. *The Political Economy of Growth.* New York: Monthly Review Press, 1957.

———, and Paul M. Sweezy. *Monopoly Capital.* New York: Monthly Review Press, 1966.

Domhoff, William. *Who Rules America?* Englewood Cliffs, N. J.: Prentice-Hall, 1967.

Franklin, Raymond S. *American Capitalism—Two Visions.* New York: Random House, 1977.

Kolko, Gabriel. *Wealth and Power in America.* New York: Praeger, 1962.

Magdoff, Harry. *The Age of Imperialism.* New York: Monthly Review Press, 1967.

Mandel, Ernest. *Marxist Economic Theory.* New York: Monthly Review Press, 1967.

Marx, Karl. *Capital.* 1867.

O'Connor, James. *The Fiscal Crisis of the State.* New York: St. Martin's Press, 1973.

Robinson, Joan. *An Essay on Marxian Economics.* London: Macmillan, 1942.

Sherman, Howard. *Radical Political Economy.* New York: Basic Books, 1972.

———. *Stagflation, A Radical Theory of Unemployment and Inflation.* New York: Harper & Row, 1976.

Strachey, John. *The Nature of Capitalist Crisis.* New York: Covici, Friede, 1933.

———. *The Theory and Practice of Socialism.* New York: Random House, 1936.

Sweezy, Paul. *The Theory of Capitalist Development.* New York: Monthly Review Press, 1942.

Williams, William A. *The Great Evasion.* Chicago: Quadrangle Books, 1964.

INDEX